MW00784340

twice-dead

PETER LANG
New York • Washington, D.C./Baltimore • Bern
Frankfurt am Main • Berlin • Brussels • Vienna • Oxford

Yoram Lubling

twice-dead

Moshe Y. Lubling,
the Ethics of Memory,
and the Treblinka Revolt

with a Foreword by
Elie Wiesel

PETER LANG
New York • Washington, D.C./Baltimore • Bern
Frankfurt am Main • Berlin • Brussels • Vienna • Oxford

Library of Congress Cataloging-in-Publication Data

Lubling, Yoram.
Twice-dead: Moshe Y. Lubling, the ethics of memory,
and the Treblinka Revolt / Yoram Lubling.
p. cm.
Includes bibliographical references and index.
1. Treblinka (Concentration camp). 2. Holocaust, Jewish (1939–1945)—
Poland—Historiography. 3. World War, 1939–1945—
Atrocities—Poland. I. Title.
D805.5.T74L83   940.53'1853841—dc22   2006029186
ISBN 978-0-8204-8815-8

Bibliographic information published by **Die Deutsche Bibliothek**.
Die Deutsche Bibliothek lists this publication in the "Deutsche
Nationalbibliografie"; detailed bibliographic data is available
on the Internet at http://dnb.ddb.de/.

Cover design by Sophie Boorsch Appel
Cover art reproduced by permission of Anne Simpkins,
Associate Professor of Art, Elon University (North Carolina)

The paper in this book meets the guidelines for permanence and durability
of the Committee on Production Guidelines for Book Longevity
of the Council of Library Resources.

© 2007 Peter Lang Publishing, Inc., New York
29 Broadway, 18th floor, New York, NY 10006
www.peterlang.com

All rights reserved.
Reprint or reproduction, even partially, in all forms such as microfilm,
xerography, microfiche, microcard, and offset strictly prohibited.

Printed in the United States of America

To my grandfather Moshe Yehoshua Lubling,
a Treblinka Revolt Leader.

To the Barmherzig and Lubling families,
my parents' murdered families.

The Grandson Remembers

And then went down to the camps
and the ghetto, the Poles spitting
on us still, blood in the snow
still from the children who were childish
and cried, machine-gunned there, my father—
survivor, plumber, Israeli now—was with me,
his own father dead,
but not twice dead if I have my way,
the selection done and there is my mother's family—
ladies before gentlemen—slaughtered
in ash, the women's breast
knifed free, held, weighed, sucked, tossed
to the fire, the men naked, whipped
until they couldn't know
what to cover, what leave undone.
And my father's family—so long, so long—
just there with his father leading
the unrest, Moshe in Treblinka,
insurrection against the Reich, insurrection
put down, or does he survive
to die in short order, sticks and bones,
until he too goes up
in the thick grease of human flame,
for how long before
his name is spelt out in the fire
and I can still read it there, aloud.
                                        —Kevin Boyle

TABLE OF CONTENTS

ILLUSTRATIONS

FOREWORD

I is my custom to comment, but rarely about a work where my name appears. I prefer to convey my thoughts in person to the author. If I have decided to go back on my own rule in the case of this exciting book by Yoram Lubling, an Israeli philosopher teaching in an American university, it is because I wish to correct an injustice committed by historians regarding his grandfather. Not being a historian myself, I express myself simply as a concerned reader who is affected by everything said about the Shoah.

The subject is a certain Moshe Y. Lubling, a Polish Jew influential in his community, who, like so many others, suffered the horrors of the Czesto-chowa ghetto before being deported to Treblinka. In the ghetto he had played an important social role. That is known. What is less known is his participation in the famous revolt in the death camp that was Treblinka.

Strange: while chroniclers and diarists evoke his name, the so-called professional experts obscure it. But why? I asked Yoram during our first meeting at Elon University. He shrugged his shoulders in despair: he did not know. Intrigued, I looked into the records. He was right: in the museum archives in Washington and Jerusalem, the heroic insurrection had unfolded under the leadership of several courageous prisoners whose names are cited. But not the name of Moshe Y. Lubling. A bizarre, unjust, and incomprehensible censure. Wished by whom and for what reason? It remains a mystery.

In truth, though exhausting all leads, Yoram does not even try to resolve it in his research. But he does even better: in more than one original interpretation of the facts, testimonies, and articles, all drawn from both new and established sources, he furnishes proof. I find it convincing.

Without wishing to blame anyone, without entering into the game of names and responsibilities, it is incumbent upon me to declare the following: having read attentively the argument of this fighter for the historical truth, I believe that yes, the grandfather of the young philosopher Yoram Lubling fought, weapons in hand, together with his companions in misfortune, against the SS and their Ukrainian collaborators in Treblinka. Yes, he died in combat. Yes, he deserves a special place in Jewish memory.

He should be, and would be, proud of his grandson.

The fair-minded reader is.

Elie Wiesel

ACKNOWLEDGMENTS

My most sincere thanks go to my wife Lynne Maurer-Lubling, for her life-long support of my work on behalf of my grandfather. In the words of Martin Buber, she is "God's helper in the ongoing work of creation." To professor Elie Wiesel, for his friendship, brilliance, recognition of my grandfather's heroism, and for first using the term 'twice-dead' to describe the double death of Holocaust survivors—once when they were murdered by the Nazis and a second time by the world that forgot about them; to my brother Moshe Lubling for sharing our unique post-Holocaust journey; to Elon University and Dean Steven House for their genuine support; to Anthony Weston, Kevin Boyle, Anne Simpkins, Martin Kamela, Jane W. Romer, and Aron Tyson Smith; Yad-Vashem Archives; U.S. Holocaust Memorial Museum Archives; and finally, to Ashi and Tommy, my Golden Retrievers, for teaching me about unconditional love, loyalty, and how to enjoy the simple things in life.

Moshe Yehoshua Lubling (1902–1943)

INTRODUCTION

Once, I had believed profoundly that upon one solitary deed of mine, one solitary prayer, depended the salvation of the world.

—Elie Wiesel, *Night*[1]

Even before I could read and write I was already capable of recognizing the phrase "Lubling from Silesia" on page 535 of *Sefer Milkhamot Hagetaot* (The Wars of the Ghettos' Book). I grew-up in Israel with the knowledge that my family's name was a matter of historical record, someone in my family acted in a way that distinguished them from others. Later I came to understand that my grandfather was a unique individual who fought the corrupt *Judenrat* in the Czestochowa Ghetto, formed the legendary "Workers' Council" which developed into the Jewish Resistance Organization in Czestochowa, and was involved in acts of resistance against the Nazis. In particular, I learned that he was among the leaders of the prisoners' revolt in Treblinka; the notorious Nazi extermination camp in Poland where nearly one million Jews have been murdered, including my father's entire family.

To be a descendent of a Jew who resisted the Nazis was of great importance in the young Israeli culture. While heartbroken over the successful extermination of European Jewry, the existing Israeli society was less then sympathetic to the survivors. As free and independent "Hebrews" they were mystified by the powerlessness exhibited by millions of Jews during the Holocaust. The Israeli writer Tom Segev described these early years as follows:

> The Holocaust came to be seen as a Jewish defeat. Its victims were censured for having let the Nazis murder them without fighting for their lives or at least for the right to 'die with honor.' This attitude in time became a sort of psychological and political ghost that haunted the State of Israel—reflecting scorn and shame, hubris and dread, injustice and folly … The resentment against victims of the Holocaust recalled the way Zionist poets, such as Haim Nahman Bialik, had depicted the vic-

tims of an early pogrom: 'They fled like mice, hid like bugs, and died like dogs over there, wherever they were found.' Even then, the emphasis was on *there*. Had they come *here* earlier, it would not have happened to them.[2]

The same emerging Israeli culture was appropriately termed by another Israeli writer as "The Cult of Toughness."

> The Israeli ideal of toughness is expressed through a distain for those who cannot match it. The Israeli slang term for 'sissy' is 'sabon.' Sabon means soap, and the term appeared after WWII when stories of Jews being made into soap by the Nazis started circulating.... The word has come to express ... a genuine contempt for the victims of the Holocaust ... the reason is that the six million were passive Diaspora victims ... not heroic fighters.[3]

As such, it is obvious why the activities that are associated with my grandfather's name were a badge of honor in my society and I accepted and internalized them. The actions of my grandfather were consistent with my nation's psychological attitude and its desired identity. My grandfather's heroic actions also provided me with a source of personal inspiration; I felt obligated and entitled to continue his legacy of resistance and passion for values over concerns for personal consequences. It gave me the inherent right to stand-up for what is just, fair, selfless, and altruistic, without compromise. In reality, I felt that my grandfather's actions directly led to the creation of the State of Israel, its culture, and its ethical image. As Dr. Binyamin Orenstein wrote in 1948, Moshe Y. Lubling was a *"lichtike gessztalt"* (a shining example) of the Socialist Zionistic Movement.[4] Unlike many other Zionist leaders in the Diaspora, he didn't escape Europe and abandoned his fellow Jews. Rather, he fought for their rights, their dignity, and he set the example for the yet un-formed breed of Israeli Jews, what the late poet Berl Katzenelson described as "an entirely new tribe."[5]

My grandfather's influence followed me throughout my life and even determined my philosophical orientation. Adopting a philosophical view of existence, the American philosopher William James pointed out, is a reaction to the world. The ideas and temperament of the classical tradition in American philosophy found me as quickly as I found philosophy, especially the naturalistic writings of John Dewey. I like to believe that my grandfather would have appreciated Dewey's writings and temperament for the same reasons I did. First, because Dewey's Pragmatism, like his Labor Zionism, was the child of the Enlightenment and was concerned with building a nation and the creation of a new type of person. Both philosophical perspectives rejected traditional religion as metaphysically false and at fault for many contemporary ills of society. Second, like the Labor Zionist A. D. Gordon, Dewey saw in education and labor the primary paradigms for individual and collective change and transformation. Third, Dewey was an anti-intellectualist and, like members of Labor Zionism, he preferred the education of experience over theoretical mastery. Like America's R.W. Emerson, Israel's David Ben-Gurion warned his fellow citizens that Israel will survive only "when it cares less about what non-Jews say, and more about what Jews do." Finally, like my grandfather, Dewey was influenced by the ideas of Karl Marx regarding community responsibility, equality, shared care, public education, and the primacy of relations over isolation and individualism.[6] Put together, these are the values I inherited from my grandfather's life and actions, and these are the values that found me in the writings of John Dewey and classical American philosophy. Adopting a naturalistic and pragmatic understanding of existence, therefore, constitutes my reaction to the world after the Holocaust.

My reaction is also underscored by the burden and unique "way of seeing" characteristic of second generation Holocaust survivors in Israel. It is a perspective that is unparalleled in contemporary discourse. How many white educated Europeans do you know who are also Hebrew natives of the Middle-East and children of slaves? For the most part we may appear as living ordinary lives to the outside world. We have careers, we marry, we become parents, and some even join social clubs and political parties. But appearance is very misleading since we really live in another world. A world that involves an irreducible history and quality of violence and violation; we see nothing enchanted about this world that we cannot trust. After all, we grew-up among those who either dispossessed or murdered our families, or among those who stood silently while they were stripped of their humanity. The Holocaust survivor Eugene Kogan expressed this sentiment when he wrote:

> As you view the history of our time, turn and look at the piles of bodies, pause for a short moment, and imagine that this poor residue of flesh is your father, your child, your wife, is the one you love. See yourself and those nearest to you, to whom you are devoted heart and soul, thrown naked into the dirt, tortured, starving, and killed.[7]

See the picture of cardboard boxes with remains of Auschwitz's inmates and their names written on them. Look at the box number 2290 with the name David Barmherzig written on it. This was my mother's older brother. Here is the person to whom she was "devoted heart and soul." Here he is "thrown naked into the dirt, tortured, and killed." This is the psychological and physical burden my generation of survivors' children had to grow up with in Israel. How can we be expected to live ordinary lives? How can we suspend the images in our minds of powerlessness and victimization? Only a fool can be overly concerned with club politics or even brilliant scholarship and literature while she has been the subject of the longest and most diabolic hatred in Western history? So we wear our masks and appear to be living in this world. We know in our soul and muscles that in the eyes of others we will always be, in the words of the poet H. Leivick, "signed and registered Treblinka candidates." Although reflecting Jewish-American sentiments, this extraordinary and forgotten poem captured ours as well. I wish to quote the poem in full for the record.

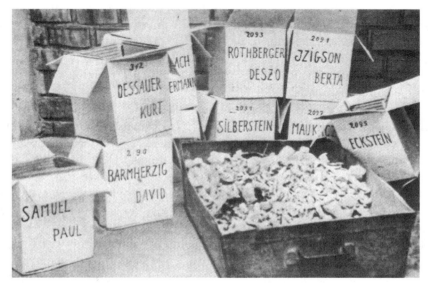

The remains of David Barmherzig, my mother's brother—Auschwitz 1945

A Treblinka Candidate
No. I was never in Treblinka.
Nor was I in Majdanek.
Yet I stood upon their edge.
The threshold is God's great world,
A still facing the world-to-come ...
I stand there and wait,
Great world, I wait for your command
You, dirty Jew, let's go—the gas chamber!

Everything I see is divine.
The forests are shaking with religious heads,
And over every mountain, over every steep
Winds are wheeling, circling and dancing.
Above, the sun is fair and pure, charged
With an overflow of flame
From whose quick flares are tearing and streaming

All the tongues of fire of Majdanek,
In this—my life—I have already had
Abundant offers promising delights
Like the Inquisition. I stand
Near the death camp of the world, on line,
A signed and registered Treblinka candidate. [8]

Furthermore, living without a fair distribution of justice is a miserable existence in which the only relief is either suicide or rationalization and denial. Alan Dershowitz, in his novel *Just Revenge* describes the return of Dori, a Holocaust survivor and an Israeli citizen, to Germany several years after the end of the war. Dori finds beautifully clean streets, coffee shops with elegant and successful men and women laughing and living a guilt-free existence. Unable to continue and live without justice, Dori commits suicide. His suicide note reads as follows:

> *Hitler promised the German people that if they killed the Jews, Germany would be better off. They killed the Jews, and Germany is better off. I cannot live in a world in which genocide is rewarded. Nor can I do what Michael Kohlhass did. I am a Jew. I cannot kill the innocent, though every fiber in my body cries out for revenge. Were I to remain alive, and were my frustrations to mount, I could become a Kohlhaas. That must not happen, for the sake of my family's name, for the sake of the Jewish people, and for the sake of my own soul. I know only one way to make sure it does not happen.*
> *I love you, and I know that you will figure out a better way.*
>
> Shalom,
> Dori[9]

In reality, many Holocaust survivors, most notably the philosopher Jean Amory and the writers Jerzy Kosinski and Primo Levy, committed suicide rather than live together with their own executioners. As a child of the State of Israel, living in a world without a fair distribution of justice is still part of my daily experience. From the senseless killing and kidnapping of Israeli soldiers and citizens to the growing anti-Semitic sentiments around the world in reaction to Israel's attempt to defend itself. It is a daily struggle for me to live with the lies, denial, false logic, and hatred exhibited towards me and my nation by the media and other apologists for Islamic lunacy. In his reaction to the almost universal condemnation of Israel's recent actions against Hezbollah in Lebanon, Israel's Prime Minister Ehud Olmert asked the world:

What is it about us, the Jews, the minority, the persecuted that arouses this cosmic sense of justice in you? What do we have that all the others don't? … I don't recall such a wave of reaction in the face of the 100 citizens killed every single day in Iraq. Sunnis kill Shiites, who kill Sunnis, and all of them kill Americans—and the world remains silent. And I am hard pressed to recall a similar reaction when the Russians destroyed entire villages and burned down large cities in order to repress

the revolt in Chechnya. And when NATO bombed Kosovo for almost three months
and crushed the civilian population—then you also kept silent.[10]

The burden of living in an unjust world also motivated me to write this book
in memory of my grandfather. I want to make sure that his death and heroism
will not be lost in the prosperity and historical amnesia of the executioners.

I will violate my grandfather's memory if I did not address my academic
colleagues' often uncritical and irresponsible defense of contemporary
Islamic terrorism and their commonplace demonization of Jews and Zionism.
Unfortunately, when it comes to the conflict between Israel and the Palestinians, academic environments proved to be one sided, narrow minded,
negligent with regards to facts and history, and dangerously close to becoming the official apologists for terrorism, killing of innocent civilians, and all
anti-Western hatred. In their "obligatory" and nearly unanimous condemnation of the Israeli position, the academia today failed to fulfill its promise as
a free thinking, fair and honest community of inquiry. Its free thinking
promise turned into an ideological blindness that allows the repetition of lies,
false accusations, and straight-out revisionism. No fair-minded individual
would recognize the actual State of Israel and its people through the images
and descriptions reproduced in academic environments all over the world.
Rather, a fair-minded individual would find a frightened and traumatized
community still fighting the cosmic attempt to exterminate them; a group of
people who would do almost everything to share in the peaceful and ordinary
lives of nations, but who are no longer willing to satisfy the world's constant
thirst for a scapegoat.

Furthermore, in its one sided response to the conflict between Israel and
the Palestinians, the academia directly encouraged the objectification of Jews
and Zionism, and by so doing legitimized intimidation, violence, and often
the killings of innocent Jews all over the world, in particular Israeli Jews.
The academia intentionally eclipsed the Zionist position by either being
indifferent or silent when false and outrageous accusations are leveled
against Israel, or by directly excluding pro-Israeli professors from professional organizations and conferences; by rejecting and ignoring their research, and most significantly, by verbal intimidation—a contemporary form
of an intellectual pogrom. Finally, it is worth remembering that in the late
1930s Harvard University's newspaper *The Crimson*, published articles
supportive of Nazi Germany and its policies. The university also hosted
Nazis officials (Ernst Hansfstaengle and the navel officers of the *Karlsruhe*),
and sent Harvard students to German universities that discriminated and
expelled Jewish professors and students.[11]

Such misguided behavior by learned individuals during the conflict with Nazism is similar to the behavior by like individuals to the conflict with radical and militant Islam. Respectable universities invite individuals with innocent Jewish blood on their hands to lecture and develop Middle-Eastern centers and foundations. The latter, we now know, are raising money for terrorist groups that kill innocent Israelis. They celebrate as diversity and free-speech the brain washing of unsuspected and impressionable young minds with conspiracy theories about America, Zionism and the Jews.

What explains the academia's consistent failure to understand historical events and their realistic dangers, as well as the permanent existence of old fashion anti-Semitic sentiments among its ranks? I suggest that it is a conscious or unconscious attachment to an intellectualistic universe. As such, it is subject to what William James called The Sentimentalist Fallacy. Here the intellectual "sheds tears over abstract justice and generosity, beauty, etc … (but) … never knows these qualities when … (she) … meets them in the street, because the circumstances made them vulgar."[12] The liberal character of the academician reflects the traditional Platonic position of the escapist who, instead of starting her inquiry from the actual conditions under which we live, begins with abstractions. And, when the empirical world of plain men and women fails to conform to these abstractions, she complains that the world is not how it should be. The next step is failure of nerve, followed by blame and scapegoating.

In this book I also address the "Holocaust Establishment," its various institutions, and the numerous scholars who appointed themselves the guardians of Holocaust memory and historiography. While their intentions are usually noble, they are no match for the corruption of creative thinking and progress that inevitably engulfs every organization and its bureaucracy. They make dialogue and open inquiry difficult for average survivors or their children to whom the event truly belong. It should be clear to the reader that this book was not written for personal self-glorification or academic recognition, but in order to correct an historical record and because there is no one else to write it. The task of retelling the story of the true leader of the Treblinka Revolt was left to me. I wrote the book in order to insure that my grandfather's name and heroic actions, as well as other forgotten names of the Treblinka Revolt, will become a permanent part of Holocaust historiography. The argument of this book should serve as a warning and a reminder to professional Holocaust scholars and institutions that the event still belongs to the victims and their families.

Finally, the book addresses the issue of courage and heroism. All things being equal, I agree with Woody Allen that courage is the single most significant quality of character and personhood. Courage tests the authenticity of the person's existential foundations as opposed to his mere verbal and cognitive commitments. To be politically on the left, for example, means much more than just the views one expresses verbally or even the way one lives his private life. It means that the lives of others and the actual lived quality of one's surroundings were affected by one's total character, by the fact that one lived among others. As an academician I am surrounded by people who think of themselves as liberals, progressives, left-wing, and open-minded; they all believe that some genuine human values are contained in the thoughts of Karl Marx. Yet, their actual lives are far from being consistent with such values. For the most part, they all live a small capitalistic life with private property(s) and a sense of intellectual and social elitism. While they intellectually champion the working men and women, they have no clue or insight into the redemptive nature of actual physical labor. Their social involvement is tokenistic at best and their narcissism would have made Max Stirner proud.

Courage, on the other hand, is the quality of character that makes it possible for the ideational function of the person to "connect" with one's muscles, i.e., in Martin Buber's term, to speak as a "whole person." To be politically on the left, to see the value and beauty of the working-class, to be Jewish, to care for others and the environment, *to be human*, to have courage, must cash itself empirically and change existing conditions. To give-up private property as the early members of the Israeli kibbutz did in order to live a genuinely shared existence, this takes courage. To give-up your safe and protected life abroad and volunteer to risk your life for the collective, as hundreds of thousands of Israelis did during the 1973 Yom-Kippur War, this takes courage. To stand-up to authority when they are wrong, no matter what the personal and political costs are, this takes courage.

Unfortunately, I haven't encountered too many acts of courage among my academic colleagues. It might sound strange to readers unfamiliar with post-Holocaust psychology, but I always wonder if any one of my non-Jewish colleagues and friends would have risked their lives to shelter me from the Nazis. Would my students, during my class on Spinoza, have stood between me and the Gestapo when they came to arrest me and refused to hand me over? Would I have the courage if tomorrow the Religion Police came to arrest my gay or atheist colleagues? Would I have the courage to stand with my body and risk it all because this is what it means to be human, or would I shrivel and settle on complaining or writing a "strong" letter to the editor?

Of course, if the reader holds that survival trumps all other considerations and that giving-up on self-interest is a sign of weakness, then the sense of courage I am thinking about would not mean much to you. If the best policy is to keep quite, always be part of the accepted majority, and always think of the bottom-line, then courage to live with one's "whole person" might be a sort of weakness. Indeed, for courage to be a virtue and not a vice, as Aristotle noted, one must always act in moderation. In fighting a war courage is necessary, but too much courage might get one killed and it usually does. Courage is a quality of character that unifies the intellectual and physical functions in a person and creates the very meaning of humanity. To be moved by nature's primitive instinctual energies might be necessary for artistic freedom and aesthetical experiences, but for humanity to live ethically, it must transcend its biology. In opposition to organisms in general, human organisms are not caught in their biology but are capable of transcending it through thoughts and see their own self-becoming. Courage, I suggest, expresses such act of transcendence and separates humanity from bestiality, and since they are both within our capacity, it marks an existential moment of choice in one's life. As Martin Buber so profoundly observed, living a genuine life is analogous to a walk on a narrow ridge in which any wrong step can cost you your life or your humanity. It is a stream of conscious choices between being human or sinking back into the unreflective instincts of animal life. The story of Moshe Y. Lubling's life and death manifest such courage and humanity in its most beautiful form.

In addition to the act itself, suggested Sidney Hook, to show that an individual is a hero one "must present the evidence that these individuals not only existed but had a decisive influence on their respective fields of activity [and] be able to meet reasonably the challenge that if these individuals had not lived and worked as they did, their work would, in all likelihood, have been done by others."[13] In what follows I hope to establish the outstanding nature of my grandfather's heroic life and actions by showing that the two basic requirements above have been met, experientially and logically. First, Moshe Y. Lubling had a decisive influence in his field of activity and second, he was uniquely situated so his work could not have been carried out by many others. I hope that his story, although it failed to be discovered by Holocaust institutes and scholars, will inspire others as it inspired me, my fellow children of survivors, and the new Jewish State.

The life and actions of Moshe Y. Lubling provide an account of extraordinary heroism in the story of the Holocaust that escaped the analysis of official Holocaust scholarship. It is a story that only I can tell, although I might not be the most qualified to retell it. It is the story of my grandfather who between November of 1939, until his death on August 2, 1943 during the prisoners revolt in Treblinka, spoke and acted in a fashion that is rare among human beings. I have lived with this story for nearly fifty years, of which the last fifteen were dedicated to convincing the Holocaust establishment of its significance. I have failed to get their attention and therefore, it was left for me to articulate it. It is with great pain, as well as extraordinary pride, that I have accepted that duty.

My hope is twofold: First, that my observations will promote a re-evaluation of the "official" account of the revolt in Treblinka as it is presented in Holocaust Museums and their endorsed accounts of history. Second, that a re-examination of the relationship between the institutional system of Holocaust documentation and the victims they claim to represent, will take place.

Indeed, the relations between Israeli-Jews and those who perished in the Holocaust constitute a paradigm case for what the distinguished Israeli philosopher Avishai Margalit, called a community of "thick relations." In such a community, the emphasis is on both the living and the dead as they define the lived presence of the nation. As Martin Buber correctly reminded the early Israeli pioneers; a nation or community that is only concerned with the living and forgets those who died in their name eventually "leads an unjustified and meaningless existence [and] deserves to pass away."[14]

Burlington, North Carolina
February 2006

ONE

Holocaust Historiography

The key to working out the program of preserving common-sense realism while avoiding the absurdities and antinomies of metaphysical realism …is something I have called internal realism (I should have called it pragmatic realism!)

—Hilary Putnam

As many thinkers have observed, the Nazi period and in particular the Holocaust, has captured the interest, reflection, and creative imagination of many disciplines. Such preoccupation resulted in unparalleled amount of works in the arts, historical research, fictional and non-fictional literature, poetry, philosophy, pedagogy, social studies, psychology, to only name a few. What motivates many to research and explore the period is two-fold: First, the period reflects the reversal of all that was accomplished by centuries of civilization and moral development; all that was taught and internalized as forbidden suddenly became possible. As identified so profoundly in Nietzsche's work, the bestial instincts that have been repressed for centuries finally overcome their oppressors and received political and even intellectual legitimization. It was a period in which modern and Western political regimes openly violated their social-contract with their citizens by endorsing rape, personal and collective theft, dispossession of minorities, murder of innocence, harvesting of human parts, gas chambers that consumed the lives of millions, open enslavement of others, human medical experiments, etc. Such events will naturally and unquestionably push human curiosity and imagination to its limits. The Nazi period in modern history provides the most recent and remembered period in which the worst of human imagination became a reality.

Second, the enormity of that which was eradicated and lost encouraged unparalleled attempts to record victims' names, stories, and their destroyed communities. As a result, the issue of Holocaust memory became central as the generation of survivors and perpetrators is petering-out. How to keep the memory of the events and their lessons alive? What should be remembered and by whom? Who determines what is remembered and how it is used? Is the obligation to remember ethically binding universally or just by specific communities? So encompassing is the contemporary preoccupation with memory of the Nazi period that Andreas Huyssen correctly described it as "The Culture of Memory."[1] In this regard, the almost surrealistic disappearance of persons, entire families and villages, whole cultures, bodies of scholarly works, libraries, and in many cases the total act of eradicating families' names from human existence still haunts many thinkers. In the Jewish community, some family names and genealogical lines have been completely eradicated from the community's collective memory; it is in fact the literal meaning of being wiped off the face of the earth. The Nazi period, its unspeakable violation of personhood and the total elimination of life, have made Holocaust research and memory one of the most burning issues of our time. How we remember, use, document, and teach this period to our students will determine the moral space of our collective future.

Anyone who ever attempted to research and narrate specific events that occurred during the Holocaust is familiar with the extraordinary difficulties facing the scholar. In my view, there are two basic areas of difficulties in engaging with and writing the Holocaust. The first involved survivors' testimonies and the second involves the method used to write historical narratives. As to the former, eyewitness accounts and testimonies are notoriously contradictory and inconsistent. In nearly thirty eyewitness testimonies of Treblinka survivors that I researched for this book, I observed many contradictions and inconsistencies. For instance, Sonia Lewkowicz, the only Jewish woman that survived the 1943 uprising in Treblinka, argued in her testimony that the prisoners in Treblinka II (the extermination area) never heard about the Warsaw Ghetto uprising, while others argued that the latter inspired them to revolt in Treblinka. Some surviving eyewitnesses of Treblinka accused Capo Kurland and Engineer Galewski (two of the recognized leaders of the uprising) of cruelty and the murder of prisoners, while others described them as leaders and dedicated Jews; some claimed that the gas chambers were destroyed during the uprising and others claimed that they weren't; some claimed that Galewski was the leader of the uprising while others didn't even know that he was part of the conspiracy; some survivors claimed that they witnessed the killing of the notorious Ukrainian guard Ivan "the terrible" Grozny, while some claimed that he escaped and others that he was captured, etc.

Eyewitness Testimonies

It obviously doesn't help the historian when survivors provide accounts that stretch our imagination and put doubts in the survivors' credibility. Take for example Ben Jacobs' account of himself as the "Dentist of Auschwitz" and some of his amazing descriptions of encounters with the notorious Dr. Josef Mengele and Adolf Eichmann.[2] The issue is not whether Mr. Jacobs was in Auschwitz or whether such encounters took place. The issue for the researcher is how to document the authenticity of such events since there are no other eyewitnesses to these meetings or any documents to support such scenarios.[3]

Even more significant are cases in which eyewitness accounts are proven to be inconsistent, incomplete, and right out false. Take the example of Eliyahu Rosenberg, a famous survivor of the Treblinka death-camp whose testimony was used extensively by Jean-Francois Steiner for his 1966 book *Treblinka,* and later by Yitzchak Arad for his 1983 book *Treblinka—Hell and Revolt*—the "definitive" scholarship on the Treblinka prisoners' revolt. Mr. Rosenberg was also a central witness during the 1987 John Demjanjuk's trial in Israel. In the trial he identified Demjanjuk, a Ukrainian auto worker from Cleveland, as the notorious Ivan "the terrible" Grozny from Treblinka. The defense alleged that in early written testimonies given by Mr. Rosenberg, first in 1945 to the Warsaw Historical Institute and second time on December 20, 1947 in Vienna, he claimed that during the revolt in Treblinka on August 2, 1943, he witnessed the killing of the monstrous Ukrainian guard, Ivan Grozny. In his 1945 testimony he wrote that, "We went out of the barracks and fell on the Ukrainians who were guarding us. Mendel and Chaim, who had pumped water from the well, jumped the *Wachmann* ... After this we broke into the engine room toward Ivan, he was asleep then, Gustav, [who] was the first, hit him on the head with a spade. Thus he was left lying there forever ...."[4]

In a fiery exchange during the trail, the prosecution attorney Paul Chumak attempted to establish Ivan's death by challenging Rosenberg's 1945 testimony:

"You wrote this and is it correct?" Chumak asked Rosenberg.

"What I said there I didn't see. I heard," responded Rosenberg, "there is a very big difference ... I did not have a chance to see. My role, along with five other people, was ... to take blankets and throw them over the fences."

"But on December twentieth you wrote," insisted the attorney.

"That's right. I wrote—but I didn't see it ... Escape. This was my purpose. The bullets were shrieking all around us."

But, "why didn't you point out what you did write and what you saw?'
suddenly asked the Judge.

> Perhaps it was a mistake. I wanted to believe and I did believe. It was a symbol for
> us. For us, it was a wish comes true. It was a success. Can you imagine such a suc-
> cess, where people who were the victims could kill their executioners? I believed it,
> and wish that it were so ... It was my fondest wish, I wanted to believe, to believe
> that this creature ... Unfortunately, to my great sorrow, he managed to survive.
> What luck he had."[5]

Rosenberg was not the only one that reported on the death of Ivan during the
uprising, there were similar reports by the survivors Abraham Goldfarb and
Shlomo Hellman. In conclusion, the Judge argued that none of the testimonies was an actual eyewitness account but rather the wishful thinking of
young survivors. As a result, he concluded that the killing of Ivan could not
be proven.

The damage such falsification and inconsistencies inflict upon the post-
Holocaust Jewish community and the historian's craft is severe. Not only
will Holocaust deniers use such unreliable testimonies to forward their cause,
but the genuine project of Holocaust historiography and memory will be
fatally compromised. This amount of damage, furthermore, does not even
start to address the implications such discoveries have on the Israeli consciousness. The latter always had its suspicion about the moral character of
those Jews who went to their death without resisting, like "lambs to the
slaughter." False, inconsistent, exaggerated, and voluntary self-promoting
testimonies about personal acts of heroism only added material support for
this national and cultural trend in Israel. Obviously, some survivors' early
testimonies were merely the bragging of young men and women who
survived the hellish experience of the Holocaust. Such cases only give
ammunition to Holocaust deniers who, by using false logic, can now argue
that if survivors can be wrong (or lie) about specific occurrences, then they
can be wrong (or lie) about mass gassing and extermination.

Consider the book *Fragments*,[6] a testimonial forgery written by Binjamin
Wilkomirski. In its praise, Jonthan Kozol of the *Nation* wrote that it is a
"stunning and austerely written work ... so profoundly moving, so morally
important, and so free from literary artifice of any kind at all that I wonder if
I even have the right to try to offer praise."[7] The book outlines Mr. Wilkomirski's memories as a three and four year-old child, starting in the Jewish
Ghetto of Riga where he witnessed the killing of his father, to his imprisonment in the Majdanek and Auschwitz concentration camps. However, after
the enormous success of the book some disturbing facts about the author
have emerged. According to official records by the Swiss government it was

established that Mr. Wilkomirski was born in Switzerland and has never been in the Jewish Ghetto in Riga or the Majdanek and Auschwitz concentration camps; in fact, he was not even Jewish. Some Holocaust deniers have pointed to the similarities between Wilkomirski's account to another supposedly "fraudulent" book of war time memories, *The Painted Bird* by the late writer and Holocaust survivor Jerzy Kosinski. What is more disturbing, in my view, is the lack of condemnation from the Holocaust research community, as seen in the remarks made by Israel Gutman, the former director of Yad-Vashem. While acknowledging the fictional nature of Mr. Wilkomirski's account, Gutman still argued that the latter "is not a fake, he is someone who lives this story very deeply in his soul. The pain is authentic ... So that, even if he is not Jewish, the fact that he was so deeply affected by the Holocaust is of huge importance."[8] In response to Gutman's perplexing view, Avishai Margalit correctly argued that "a mere act of identification with children in the Holocaust does not establish identity as one of them."[9] Unfortunately, the result of such controversies is that those who use survivors' testimonies to make claims about Nazi brutality and genocidal intentions are now being accused of conspiracy to cover-up the "lie of the Holocaust."

In the case of the Treblinka revolt, the inconsistency between survivors' accounts as well as writers on the subject is especially astonishing. Consider the event surrounding Dr. Chorazycki, the prisoners' physician in Treblinka, who committed suicide in April of 1943 and the consequent torture of the *Goldjuden*. As a researcher, it was never clear to me how and when my grandfather was killed. According to the obituary in the book *Hurban Czenstochow* he was killed during the actual uprising in August 1943. However, in the survivor Stanislaw Kon's account of the revolt, after he initially names him among the original four plotters, Moshe Y. Lubling's name disappeared. Of course, many other names disappeared from records due to the ensuing chaos. At the end, none of the leaders survived to record the activities of the various members. However, a suspicion was starting to build inside me after I read Steiner's 1966 book *Treblinka*. It is agreed upon by all scholars that the Organizing Committee attempted to buy weapons from the Ukrainian guards and bribe others. According to Kon, Dr. Chorazycki was caught with a large sum of money by SS Untersturmführer Franz who demanded to know who transferred the money and for what purpose. Knowing that he was discovered, Dr. Chorazycki attacked Franz with a surgical knife and immediately swallowed a large portion of poison; he died within seconds. The Nazis attempted to revive him but to no avail; his body was mutilated and finally burned.

It was clear to the Nazis that the money could have only been obtained by the *Goldjuden* who had access to the property of hundreds of thousands of victims. The task of getting the information out of them was left to another SS member Küttner, nicknamed Kiewe/Kiwe. At that time it seems completely possible to me that Moshe Y. Lubling was among the men who were questioned. The following is the way Steiner depicted the event:

> He (Kiwe) had decided to continue the investigation at the other end: the origin of the gold. The size of the amount, the round number, and the fact that it was in dollars suggested that it could have been collected by the *Goldjuden*. To make them confess, Kiwe had a plan.
>
> ...Kiwe took the first man to the "hospital," where he had the fire stirred up. When they reached the edge of the ditch, he made him an offer: the ditch or a name. The first man chose the ditch without hesitation. As he fell into the fire he gave a terrible cry, which was heard distinctly in Roll call Square. All the prisoners gathered there had understood, and they looked at the seven others who waited motionless. The second made the same answer, as did the third. Then the last five were led away together. ... On the night of its first battle the Committee had lost eight men, one member, and its leader.[10]

The "one member" of the Committee could have been Moshe Y. Lubling who, according to others' testimonies, was also a *Goldjuden*. However, this account was contradicted and challenged by other accounts. In fact, Steiner's entire book was challenged immediately after its publication in 1966 and later in 1987 as the result of the John Demjanjuk Trial in Israel.[11] Steiner claimed that his book is based on the eyewitness testimony of prisoners who survived the revolt. The authenticity of Steiner's account was also supported by the French philosopher Simone De Beauvoir, who in the preface to the book wrote that "each detail is substantiated by the written and oral testimony he has collected and compared."[12] Also in another introduction written by the historian Terrence Des Pres, he claimed that the descriptions in the book are "as close to the facts as we are likely to come."[13]

Consider the exact same episode as it was depicted by the Treblinka survivor Tanhum Grinberg in his 1945 testimony.

> 'The Doll' was still trying to find out the source from where the doctor had obtained his money. The men of the gold detail had not been present at the time the money was discovered; they were now gathered and received a full measure of beating, but they denied that they had ever had any contact with the doctor. The Germans took the eight most likely suspects, one of whom had indeed been involved in the affair. They were ordered to undress, were beaten savagely, and then were forced, one by one, to do 400 meters of frog-leaps. 'The Doll' accompanied the first one, then led him to the fire ditch and fired a shot in the air; he threatened to shoot him if he would not tell all he knew. Then he left him there. After he had gotten through with the first one, 'The Doll' went back to the seven others and ordered a second man to

do frog-leaps. After they had gone a certain distance, he told him that the first man had been killed, after confessing that not he, but the second, had turned over the money [to the doctor]. The Jew replied that he was innocent of any crime and if were killed, he, too, would be killed for no cause. All eight of them were tortured in this way and they finally met at the incinerator. They were all subjected to additional torture in a similar manner, but not one of them gave away the secret, **and the men were finally released.**[14]

There is no doubt that the two accounts have some converging ideas. First, both suggest that one of the eight *Goldjuden* was a member of the organizing committee, which combined with other information, could have only been Moshe Y. Lubling. Second, both accounts involve the *Lazaret* and some sort of mental manipulation by Franz, 'The Doll'. However, Grinberg's account contends that the eight Goldjuden were not killed but released.

Furthermore, only if the above individuals had been released and later communicated their conversations with 'The Doll', Grinberg seems to have the same problem as Steiner. How did he know what Franz told the first prisoner while he took him away? According to Grinberg and others, they were all standing at the Roll Call Square motionless. It is also unclear what the term "savage beating" means. Can someone survive continuous torture by the SS? And, why did Franz release the prisoners? The Nazis were killing prisoners for as minor a violation as walking in camp with their head erect, or for having an unauthorized piece of bread. Stealing gold and money should have required the immediate killing of the prisoners. Finally, if they remained alive and communicated their conversations, why is it that no one knows who they were?

In another description of the episode by the survivor Samuel Willenberg, he seems to suggest that it was he who delivered the money to Dr. Chorazycki and that the money was given to him by his friend Alfred Boehm. The latter originally received it from the Organizing Committee member who worked as a *Goldjuden*. This fact was never supported by anyone else, nor did Willenberg know where the money originated from. It also seems illogical for Willenberg to claim, on the one hand, that he was deeply involved in the resistance in Treblinka as to be the liaison between the *Goldjuden* and Dr. Chorazycki, and on the other hand, that he had no idea who was the former. Willenberg's testimony can make sense only if he was really a marginal figure in the uprising and the identity of the organizers was concealed from him, as was the case with most surviving fighters.

> The camp authority suspected that the money had been supplied by the *Goldjuden,* and therefore put them through a thorough search. But the Jews were careful and did not let themselves get caught in the trap. Nothing was found on them. All that time I feared for my life, for it was I who had gotten the money from the *Goldjuden.*

> Many of the prisoners knew that I had given [Chorazycki] the money and also from
> where I had obtained it, but our solidarity stood the test and no one betrayed me.[15]

Here we are offered the proposition that the eight prisoners were merely searched, but they were not "caught in the trap." Nothing further is said about their fate as if nothing dramatic has taken place. Also, if others knew who Willenberg got the money from, and that he was the one to deliver it to the Doctor, then why is he calling the individuals "Jews"! And, why is it that no one else ever mentioned that Willenberg was involved in this event? For example, Stanislaw Kon, who is mentioned in Mr. Willenberg's account, in turn does not say a word about Willenberg's claim that he was responsible for getting the money, nor that some *Goldjuden* were tortured or killed. Most significantly, however, he doesn't mention Mr. Willenberg at all in his testimony.

> 'Give me the money!' the SS man roared. He suspected that the doctor was planning
> to escape from the camp. Chorazycki attacked him with a surgical lancet, stabbing
> him in the neck. Franz was able to jump out of the window and call for help. Well
> aware of the torture which would await him, and realizing the threat to the entire
> conspiracy, Chorazycki swiftly swallowed a large dose of poison which the con-
> spirators always carried on their persons. The SS men rushed up and tried to revive
> him in order to take their revenge, but to no avail.
>
> In this way the initiator of the revolt died, but his death did not put an end to
> the matter. On the contrary, it encouraged the others to continue.[16]

Finally, another survivor, Samuel Rajzman, in his testimony does not mention anything about the Chorazycki episode, his suicide, the resulting torture, or the killings and torture of the *Goldjuden*. If everyone was standing motionless in Roll Call Square, why is it that he doesn't even mention that the Doctor committed suicide, or that there was a resulting torture or killings of *Goldjuden*? How can this event, which challenged the foundations of the organizers and the conspirators, be simply ignored? Is it possible that Mr. Rajzman was not aware of the episode at all?

The issue is significant since, for the researcher, it might have explained why Moshe Y. Lubling's name suddenly disappeared from Kon's account. What is the researcher to do when Steiner's account claimed that my grandfather was killed by jumping into the fire pit, while Grinberg's account claimed that he was "savagely beaten" and made to jump like a frog for 400 yards. Furthermore, what is the researcher to conclude by the scenario in which an individual who is starving and naturally weak from hunger and thirst will survive such a brutal ordeal, or will survive and immediately resume the hardship of the camp? Finally, what are we to make of eyewitness testimonies that do not say a word about this episode at all? Is it possible that the prisoners were merely searched, nothing was found, and then released? Very unlikely!

I long ago gave-up hope of ever discovering the truth about the nature of my grandfather's death. Imagine my surprise when I discovered Richard Glazer's 1995 account of Treblinka. Not only does Glazer confirm the role of Moshe Y. Lubling as a member of the Organizing Committee from the start, but he also describes his actions *during the uprising*! In fact, he was not killed during the above episode involving Dr. Chorazycki's suicide but lived until a bullet from a Ukrainian guard ended his life. I will return to Richard Glazer's amazing testimony later.

Such contradictions in some survivors' testimonies led Shmuel Krakowski, another former director of the Yad-Vashem Museum, several years ago, to defend such testimonies by suggesting that "only few" testimonies in Yad-Vashem's archives are false or inaccurate. As anticipated, the question regarding what percentage of the 20,000 archival testimonies is inaccurate became fresh ammunition for a new wave of claims by Holocaust deniers. In a 1986 front page article by Barbara Amouyal in the Jerusalem Post, Krakowski was quoted saying that "many (survivors) were never in the places where they claim to have witnessed atrocities, while others relied on second-hand information given to them by friends or passing strangers…A large number of testimonies on file were later proved inaccurate when locations and dates could not pass an expert historian's appraisal."[17] In a letter to the Editor on August 21 of the same year,[18] Shmuel Krakowski rejected the content of Amouyal's article, but the damage was already done.[19] Aside from rejecting the misrepresentation of his remarks by Amouyal, Mr. Krakowski should have also pointed out that the mere fact that an eyewitness account cannot stand the scrutiny of the historian, does not necessarily prove the account useless or false. In fact, it usually proves the poverty of the historian's methodology which attempts to prescribe an account rather than describing its multi-layer experiences.

Let me make it clear. As a second-generation Holocaust survivor and a native of the State of Israel, I have nothing to do with those who use such discrepancies in survivors' accounts and testimonies to deny the Holocaust or question the reality of its events. Neither do I wish to give Holocaust revisionists any legitimacy by addressing their concerns as if they were ordinary academic or research issues. As an academician, I have encountered many revisionists and I can only conclude that they are driven by an irrational passion and not scholarship as are all forms of xenophobia. Their so-called historical "scholarship" gives new meaning to Woody Allen's description of anti-Semitism as "sub-mental". In their passion to continue the demonization of the Jewish people they have failed to follow the first and basic rule of all legitimate research. That it is legitimate to draw a specific conclusion from a universal proposition, but it is not legitimate to draw a universal conclusion from a specific proposition. It is valid to infer from a true proposition such as 'All ravens are black' that if x is a raven, then x must be black as well. It is not valid, however, to infer that if x is a black raven, then *all* ravens must be black. From the true fact that some testimonies have been found to be inaccurate, it does not logically follow that all testimonies are inaccurate, and therefore, that the Holocaust never happened. However, a genuine attempt to narrate or correct previous narratives about the Holocaust must take such discrepancies and youthful imagination seriously. In some important cases, such as the prisoners' revolt in Treblinka, inconsistent and imaginative testimonies may have denied some individuals' their rightful place in our collective memory.

In the last two decades, extraordinary attempts by public and private individuals and organizations were made to document survivors' personal accounts. The United States Memorial Holocaust Museum in D.C.; the Yad-Vashem Institute in Jerusalem; the new Holocaust Museums in New York, Los Angeles, and Europe; Yale University Testimony Archives; and most notably is Steven Spielberg's Holocaust Documentary Project, among many others. In addition, an unprecedented number of testimonial books by survivors, "vicarious witnessing" by second-generation survivors (as this book), scholarly research, and educational initiatives are produced daily. All efforts to document this still incomprehensible event reflect the enormous significance given by contemporary educational and research institutions to correctly understand its implications and lessons. However, given the reasons outlined above, it is not surprising then, that for some professional Holocaust historians personal testimonies carry very little "scholarly" value. Such testimonies, some scholars insist, are mostly therapeutic in nature for the survivors, i.e., "empathetic reliving."

For professional historians, testimonial accounts present both a wealth of information, as well as endless complications in their attempt to write a correct narrative of the Holocaust and its many specific events. In addition, some Holocaust scholars lack any existential connection to the Holocaust, resulting in a detached form of inquiry based on analytical reasoning and the writings of other historians. Very often, however, their narratives of events fly in the face of survivors' experiences. Like many academic fields of inquiry, contemporary Holocaust scholarship is slowly becoming irrelevant to those who, in their name, the scholarship and the institutions have been established in the first place. As some philosophers have long observed with regards to the positivist's detached approach to the study of human events, it "appears to much of the world as an ash-gray mortician to whom no one in his right mind would entrust a living thing...it employs language others cannot understand, and it works at problems which are such to no one but fellow specialists."[20]

Methodology

The second area of difficulties in writing the Holocaust involves the method used to validate historical representations of past events. It should be noted, however, that it was the attempt to provide narratives of the Holocaust that challenged the academic community and that led to a vicious contemporary debate over the historian' craft. The enormous significance of the event, the extraordinary need to get it right, and the desire to keep alive through memory the lost world of European Jewry, all forced a re-examination of the historian's craft. The debate is over the proper meaning and validity of the profession's traditional understanding of the terms 'fact,' 'representation,' and 'reality'. The feuding parties are, on the one hand, practicing historians who follow the constraints and guidelines of academic research, and on the other hand, those critics who usually do not write history but challenge the validity of the former's project. The historian who writes history shares the traditional realist and positivist philosophical assumptions under which an objective representation of reality is possible, what John Dewey called the "spectator view of knowledge." The historian who engages in metaphysical criticism of practicing historians usually shares in the post-Modernist/Deconstructionist philosophical tradition. The latter maintains that historiography ('fact,' 'representation,' and 'reality') should not be understood as a copy of reality, but merely as "the relationship between past 'reality' as construction of mind in the present *and* in the past."[21] This challenge to traditional historical method of representation is associated with the thoughts of the noted historian of consciousness Hayden White.[22] His argument, it seems clear, follows the revolution in the philosophical realists' theory of knowledge caused by the introduction of Heisenberg's Principle of Indeterminacy. The principle's revolutionary claim was that the observer's irreducible presence (our intentional existence), changes the phenomena to be known. As a consequence, the present can never be known with certainty and therefore, future predictions cannot be known with certainty either. This challenge to epistemology was already observed in 1927 by John Dewey, who argued that as the result of Heisenberg's physical proof of epistemic indeterminacy, philosophy must surrender its "theory of mind and its organs of knowing which originated when the practice of knowing was in its infancy."[23] With regards to historiography, the principle puts an end to the claim that our propositions about the world, in particular past historical events, can "truly" represent reality. The principle shows that the very act of knowing—historiography itself—is an intentional, existential, and interactive activity that modifies "that pre-existing something." As Dewey puts it, "the principle of Indeterminacy ... is proof that the act of knowing gets in its own way, frustrating its own intent.[24]

The implications of the principle, therefore, challenged the very metaphysical and epistemological foundations of the realist' positions which rests on the notion that objective reality, in being independent of the inquiry's operations, is the standard and measure of anything to be known. The realist still holds the discredited view that a mind beholds or grasps objects from outside the world of things, physical and social, rather than that a mind is a functional and intentional participant in the process of knowing, as Heisenberg's principle implies. In other words, the historian as the researcher "modifies that pre-existing something" (the Holocaust), and gets in the way of knowing, "frustrating" the historians' intent of providing an objective representation of past events.

The Philosophical Debate behind Historiography

The writing of historical narrative is a paradigm case for the examination of two central philosophical issues; the nature of our interaction with the external world, and the consequent debate regarding the nature of truth. As the reader can assume, these questions are essential to modern philosophy's metaphysics and epistemology, and to the historian's attempt to represent the past through propositional language that is subject to "truth conditions." Activities, events, and doings, on the other hand, are not subject to "truth conditions" but to "adequacy" conditions. As such, one can not wonder whether the Treblinka revolt was true or false, but only examine what people *say* about the revolt as true or false. Finally, for a proposition to be true or false requires an imaginative correspondence between the proposition and the way things actually are, or in the case of historiography, the way things actually happened in the past. However, imagining such a correspondence, as working historiographers and modern positivists do, involves accepting some seriously challenged metaphysical assumptions and common sense view of existence.

For the purpose of our discussion we may group together several diverse, and seemingly unrelated, schools of thoughts. What connects these diverse perspectives, however, is the shared metaphysical view of existence. As such we can describe the parameters of the debate as follows. On the one hand of the philosophical spectrum is the naïve realist for whom the world is irreducibly dualistic. One realm of existence involves an objective world full of buildings, mountains, cars, etc., and the other realm involves man's inner mind and cognitive powers that are capable of capturing and representing the former realm through language. Knowledge for the realist is a "go-between" undertaking in which direct correspondence must be established between propositions about the world and the external and objective world, that is to say, the world independently of its being known by us. Hence, under such metaphysical structure, the proposition: 'The plans for the prisoners' revolt in Treblinka started when Moshe Y. Lubling arrived in October 1942' will be true, if and only if, the plans for the revolt *actually* started when Moshe Y. Lubling arrived at Treblinka in October 1942. The naïve realist obviously assumes the existence of legitimate means by which one can actually know objective reality. In other words, it assumes that a method exists by which the realist can transcend his/her intentionality in the act of knowing and somehow touch, as it were, objective reality. The latter is to be understood as the way things are prior to them being known by us since the act of knowing "gets in the way" of touching objectivity.

Since the historian always presents narrative in the form of linguistic propositions, such correspondence is necessary if the account is to be considered legitimate. In the case of the Holocaust, the historian will usually look at documents, eyewitness accounts, etc., to establish the truthfulness of various propositions. In other words, evidence such as testimonies and authentic documents furnishes the historian with the realm of reality; the Holocaust prior to its being known by us. The historian will also develop formal methodologies to support cases in which evidence is lacking or involves contradictions in eyewitness accounts or documents. For example, in order to establish and represent as an historical fact the names of the people who plotted the Treblinka revolt, the historian is required to show two "primary sources" naming such a person. Such formal rules for historical research constitute the basis for all academic disciplines and for very good and obvious reasons. As with the practice of Law, one eyewitness account is not sufficient to establish the prosecutor's proposition that x committed the crime; especially if the account can be legitimately challenged by questioning the eyewitness character, whereabouts, and grasp of reality. Hence, Carlo Ginzburg has concluded that "the tasks of both the historian and the judge imply the ability to demonstrate, according to specific rules, that x did y, where x can designate the main actor, albeit unnamed, of a historical event or a legal act, and y designate any sort of action."[25]

What is challenging about the naïve realist's position is two-fold. First, it does not explain how the necessary "go-between" the propositions and the objective world works or even possible. Second, it does not show how ordinary individuals get to know things prior to them being known by us, i.e., objective reality. The first issue involves the assumption about the dualistic nature of existence and the second issue the assumption about the nature of knowledge. The assumption about the dualistic nature of existence is as old as Plato and has been endlessly repudiated. Dualism exists only as a function of language—a distinction in thought—and is not descriptive of actual ontological realities. As Aristotle observed, Plato's dualism was the result of confusing intellectual analysis with ontological facts. The fact that Plato could *intellectually* separate existence into a duality between Reality and Appearance does not mean that existence is thusly divided. With regards to knowledge about history, the issue is not less troubling. To know things as they are prior to being known by us is absurd since it assumes that persons can adopt a "view from nowhere," or a "God's eye viewpoint," as described by the philosophers Thomas Nagel and Hilary Putnam respectively. How does one achieve such metaphysical separation from his natural uniqueness is beyond the framework of common-sense philosophy. It usually involves the acceptance of unsubstantiated assumptions as necessarily self-evident, and the preference to converse only with individuals who also accept as true such basic assumptions about the structure of existence. Such avoidance of critical reflection regarding basic metaphysical and epistemological assumptions in academic research sometimes resembles the unspoken alliance that exists among members of a religious group; all is clear as long as no one challenges the rationality of believing in things without sufficient evidence. As can be expected, neither philosophy nor religion has yet to provide a satisfactory answer to the question: "How do human organisms achieve total separation from human intentionality?"

Contrary to the spectator view of the mind is the anti-realist's position which sees the mind as an intentional function within the world and not as an objective recorder of facts. Influenced by Heisenberg's principle, the anti-realist's conception of the mind leads to a situated or contextual view of knowledge since it recognizes the intentionality of the knower in the representation of the thing known. This side of the philosophical spectrum is represented today by the post-Modernists and Deconstructionists variety. The latter hold that all access to the objective world is blocked and that propositions about the world will never achieve the correspondence that the realist requires for true knowledge. As such, no exact historiography is practically possible. The objective world, or the truth, is forever blocked due to the fact that, for us, the world is irreducibly linguistic (as meaning), intentional, and perspectival. In my judgment, these are warranted and justified claims insofar as they are supported by contemporary scientific knowledge, i.e., Heisenberg's Principle and quantum physics. As we observed with John Dewey earlier, the challenge of Heisenberg's principle leaves philosophy, and the historian's attempt to provide true historiography, as a self-defeating program.

For historians working within this tradition (and there are very few), all historiography should be viewed only as interpretations or personal/ literary "signatures." The extreme anti-realists will not acknowledge that there are fixed realities, facts, and evidence, and would go so far as to conclude that all realities are nothing but linguistic and interpretive accounts. This conclusion, of course, is as absurd as the realist's conclusion that one can know things prior to them being known by us. Both conclusions are unacceptable to common-sense and to the experience of ordinary men and women. This absurdity is shown by the simple fact that both theories were used to challenge the reality of the Holocaust and survivors' testimonies. The naïve realist will demand that claims about the Holocaust ought to correspond with the event itself, although he himself is in no position to know what the event was like "prior to being known" by researchers. Many have challenged the events of the Holocaust by arguing that claims of mass killing and gassing of Jewish victims cannot stand the minimum legal requirement to be establishment as facts of history. Under such constraints by truth conditions, an historian will hardly be able to establish any facts about the Holocaust or write its historiography. Since they must write nonetheless, their accounts are always open to epistemological challenges that ultimately lead to doubt and abuse of history itself.

On the other hand, the Deconstructionist's position that truth and objectivity are forever blocked also supported many deniers' claims that all Holocaust historiography and survivors testimonies are subjective, contextual, and reveals nothing about what actually happened. They are merely personal expressions that only expose the inner and interpretive narrative of the individual. Testimonies, then, should never be taken as propositions which collectively meant to mirror the objective nature of reality. Furthermore, documents will not fair any better under the deconstructionist lens since documents too are subject to interpretations, location, linguistic constraints, and context. Indeed, many Holocaust deniers have used such

26   TWICE DEAD

post-modernists assumptions to challenge and discredit traditional Holocaust historiography.[26]

Such intellectual conclusions motivated the distinguished Harvard's philosopher Hilary Putnam, to correctly admonish his colleagues for holding the position that all philosophical perspectives, assumptions, methods, and values are "just as good as the others."[27] Such a conclusion will negate any common-sense inquiry into past events including the possible lessons that can be derived from them. It will make the very definition of an academic discipline meaningless. Every college professor who received a Ph.D. prior to the post-Modernist revolution will be familiar with the ensuing behavior of its students and young scholars. These are the individuals for whom terms such as 'terrorist,' 'truth,' and 'genocide' are ambiguous since one person's terrorist is another person's freedom fighter; one man's truth or reason might not be another's; and one person's genocide is another person's justified revolution, who is to say?

My personal view of post-Modernist epistemology and metaphysics is analogous to the one I have about religious converts. The latter always seem to be more extreme, more zealot, and more literal in their interpretation of Heisenberg's principle and the new scientific paradigm. First, there is nothing novel in the post-Modernist's position regarding the contextual, contingent, linguistic, and interpretative nature of knowledge. All these issues have been recognized and dealt with successfully through the work of John Dewey and other pragmatists. The reason why post-Modernists and not pragmatists reached absurd conclusions regarding the nature of knowledge is because the former only adopted the deconstructive aspect and overlooked the reconstructive, e.g., Richard Rorty.[28] The interactive nature of knowing ought to viewed as a proletarian activity directed at the reconstruction of daily experience—"as the artist that works from within"—and not as an aristocratic preoccupation with doubting and re-doubting.

Furthermore, that which distinguishes knowing from being ignorant is our ability to categorize and construct methods that channel spontaneous change into controlled changes. More specifically, knowledge is by definition the outcome of our intentional attempt to channel experience, data, information, and intuitions through categories that we agreed upon in advance. Without such an intentional human channeling, all cognitive events will just be a collection of disjointed data that amount to nothing in particular. Knowing, Dewey correctly argued, *is* the consequences of operations purposely undertaken, provided they fulfill the conditions for the sake of which they are carried on.[29] Events that are not subject to purposeful operations, the very constructed field of inquiry that defines a discipline, are merely meaningless movements and processes of natural energies. Even the existence of signs might be controversial since signs (linguistic or experiential) require *something* to be the sign of, and if the sign is to have meaning at all, it requires "operations purposely taken." This acknowledgment might assume the existence of a reality behind the sign—a post-Modernist sin.

The mere intellectualist nature of the post-modernist position can be easily seen when one considers the famous case of Paul de Man, a modern prophet of the deconstructionist movement, a literary critic, and academic scholar. While a young man in Nazi occupied France, de Man worked for the Nazis by contributing anti-Semitic articles for their publications. He moved to the United States during the 1940s and never revealed his Nazi and anti-Semitic past. It was only in 1987 that his past writings and activities were discovered and generated a debate regarding the meaning, truth, and character of de Man's contribution to the deconstructionist movement. The point to emphasis here is that despite all challenges to historical truth by the deconstructionists, Paul de Man, a founding member of the movement, made every attempt to conceal and re-invent his personal history. If post-Modernists really believe that there is no reality as such, no facts as such, no difference between one interpretation and another interpretation, then why did de Man attempt to conceal his *true* past? In my judgment, it is because much of what passes today as serious deconstructionist work is merely an exercise in rhetoric and criticism of existing texts. Its strong association with French intellectuals led one classical American philosopher to label the former's fleshy and sexy approach to philosophy as, "the Liberace of contemporary philosophy."[30]

Towards a Common-Sense Historiography

From the above philosophical discussion it is easy to see the difficulties facing those who attempt to narrate the Holocaust. If followed, both the realist and anti-realist positions would make it impossible for the historian to write an acceptable and coherent account of the Holocaust. But like everything else in philosophy, there is a middle position between the realist and the anti-realist, what John Dewey simply called Naturalism and Hilary Putnam named Pragmatic Realism. Such a position, I suggest, provides the most common-sense philosophical position when dealing with the nature of objects, justification, evidence, and ultimately truth. It is a position that accepts some of the main claims of both positions within a reconstructed and common-sense view of existence. "Genuine Naturalism," Dewey writes, "supervened when the *un-fixity* of human features *under the influence of*

emotion was perceived; when their own variety of rhythm was reacted to."[31]
In other words, a genuine and coherent realist position must be continuous
with the lives human organisms live and the way they interact with the
surroundings, which is always existentially intentional and "under the
influence" of emotions.

More specifically, naturalism requires us to first reject the philosophical
conception of things in-themselves (of objectivity) since, as Putnam correctly
argued, "the notion of a 'thing in itself' makes no sense; and not because we
cannot know the things in themselves … (but because) we don't know what
we are talking about when we talked about 'things in themselves'.[32] It means
that the notion itself is logically meaningless since it requires a perspective
that we do not, and never will, posses. Second, the genuine realist must give
up its attempt to shove aside the ordinary human organism from its understanding of the act of knowing. By ignoring the contributions of the person to
the act of knowing, the realist creates an account of truth and knowledge that
seriously lacks any comprehensive analysis of human intentionality. Truth
comes to be viewed in a way that simply omits the individual's own position
in the analysis or the historian in her attempt to narrate and represent an
historical event.

Truth must be understood and defined in terms that are consistent with
ordinary experience. Instead of viewing knowledge from the universal
standpoint of *truth conditions* which ignores the intentionality of ordinary
people, knowledge should be viewed from the standpoint of *assertibility
conditions*. Here the historian weighs the validity of the narrative based on
how well it is supported by the **existing documents and knowledge,** and not
in relation to the event as it was *prior to it being known by us.* Under such
conditions an historical account can achieve warranted assertibility, but not
Truth. Instead of a correspondence between the written historical narrative
and objective reality, it only requires a correspondence between the historian's narrative and the empirical evidence. If the latter "supports" our
written narrative, then our assertions and interpretations within that narrative
are warranted if only to approximation. Furthermore, by accepting only
approximations of objective reality we are not doing away with the existence
of the objective world. On the contrary, we only wish to acknowledge the
fact that knowing is an intentional activity by the person and therefore,
shapes our final understanding of the world. The fact that we cannot touch
naked objectivity does not negate the existence of such objectivity; it merely
accepts the limitations imposed by the person as the knower.

Warranted assertions are consistent with the kind of knowledge that
ordinary people with ordinary capacities and in ordinary situations have, and

historians are no exception. Knowledge based on "operations purposely undertaken" acknowledges both the researcher's need for formal require- ments of evaluation which defines every academic discipline, as well as the realm of intentionality that is inherent in the historian, the testimonies, and even the documents. Furthermore, for those who wish to claim that natural- ism simply got rid of the concept of truth altogether, we may argue with Putnam that what grounds a proposition as true or warranted is merely "a preconceived idea of what is and is not 'ontologically queer', that is, what is and is not capable of being a part of the world as the world is 'in itself.'"[33] We must also acknowledge, as Thomas Kuhn did with regards to scientific theories, that the very practice of a discipline is theory relative. It does not diminish the historian's process of inquiry into the Treblinka Revolt, for instance, that the account is affected by his own intentionality and methods of inquiry, or by the intentionality of testimonies and documents. On the contrary, **this is what knowledge in human hands means!** Knowledge in human hands is nothing other than the process of inquiry itself with the researcher's intentions, methods, language, and anticipated goals all there to examine. Any other type of knowledge will be outside what is available to ordinary men and women and therefore, belong to "something" trans- empirical. I will leave the reader to draw her own conclusions.

To be sure, however, I am not suggesting that because of the above philosophical difficulties one can never provide an adequate or warranted narrative of an event. What I want to suggest is that for the historian, detachment from the events does not sharpen objectivity, on the contrary, engagement with the emotions, the imagination, the common space, and the interpretations of the events by the survivors; helps sharpen our total under- standing of the events. The existing documents, including survivors' testi- monies should be considered as an "open window" to direct engagement with the event, as Carlos Ginsburg suggested.[34] I also suggest that what happened during the Holocaust does not lend itself to academic "cold- blooded" analysis; not only because the Holocaust is incomprehensible, inexplicable, or inexpressible, as Elie Wiesel argued, but also because it was inexperience(able). Extraordinary cruelty, loss of family members, starva- tion, hopelessness, and the existential knowledge that others will not help, happened so quickly and were experienced differently by different individu- als in the same place, that an objective account is impossible. To demand objectivity in narrating the Holocaust is, as my friend and historian Robert Frey suggested, plainly immoral.[35] Also, Martin Broszat, the noted German historian, observed that the Holocaust does not lend itself to a "unified" historical narrative due to the ambiguous nature of the Nazi criminality (juxtaposing normalcy and criminality).[36] In fact, an "objective" narrative usually violates and negates the actual experience of the survivors themselves. One should remember that there were very few opportunities to report and document actions taken against Jews, especially in circumstances in which no one was left to tell the story. My suggestion is that we understand Holocaust testimonies and text as "events" in which the historian "may occasionally have to study certain important 'incidents' of thought, occurrences not simply internal to the individual mind but ones defined by public and collective dynamics."[37] As with the case of Moshe Y. Lubling's leadership in the Treblinka revolt, the historians failed to study the public and collective dynamics existing during the period among ghetto resistance organizations and partisans. Over and over again, former residents of the ghetto in Czestochowa, as well as former escapees and survivors of the revolt in Treblinka, all knew and reported on Moshe Y. Lubling's actions. The historians researching the event, however, usually ignored this public knowledge and sentiment. For example, all researchers of the Treblinka uprising have suggested that it is not known when and by whom the idea of the revolt started. As I will show later, correspondence with Moshe Y. Lubling started immediately upon his arrival at Treblinka in October of 1942. Through letters that were smuggled out of Treblinka, meeting with individuals who escaped the camp, and survivors written accounts, it is more than clear when and who started the organization of the revolt. Historians, however, again and again ignored this public dynamic and relied only on "official" testimonies voluntarily provided to commissions of inquiry and research institutions. As we observed earlier, such volunteerism does not necessarily guarantee the accuracy of the testimony.

My intention in raising the issue of survival testimonies, however, is to suggest that writing the Holocaust's history presents unique challenges to the historians and the institutions because only the survivors know what really happened to them. Sadly enough, in many cases these challenges were not met properly by the historians' community. In part it was due to the impersonal nature of the Holocaust researcher, and in part it was due to bad research methods that ignored existing documents and public dynamics. Finally, it was due to strict and formal research rules that at times are inappropriate in documenting such an event. The historian, Benjamin Nathans, describes his craft, among other things, as an attempt at "detaching oneself from the historical actors, their categories and claims, interpretations, and obsessions, and arriving at one's own analysis of causation and meaning."[38]

While the historian's craft is a noble one, it clearly presents some serious philosophical, intellectual, and moral difficulties. The attempt to detach oneself from the actors' categories and obsessions in order to, "arrive at one's own analysis of causation and meaning," is nothing short of a philosophical act of suicide. Such an attempt echoes the philosopher C.L. Stevenson's erroneous admonishing that engagement endangers objectivity, and supports John Dewey's claim that objectivity is actually "sharpened" by continuing attention to exigent social and moral realities. The noble craft of the historian, I suggest, ought not to be the imposition of a "detached" view of history over the categories, interpretations, and obsessions of the historical actors. Rather, such categories of thinking, interpretations within a particular language and period, and the obsessions of emotions and feelings, are all there as history. The illusion of an "objective" account supernally imposed upon the actors (in our case they are living Holocaust survivors), is metaphysical nonsense and belongs to a long Western pre-occupation with truth and certainty. In practice, it is an elitist intellectual engagement that imposes an artificial account upon the survivors, their families, and the event itself. It is a practice that rejects discovery through the layers of experiences and texts in favor of consistency of logic and the aesthetics of a well structured account. The Holocaust was many things but it was never structured, logical, and rational.

Historical accounts, I suggest, ought to be what all forms of expressions are, that is, a reaction to the world guided by a perspective, method, and pre-reflective intentions. Its final goal ought to be to inspire further inquiry, and not to settle questions about the "true" nature of reality. Let the inquiry and its stated methodology be the account itself and let the evidence provide warranted support rather than proofs. A fixed method for historical inquiry should not be imposed in cold-blood upon all historical events and periods. Holocaust historiography cannot be a matter of merely calculating the number of primary sources in order to establish something as an historical fact. Drawing such a distinction in the area of ethical analysis, John Dewey argued that deliberation or analysis, like ordinary life, cannot simply be "a cold-blooded setting down of various items … and then striking an algebraic balance." On the contrary, "deliberation is dramatic and active, not mathematical and impersonal; and hence it has the intuitive, the direct factor in it.[39] The same understanding should also guide the writing of historical narratives; it should not be an "algebraic" process in which events or persons are being written off the pages of history for technical or methodological reasons. The historian should also be intuitive and recognize the "public dynamics" and the dramatic nature of the event itself. The historian should not function as the ultimate judge for historical representation but only function as the judging-inquirer.

In giving up the spectator view of knowledge it becomes very important to understand what is involved in experiencing/knowing a thing as belonging to the past. In other words, from the agent's point of view to assert that things exist prior to encounter (not prior to knowing them) is to rely on what is given to the agent in the immediate experience. Things in the past are never experienced directly, we only experience or know immediate things as things *that belong to the past*. There is clearly an intellectual element involved in experiencing or knowing objects as belonging to the past. When we point to the remnants of Treblinka and say, "mass killings took place here," surely what we mean by that is not that we are experiencing the past, but rather that our immediate experience or knowledge is informed in such a way that we experience or know what happened in Treblinka as belonging to the past. Indirect information about the existence of the camp, as well as memories and mental images, become part of the intellectual elements that are involved in the experience of the camp.

All knowledge is acquired as a direct result of inquiry and not by constructing theoretical maps that suppose to mirror reality. Knowledge is a function in the total interaction between the organism and the environment, not the act of peeling away the layers of appearance until true reality reveals itself. The knowledge that we acquire through inquiry where the intentionality of the human organism is acknowledged, is always purposeful and functional. This is what knowledge means for agents like us, absolute and unaffected knowledge is only available to God or individuals with privileged access to the former. From the standpoint of ordinary experience in which unaffected interactions are impossible, neither an objective position nor a mirroring activity can be accomplished. When historiography gives up its notion of representation as a mirroring activity, the special problem concerning the relation between thought and reality, theory and reality, or how words "hook onto" the world disappear. The relation is not that of "mirroring" but one between thought as an eventful function and the continuous changing nature of the environment. Historiography ought to be viewed as a process of inquiry that can establish warranted assertions and approximated truths. If historiography continues to insist that its narratives must "correspond" to things before they are being known by us, then it defeats its own best efforts in representing the past. Nor are we going to be successful if we consider historiography as merely a web of linguistic meanings and systems without any connection to an objective reality, thereby negating the very notion of knowledge by discipline.

In the next chapters I will narrate the life and death of my grandfather Moshe Y. Lubling, a Treblinka Revolt leader, as a human expression that can only be provided by a proud grandchild. As such, my narrative does not only acknowledge the unique perspective that motivates the narrative but celebrates it; it is one layer of experience in the general inquiry into this important event in Jewish history. However, my account of the Treblinka Revolt is also heavily grounded in the existing documentation available to all researchers of the prisoners' uprising, as well as documents that are presented for the first time in connection with the uprising. More specifically, the latter documents establish a direct relationship between the Workers' Council, the precursor of the Jewish resistance organization in the ghetto of Czestochowa, and the Organizing Committee of the Treblinka Revolt. My goal is not to settle the questions involved in knowing the past but only to inspire further inquiry.

TWO

Twice-Dead

Moshe Lubling, the former chairman of the Workers' Council in Czestochowa, established the revolt's Organizing Committee, and this is how the idea for an armed uprising in Treblinka was born ...The idealistic and practical organizer of the uprising, Moshe Lubling, fell in an heroic struggle in the camp during the uprising.
—Dr. Binyamin Orenstein, *Hurban Czenstochow*

On January 20, 1942, the Wannsee Conference met to determine the policy for the total destruction of European Jewry by the Nazi regime. The outcome of the policy came to be known as the Final Solution to the Jewish Problem in Europe. In Nazi Occupied Poland the Final Solution was organized under the name Operation Reinhard. In implementing the operation the Nazis built several death-camps north of the largest concentration of Jews in Poland; Czestochowa, Lodz, Lublin, Warsaw, Bialystok, and many others. These camps came to be known as Belzec, Sobibor, and Treblinka. The latter death-camp was erected next to the agricultural Polish town of Malkinia; in fourteen months of operation it systematically murdered nearly one million Jewish men, women, and children. It is important to remember that Treblinka was not a concentration camp but purely a factory of death. Thousands of Jews were transported to Treblinka from as far as Greece and were processed through an execution assembly-line in a matter of hours. The distinction between a concentration or labor camp and death camp was not always made clear when scholars reflected on the responsibility of the prisoners in the actual process of killing.[1] In concentration or labor camps the prisoners had a chance to survive and they were not necessarily involved in the process of killing other prisoners themselves. In death camps like Treblinka, however, there was hardly any work assignment that was not directly involved in the killing process. The prisoners built the camp, the gas chambers, the guards' barracks, the watchtowers; they unloaded the trains, cut the prisoners hair, dragged the bodies from the gas chambers, extracted the victims' gold teeth, sorted the victims' possessions, packed the possessions for shipment to Germany, and assisted in burning the "bodily" evidence. The conditions under which prisoners in concentration or labor camps lived, although hellish enough, were not the same as the ones under which the prisoner lived in a death-camp. This difference should be kept in mind as we continue with our analysis of Treblinka and the prisoners' revolt on Monday, August 2, 1943.

The construction of the camp started in April 1942 with the help of both Polish and Jewish slave laborers. We know that the murder of Jews started even during the construction work period; not a single Jew who worked on the site survived.[2] The camp started its operations on July 23, 1942, and by September of the same year an estimated 310,000 Jews were murdered, mostly from the Warsaw area. It should be noted that the gas chambers in Treblinka used Carbon Monoxide and not Zyklon-B poison to murder the Jewish victims; the result was a slow and painful death, up to 45 minutes of agonizing suffocation. Much of the operation was supervised by Ukrainian guards who exchanged their status from prisoners of war to Nazi- camp guards. Their unique hatred of the Jews, in addition to their basic brutish character, inflicted endless misery on the Jewish victims. Among the Ukrainian guards in Treblinka was the previously mentioned Ivan "the Terrible" Grozny. Together with Nicolas, another Ukrainian guard, they were known to stand at the entrance of the gas chambers with dogs and a big knife; the dogs were trained to lock their Jaws on the males' genitals while Ivan used the knife to cut women's breasts off when they were pushed into the gas chamber. Through deception and brutal force, Jews from all over Poland, as well as Jews from France and Macedonia, were deported to Treblinka until the summer of 1943 when the camp was burned down during the Jewish prisoners' uprising.

Our case then, involves the above famous prisoners' revolt in the death-camp Treblinka in Poland on August 2, 1943. We know that around 600–700 prisoners existed in the camp during the uprising. The prisoners were divided into different groups that carried different responsibilities in the process of killing. There were the "Blues" who worked near the ramp when transports arrived at the camp. Their job was to clear the dead bodies inside the trains and unload their belongings; the "Reds" assisted in processing the victims by taking their clothes under the deception that next they will be ordered to take a shower; the *Lumpenkommando* (Commando of Clothes) were in charge of sorting the clothes of the victims into separate piles; the *Goldjuden* were responsible for collecting and sorting the money and precious valuables left in the sorting area by the victims; the *Tarnungsgruppe* workers' job was to help with the camouflage of the camp's barbed wire fences; the "Yellows" included professional Jews such as carpenters, physicians, etc.; the "Potato Commando" was in charge of the supplies of potatoes stored in the camp; and the "Court Jews" served the immediate needs of the Nazis in the camp. There were also groups of "professional" Jews working in the extermination camp (Treblinka II), extracting gold teeth and burning the bodies.

On Monday, August 2, 1943, a selected group of around 60 prisoners led by four or five plotters attacked the Ukrainian and SS guards and succeeded in burning most of the camp down. Of course, by that time, nearly a million Jews have had been exterminated in Treblinka; among them were Moshe Y. Lubling's family. From the existing 600–700 prisoners around 200–300 survived the uprising, however, most were either killed or captured by Polish peasants, returned to Treblinka and were later gassed in the nearby camp of Sobibor. In the end, around 40–70 prisoners survived and lived to tell the story. The number of the survivors also includes prisoners who escaped Treblinka before the uprising. To the best of my knowledge there are no more than 27 to 30 survivors who experienced the death-camp Treblinka and provided eyewitness testimonies. Some eyewitness accounts were submitted to the Jewish Historical Institute in Warsaw, Poland, some were written as articles in newspapers and magazines, some as books, some as testimonies in Nazi trials, and others as interviews conducted by different Holocaust Institutions.

On May 10, 1945, the Polish-Jewish newspaper *Dos Naye Lebn* (New Life) in Warsaw published an eyewitness account of the Treblinka revolt by Stanislaw Kon. Mr. Kon was involved in the organization of the revolt and succeeded in escaping during the ensuing chaos and ultimately survived the war. Mr. Kon arrived in Treblinka on October 1, 1942, only two months after it started its killing operation on July 22, 1942. By October, the majority of all previous prisoners that assisted in the process of killing the Jews of Warsaw were also executed by the Nazis. Only a few prisoners remained, most notably among them were Dr. Chorazycki, the camp physician, and Kurland, the Capo of the *Lazaret*, both from Warsaw. Starting on September 22nd 1942, with the transports from Czestochowa and its surrounding areas, a prisoners' work force of 1000 to 1500 prisoners were kept alive mostly from the above area. As part of Treblinka's second commandant Franz Stangl's diabolical plan of turning Treblinka into an independent moral universe, the Germans decided not to continuously kill the workers after the end of each transport. They started to keep a permanent and experienced working force that was controlled and led by Jewish Capos and foremen.[3] The arrival of Kon in Treblinka on October 1, 1942, therefore, marks the first time in which prisoners were kept alive and were able to start organizing the uprising. In other words, Kon was there from the beginning of the organizing activities and was privileged to the planning and execution of the revolt in 1943. In his famous and often cited account of the Treblinka revolt he writes the following:

> After the gruesome experiences of the day, the four plotters of the revolt met by night around his (Dr. Chorazycki's) plank bed and discussed the plans. Their first problem was how to get hold of weapons and explosives which were needed. The four men were the above mentioned Dr. Chorazycki, the Czech army officer Zelo— a Jew, of course, Kurland from Warsaw and Lubling from Silesia.[4]

Several points should be made immediately. Neither Mr. Kon nor any other survivor of the Revolt knew the full names of any of the organizers. No one knew what Dr. Chorazycki's first name was or even the well mentioned Capo Kurland's first name; Zelo is a partial name, as well as "Lubling from Silesia." It is believed that the doctor's first name was Julian and Kurland's first name was Zev. We now know that Zelo's last name was Bloch and Lubling's first name was Moshe. In the camps, the identity of individuals was often marked by their places of origin, profession, or physical features. This fact is significant since it allows the historian to understand some of the modalities of relations that existed among the prisoners in Treblinka. For Mr. Kon to be in Treblinka for eleven months, to be directly involved in the planning and execution of the revolt, and not to know the full names of those with whom he organized the revolt means that such information was restricted for obvious security reasons. As we will show later, from among the 60 revolting prisoners, not a single individual either knew all the others, or more than one or two partial names of the "Organizing Committee." Some participants in the uprising such as Samuel Willenberg knew Engineer Galewski (no first name) but did not know that he was a member of the "Organizing Committee."[5] Such lacunas, furthermore, are present in all survivors' accounts of the Treblinka Revolt, as well as in all later narratives and interpretations.

The problem with historical scholarship, and the very notion of being *killed twice*, can be seen immediately when one reads the introduction to the 1979 Alexander Donat's book, *The Death Camp Treblinka—A Documentary*. In a reflective mode Donat writes:

> We see them all in their grim, macabre heroism: the physician from Warsaw, Dr. Julian Chrazycki, the heart and brain of the revolt, who unhesitatingly offered his life when he was discovered by Kurt Franz; ...Zev Kurland , the tragic kapo of the

Lazaret, to whom the plotters made their vow of secrecy and who, under cover of darkness, tearfully recited the mourner's Kaddish for the countless victims of the day; the heroic Czech officers Zelo Bloch and Rudolf Masarek, the military brains of the conspiracy... [6]

What Happened to the heroic and tragic death of "Lubling from Silesia"? Who was he? How did he become, according to Kon, a member of the original four plotters of the revolt? Why didn't anyone attempt to find out? Is it because no one was left from his family to report on his life and death? Is it because no one in Treblinka knew him either before or after the revolt? For the sake of narrating the Holocaust, if you undertook to understand the only successful act of resistance by Jews during the Holocaust, wouldn't you be interested in such a person whose life and deeds can be of significance in understanding the revolt? Do we know whose idea it was to organize the committee and the resistance? Is it possible that it was Mr. Lubling from Silesia? After all, individuals who participated in the planning of resistance against the Nazis were no ordinary individuals. In fact, other than Jews, the only other group that staged armed resistance against the Nazis in the camps was that of Soviet prisoners of war. The latter were both militarily trained and ideologically motivated against fascism and capitalism. These Jewish individuals who revolted usually shared some of the characteristics of the Soviet prisoners and in the entire account of Jewish resistance to Nazi persecutions only a handful of individuals are mentioned. Although many of the Zionist leaders in Eastern Europe escaped the Nazi occupation, their trained followers and youth movements carried on the practical vision of secular and political Zionism.[7] They were mostly military trained, socialists, and motivated by a vision larger than their concern with immediate survival. Such few individuals succeeded in maintaining a degree of rationality and courage that escaped many within the torturous reality of the death-camp Treblinka.

While it is true that exceptional circumstances creates or brings forward exceptional individuals, even such individuals' ability to lead other men was not created *ex-nihilo,* that is, out of nothing. It is a failure of historiography not to look into the logical process through which such exceptional individuals traveled in order for the account to make logical sense. Seventeen year-old prisoners, no matter how brave they were under the circumstances, could not have organized and maintained the passion and energy for revenge in Treblinka for over a year. As we can see in almost all accounts of Jewish resistance to Nazi prosecutions, the leaders indeed were members of ideological movements, in particular, Zionist ideology. Such individuals were trained from childhood to become leaders and usually were involved in acts of organized resistance before their arrival to Treblinka.[8] However, not much was researched into the backgrounds of the Treblinka revolt leaders, in part because no information was available and in large part because the historians didn't do their job well. Most accounts seem to describe the revolt and the energy it took to keep the spirit and concentration alive for over a year, as a magical or at best spontaneous event. Individual acts of revenge were spontaneous but not the organization of a revolt against the overwhelming power of the Nazi run death-camp Treblinka. It is estimated that on a regular basis there were around 150 armed guards in Treblinka against 700–1000 traumatized, starving, and unarmed Jewish prisoners. Three times a day during roll-calls, prisoners could have been selected to die in the "field-hospital" at the hands of the Nazis and at times, even by their fellow prisoners. In more vivid terms, every eight hours, three times a day, every day, you were subject to selections that could have ended your life immediately. In response to such pressure, one can either become indifferent and welcome death by injection or commit suicide. Very few kept their reason together through three roll-calls a day, continuous starvation, loss of family members, total humiliation, and impossible work.

The difficulties in extracting a coherent account of the plotters' activities are also due to the fact that very few individuals survived the revolt in Treblinka, and even fewer survived who possessed any knowledge of the inner workings of the revolt plotters who didn't survived the revolt. Who would make sure that their lives and heroic deaths would not be forgotten by those who survived? How does one account for the lack of academic integrity when a major research work on Treblinka, such as Alexander Donat's, can print Stanislaw Kon's account of the revolt in full, including the reference to Lubling from Silesia, and yet not mention Lubling's name in the body of the work, or attempt to find out who he was? This negligence is reflective of all research on the revolt in Treblinka.

A month after the publication of Mr. Kon's account of the Treblinka revolt in *Dos Naye Lebn,* a typed and signed copy of the account was submitted to the *Zydowski Instytut Historyczny W Polsce* (The Jewish Historical Institute in Warsaw, Poland). The institution's archives contained a handful of eyewitness accounts of the revolt in Treblinka that were submitted immediately after the end of the war. Every major research work on Treblinka used the above institute as their main research source, in particular, the works done by Jean-Francois Steiner's 1966 *Treblinka*, Alexander Donat's 1979 *The Death Camp Treblinka: A Documentary*, Yitzhak Arad's 1983 *Treblinka—Hell and Revolt*, as well as more general works on Jewish resistance during WWII such as Isaiah Trunk's 1979 *Jewish Responses to*

Nazi Persecution and 1974 Reuben Ainsztein's *Jewish Resistance in Nazi-Occupied Eastern Europe.* In all cases, the authors make reference to Mr. Kon's testimony as one of their main sources, yet neither makes any reference to "Lubling from Silesia" which is contained in Kon's account. What made researchers of Jewish resistance during the Holocaust decide that it would make no difference to our collective understanding of the Treblinka revolt if Mr. Lubling was simply omitted from the account? Why would Yitzhak Arad, a former general in the Israeli army, a former partisan, and the former director of Yad-Vashem Holocaust Museum and Research Institute, ignore the reference to Lubling from Silesia? After all, the very existence of the Yad-Vashem institution is based on creating a home for the names of those who died in the Holocaust. The institution's name literally means in Hebrew, *a place and a name,* and was based on a verse in Isaiah 56:5 that reads as follows:

> Even unto them (those who have no one to carry their names) will I in mine house and within my walls *a place and a name* [Yad-Vashem] better than sons and of daughters: I will give them an everlasting name, which shall not be cut off.

It is then, not the role of Holocaust institutions to "cut off" the names of those who have no one to carry their names or tell their story, the contrary is their role. It is to inquire, investigate, and never let a name be "cut off" from memory, especially when a survivor such as Mr. Kon takes the time and effort to formally testify to the heroic life of a person other than himself. In a time in which all survivors wanted to take credit for past heroic involvement, Mr. Kon's account points to the heroic life of another, and is ignored nonetheless. This selfless act alone should have compelled Yitzhak Arad and Holocaust institutions to find out as much as they could about the mentioned, but not alive, plotter of the revolt in Treblinka. It should also be clear that Arad's work was done while he worked and used the resources of Yad-Vashem, a national Holocaust institute in Israel. His responsibility was not, as Jean-Francois Steiner's was, to himself and his publisher alone. Yitzhak Arad's account carries with it the force of the State of Israel, its national institutions of memory, and its ethical obligations towards Holocaust victims.

Early Voices from Czestochowa

In 1948 the book *Hurban Czenstochow* (The Destruction of Czestochowa) was published in West Germany by Jewish survivors of the destroyed community.[9] Under the article *"Di role fun di Czenstochwer in Treblinka"* ("The Role of the Czestochowean in Treblinka") a long account of one, Moshe Y. Lubling's activities in the Ghetto are described. Can that be the same person mentioned in Mr. Kon's account of the revolt in Treblinka? Those who knew him in the Czestochowa Ghetto and survived the war tell of a fearless individual who not only fought the Nazis but risked his life on behalf of the 8,000 slave workers and their families. The article suggests that Moshe Y. Lubling, through his connections with the Polish left-wing underground, was offered to be smuggled out of the Ghetto the night before the liquidation. He refused and remained in the Ghetto with his wife, two children, and 50,000 doomed Jewish souls. Even more surprising to the historian would have been the description of Moshe Y. Lubling's activities in Treblinka and his heroic leadership in the revolt. Dr. Binyamin Orenstein, the author of the book and a survivor of the Czestochowa Ghetto, writes that Aron Gelberd, another member of the Czestochowa Jewish community who was deported to Treblinka but escaped nineteen days later, "*sztejt in kontakt mith Mojsze Lubling, organizator fun ojfsztand in Treblinka*" [stayed in contact with Moshe Lubling, the organizer of the uprising in Treblinka].[10] Furthermore, Mr. Tzvi Rozenvayn, another member of the Jewish community in Czestochowa who participated in the writing of a later book on Czestochowa, not only testified that the underground organization kept communication with Moshe Y. Lubling while in Treblinka, but that the latter was "the leader of the uprising in Treblinka," not merely one of the organizers.[11] The article also sheds light on the beginning of the organization in Treblinka that so far escaped the researcher's attention. It is the unique role of Czestochowa Jews who were deported to Treblinka in early October 1942, and who previously were among the leaders of the Jewish resistance organization in the Czestochowa Ghetto. Dr Orenstein writes the following:

> After the Jews of Czestochowa saw the tragic reality of the [Treblinka] camp, they started to look for ways out of this situation. All hopes for truth and justice from the larger world were shattered. The dreams that an end to the mass murder of European Jewry will be forthcoming and that the death camp will be destroyed by allied bombing or by the landing of paratroopers, disappeared.
>
> Despite the heavy security in the camp several Jews from Czestochowa succeeded in escaping. Those from Czestochowa were considered experts in escaping from death's nails. Among those who successfully escaped were Aron Gelberd, Fischlwitz, Abraham Bomba, Ya'akov Eisner, Moshe Rappaport, Kudlik, and others.
>
> Gershon Prentki, a public figure from Czestochowa started to organize a resistance cell that later developed into the revolt movement. Despite the fact that he lost his wife and ten year-old son in Treblinka, his spirit was never broken and he remained loyal to his fighting spirit. The first members of the cell were Gershon Prentki, Moshe Lubling, Aron Gelberd, and two others, one from the town of Vilon, Poland, and the second from Lodz. The first three were from Czestochowa.
>
> The cell's missions were: 1) to investigate the camp's conditions; 2) to escape; 3) to look for ties with the outside world. The first consultations took place in com-

plete secrecy so no one would find out about their plans. The reason for the secrecy, aside from the obvious, was the presence of the Jewish camp-elder, a corrupt Jewish engineer from Warsaw, who acted brutally towards the Jewish workers; for every small "sin" he landed 50 lashes. Later on he experienced a re-birth and joined the revolt organization.

The first cell decided to send Aron Gelberd to Czestochowa in order to tell others the horrific truth about Treblinka. The plan worked: Gelberd whose job was to cut pieces of rope to tie-up the shoes of the murdered Jews, escaped after a stay of 19 days in Treblinka. He escaped on October 21, 1942, and after a dangerous journey in which he was hunted and threatened by Poles, he arrived in the Small Ghetto in Czestochowa on November 9, 1942. He joined the active underground resistance organization in Czestochowa and communicated to them the cruel truth about Treblinka. The majority of the Jews still refused to believe the truth of his account.

Aron Gelberd stood in continuous contact with his friends in Treblinka. He sent letters with the help of train drivers who drove the transports to Treblinka. *Following these letters, Moshe Lubling, the former chairman of the Workers' Council in Czestochowa, established the revolt Organizing Committee, and this is how the idea for an armed uprising in Treblinka was born.*

Until the liquidation of the Small Ghetto, eight letters were sent to Treblinka, but because of the difficulties in making contact, only three responses arrived. The first letter from Treblinka to be received by Aron Gelberd arrived in the Small Ghetto of Czestochowa in May 1943 and was written by Moshe Lubling … after arriving to the Small Ghetto he [Gelberd] engaged in technical preparations for revolt. He stood in contact with Moshe Lubling, the organizer of the Treblinka Revolt, until the liquidation of the Small Ghetto.

… New volunteers determined to fight back joined the organizers of the armed uprising daily and far reaching preparations were made. By making a duplicate key to the German armory, the Organizing Committee succeeded in securing weapons, explosives, and gasoline in order to burn-down the camp. In the meantime, the underground organization in the Czestochowa Ghetto was preparing an Aryan identification card for Moshe Lubling so immediately after the revolt he could return to Czestochowa and move freely on the Aryan side.

… The majority of the conspirators did not survive the revolt … *Moshe Lubling, the spiritual leader that in fact organized the revolt fell as a hero during the uprising.*[12]

Indeed, Dr. Orenstein is talking about the same "Lubling from Silesia" pointed out in Mr. Kon's official published testimony of the Treblinka Revolt. I should also point out that the above 1948 document was never read by any former researchers of the Treblinka uprising. The document is significant since it claims that the Organizing Committee in Treblinka was in continuous contact with other resistance organizations on the outside world. It might even suggest that the Organizing Committee was expecting help from the outside. It also means that individuals, other than the prisoners themselves, had information about the preparations for the uprising. In fact, since none of the revolt's leaders survived and none of the survivors were aware of the inner workings of the Organizing Committee, the above document may provide the only insight into the uprising's time-line and plans. Most significantly, however, is Dr. Orenstein's above categorical claim that *"Der idejiszer bagrinder un praktiszer organizator fun ojfsztand, Mojsze Lubling iz gefaln in heldiszn kamf, in cajt fun ojfsztand."* [13]

How did Dr. Orenstein know about Moshe Y. Lubling's involvement in the Treblinka uprising in 1948, while he was in West-Germany in the American Zone? The State of Israel did not yet exist, many survivors were still looking for friends and family members, no "research" was yet done, and no Holocaust institutes existed anywhere. There was no internet, television, or publicly accessible phones. How does a group of survivors from Czestochowa know in 1948 that Engineer Galewski, the Jewish camp-elder, was initially cruel to Jews and that Moshe Y. Lubling was the leader of the Treblinka uprising?[14] Even more interesting, at the same year the book *Kiddush Ha-Shem* (Martyrdom) was published in New York and it includes a 1946 testimony by Y. Dorsman who also names "Lubling from Silesia" as among the leaders and heroes of the Treblinka uprising.[15] Mr. Dorsman's 1946 testimony is even more challenging and suggestive since in 1946 conditions were even worse for communication among survivors. How did he learn about Moshe Y. Lubling? The truth is that I do not know. However, it is becoming clear that "Lubling from Silesia" mentioned by Mr. Kon in 1945 is the same person as Moshe Y. Lubling from the Czestochowa Ghetto who is mentioned in the above 1946 and 1948 accounts. Again, keeping in mind that no internet, public phones, and 24 hour TV news channels existed at that time, three sources that knew nothing of each other in two different continents, point to a one, Moshe Y. Lubling, as the organizer of the uprising in Treblinka. This was not just an extraordinary coincidence, it was established knowledge. Yet, the historiographers of the Treblinka revolt were never interested enough in knowledge that emerged out of the "public dynamics" after the Holocaust, and thereby failed to inquire into the texts of the survivors' collective knowledge. The historian failed to look at the revolt as an "event" that had its beginning before and after the actual uprising. The inquiry should have started with the background and individual characteristics of the plotters and end with their sacrifice on behalf of others.

The Unforgettable Chairman of the Workers' Council

At the same year of the publication of *Hurban Czenstochow* another book, *Tshenstokhover Yidn* (The Jews of Czestochowa) was published in the United States naming Moshe Y. Lubling as a Treblinka Revolt Leader.[16] And in 1958 a new supplement to *Tshenstokhover Yidn* was also published in the U.S. with an astonishing article on *"The Hunger Strike in the Czestochowa Ghetto"* by Tzvi Rozenvayn (a survivor and member of Moshe Y. Lubling's inner circle in Czestochowa).[17] The article is so astonishing that parts of it must be quoted in full.

> Every historian who will ever research the inner life of Jews in the ghettos will have to stop on the very unique workers institution, "the Workers Council" that existed in the time of the Second World War in the city of Czestochowa.
>
> The Worker Council was an illegally organized administrative body that represented more than five thousand slave workers in the ghetto and conducted great social, political, and cultural work among the workers in the Czestochowa ghetto.
>
> Let us recall here one wonderful chapter of that heroic era. The hunger strike that was organized through the Workers' Council and was successfully carried out.
>
> The strike was conducted against the *Judenrat* which had in its possession the distribution of the means for living for the entire Jewish population. The *Judenrat* ostensibly had to care for the slave workers, for those who worked for the well-to-do Jews that had, through a payment to the *Judenrat,* freed themselves from the work.
>
> As someone who actively participated in the societal life of the Czestochowa ghetto, I want to go over those stormy moments of the mass-gathering of the workers on the day of the hunger strike. There, where the bitter complaints and the demands of the workers come to express the causes of the strike.
>
> It was a day in December 1941. Hundreds of Jewish workers streamed into the Maccabee auditorium which contained one of the workers' kitchens. They come after a hard day of slave labor, tired, frozen from the biting cold. Jewish workers from the water work, from the railroads, from Rakov, and other forced labor factories. All have wooden shoes on their feet and paper suits on their bodies, old, torn rags that were once coats. By many, the paper clothes are ripped and one can see their naked bodies.
>
> The auditorium, which can hardly hold several hundred persons, is quickly filled by a crowd of over a thousand. In the kitchen, which distributes more than two thousand meals every day, there is no eating today. A crowded together, hungry mass sits here faint, with pale, sick faces but deeply resolved to win their demands.
>
> First speaks the chairman of the Workers' Council, Moshe Lubling *(who died later as the leader of the uprising in the death camp Treblinka)*. He gives a report on the course of the strike.
>
> He reminds us how difficult it was for everyone to agree on the hunger strike. Nevertheless, everyone knows how difficult, inhumanly difficult are the conditions of the workers. Those that work in the water or laying railroad tracks under the whip lashes of the Nazis, without human clothes on the body, and while being hungry and not eating to satiety, they come home to see the suffering of wife and children. Lubling reminds that there was indeed the danger that, because of the hunger of the workers' families, the strike would be broken. Plain, because the wives and children would hurry to take the piece of thrown bread from the Nazi murderer. The strike, however, exceeded all expectations. None of the thousands of starved workers' families attempted to break the strike.

Lubling also reminded us that the threats of the *Judenrat*, that those who don't take the bread would no longer receive it, did not work. At this remark, the female strikers called out, "we would rather die than break the strike."

…..It surely would have come to serious events if the representatives of the Workers' Council with Comrade Lubling at their head did not arrive right away. Comrade Lubling immediately stood on a table and with his thunderous voice asked the workers to control themselves. And here was again shown the immense influence of the workers' representatives. In the middle of the stormy feelings, when the workers heard the voice of their representative, Comrade Lubling, to calm themselves, it immediately became quite. All listen to his speech.

"Comrades", Comrade Lubling said, "I well understand your feelings and your anger! I want you to know that for a long time before we proclaimed the hunger strike, we already had negotiations with the gentlemen of the *Judenrat*. And we appealed to them to comply with our minimal, fair demands but they cynically rejected all of our words. 'The Gestapo is behind us', they answered us. We will go on with our strike though we know what the consequences may be because of it. *Aside from death, we have nothing to lose*. I ask of you one thing, comrades, in the present, serious moment. And that is 100% worker discipline…[18]

In a further article "Concerning the Workers' Council in Czestochowa", Mr. Rozenvayn replies to accusations made by Liber Brener (a devoted Bund member and resident of the Czestochowa Jewish Community) who in a 1955 article titled "The Truth about the Czestochowa Ghetto" in *Bleter Far Geshikhte* [Pages of History], charged the Workers' Council with collaboration with the *Judenrat,* and that the Council "came into being as an institution with the aim of mediating between the *Judenrat* and the workers and, in such a way, to restrain their anger toward the *Judenrat*."[19]

Mr. Rozenvayn points out to Mr. Brener that "the truth is, as you know, that from the rise of the Workers' Council until the liquidation, this institution was dominated and led by *active members of the Labor Zionists* such as Moshe Lubling…and others." He further points out, that "the chairman Moshe Lubling … and others were arrested many times on the command of the chairman of the *Judenrat* at the time Brener wants to create the impression that the Workers' Council was instituted on the chairman's command." Finally, he reminds Brener that he himself, "together with the *unforgettable Moshe Lubling*, often came to the office of 'Taz' and held conferences…and you were present occasionally. You will certainly recollect our joint worry about organizing medical help for the slave laborers. For a moment, be honest with yourself and recollect our anger then about the members of the *Judenrat* and their wantonness…It would indeed be an act of justice that you print a public declaration and take off from yourself this mark of shame and withdraw the untrue claims that you have made against virtuous Jewish martyrs."[20]

Here we find out that both Liber Brener and Tzvi Rozenvayn were familiar with Moshe Y. Lubling and both knew about his leadership in the Treblinka uprising. In fact, it is possible that both Liber Brener and Tzvi Rozenvayn contributed information for the obituary written about Moshe Y. Lubling in the 1948's book *Hurban Czenstochow*. How did they both know about Moshe Y. Lubling's involvement in Treblinka before any organized account of the Treblinka uprising had been researched or published? Again, it seems that it was common knowledge among those who lived through these difficult days; knowledge that none of the scholars about Treblinka sought or even had interest in. What is most surprising, I must repeat, is that the testimony was given on behalf of another person, a dead person. I would venture to say that when decent individuals choose to single-out another's unique contribution it usually comes from deep respect, admiration, and a deep need to keep the individual's essence as part of the post-Holocaust collective memory.

Again one must ask why, immediately after the war and in different countries and continents, different individuals, all rational and passionate idealists, would take the time to voluntarily provide information about Moshe Y. Lubling's heroic life? They could have easily omitted his name and take credit for his activities. Is it possible that Mr. Rozenvayn's description of Moshe Y. Lubling as "the unforgettable" might have been accurate, and should have been followed-up by imaginative and creative scholars interested in the Treblinka uprising? Doesn't it look peculiar when several different individuals, some who never knew each other, all took the time to single out Moshe Y. Lubling's activities during the Holocaust? What are the chances that within a year or two after the end of the war, and before the establishment of the State of Israel or any Holocaust Museums, these individuals took upon themselves to deceive future Holocaust scholars by referring to Moshe Y. Lubling as the "unforgettable" Chairman of the 'Workers' Council" and the leader of the Treblinka revolt? Yet, omitting his name from Holocaust scholarship was, without doubt, motivated by the scholars' conviction that survivors' accounts are not to be trusted. Not necessarily through a conscious attempt to deceive, but through ignorance of facts and delusional enthusiasm.

Furthermore, in 1956 a major work was published in Israel under the title of *Sefer Milchamot Agetaot* (The Wars of the Ghettos' Book). The book combined eyewitness accounts, as well as first hand accounts of resistance acts by Jews across the Nazi occupied territories. Mr. Kon's account of the Treblinka revolt was translated into Hebrew and was quoted in full, including the reference to "Lubling from Silesia." Also in 1956, the Holocaust

Scholar and former partisan M. Bakalczuk, published an article in the Polish magazine *Przeglad* (Reviews) in which he also named "Lubling from Silesia" among the original four plotters of the revolt in Treblinka.[21] Even more, in 1962, *Volbrom Irenu,* a Yizkor (memorial) book on the Jewish community of Wolbrom, Poland, was also published in Israel with many references to the Lubling family, in particular, Moshe Yehoshua Lubling. The book contains an obituary for Moshe Y. Lubling which is a direct translation of the 1948 obituary published in *Hurban Czenstochow* by Dr. Benjamin Orenstein. The writers of the obituary recall Moshe Y. Lubling as a dedicated Labor Zionist and a founding member and chairman of *Ha-Oved* (The Worker), a Zionist workers' group in Sosnowiec, Poland.

He is remembered as a serious individual who devoted all his efforts to improve workers conditions and was arrested several times by the Polish authorities for his ideas and activities. The survivors also recollected his heroic leadership in the Czestochowa Ghetto until its liquidation on Yom-Kippur 1942. Finally, the obituary points to Moshe Y. Lubling's heroic leadership in the Treblinka revolt. It describes his life in Treblinka as a *Goldjuden* who sorted the property of gassed Jews. It was he, the article suggests, that supplied the plotters with the money necessary to bribe the guards. It was this money that was discovered in the hand of Dr. Chorazycki and that led to his heroic act of suicide. It is also clear that in 1948 these individuals believed that no one was left to remember Moshe Y. Lubling's name since the original obituary asserts that Moshe Y. Lubling's wife and daughter were murdered in Treblinka and that his son Pinchas (my father), died in the Czestochowa Ghetto. In the 1956 book *Wolbrom Irenu* (Our Town Wolbrom), the obituary was corrected to include the survival of his son Pinchas.[22] Finally, in 1967 *Sefer Czestochowa* (The Book of Czesto-chowa) a two-volume Yizkor book was published in Israel in which a Hebrew translation and a revised edition of the original obituary for Moshe Y. Lubling appeared:

Moshe Y. Lubling—Bless his Memory

Born in 1902 in the town of Wolbrom in the Kielce region where he received traditional Jewish education in the *Cheder* and Yeshiva. During the First World War, under the Austrian occupation, he joined the Zionist youth movement Ha-Shomer [The Guardian]. As he matured he joined Poali Zion Yamin [The Workers of Zion Right] where he occupied a central position in different cities in which he resided. In 1929 he was arrested by the Polish police for taking part in a demonstra-tion against the British Consulate in protest of the events in Palestine. During the Second World War, while living in Sosnowiec, he was the chairman of the League for a Working Eretz-Yisrael but with the Germans' invasion into Poland he was forced to escape. In November 1939 he arrived with his family to Czestochowa and, since he had no economical base, he found himself in deep poverty.

In Czestochowa he began to organize the workers, an activity that resulted in the formation of an organization known as the Workers' Council. Moshe Lubling, who was the chairman of the organization, was not satisfied dealing with economical issues alone and soon took responsibility for the organization of the Ghetto's cultural life and the creation of kibbutzim by different Zionist youth movements in Czestochowa. Moshe Y. Lubling attracted around him the radical intelligentsia of Czestochowa from within which grew the resistance movement in the city. As a result of his activities he was persecuted by the *Judenrat* and was arrested numerous times by the Jewish Police. When the first information came about the destruction of entire Jewish communities he called for an armed revolt against the Nazis as a way of saving the honor of the Jewish community. Only the vague nature of the information and his inability to obtain weapons prevented a wide-scale operation. On Yom-Kippur, when the end of the Jewish community in Czestochowa arrived, a last meeting of the Workers' Council took place in Moshe Y. Lubling's house in the presence of the writer Zytnetzki. During this meeting, Moshe Y. Lubling was offered the opportunity to leave the Ghetto and connect with the Polish Underground Movement with which he was in contact. He refused to leave the Ghetto. Despite the fact that during the Aktion he had good chances of staying in Czestochowa, he decided to go with his wife and daughter to Treblinka where he worked in sorting the clothes of the victims. When he witnessed the slaughter in Treblinka he dispatched a letter to Czestochowa where he encouraged the people to launch an armed resistance against the Nazis. Once he was offered to escape Treblinka with a counterfeit ID, but he preferred to stay in the camp in order to organize the uprising. Indeed, at a later date, the revolt in Treblinka took place as Lubling stands at the head of the revolting prisoners in the camp and falls as a fighter on August 2, 1943.[23]

This obituary was published 16 years before Yitzhak Arad published his comprehensive study of the revolt in Treblinka. The book was available in Israel and was surely part of the library at the Yad Vashem institute. The editors and those who submitted testimonies were all alive and available for inquiry and clarification of facts. Furthermore, the account confirms my previous suggestion that leaders of men are not created *ex-nihilo* but have a logical process of self-becoming. These are individuals who can make genuine choices about life and death and on behalf of an honorable death rather than powerless survival. These are individuals who are willing to risk everything, not for the chance of survival, but for the sake of a moral principle. Do we know many individuals who would have twice refused to save themselves because of their unique position and connections, especially under the brutal circumstances of the Holocaust? Normally, survival meant the opportunity to become a witness to the unspeakable crimes of the Holocaust, not the willingness to die for a moral principle or collective honor. It should also be observed that in all accounts about Moshe Y. Lubling, his extraordinary organizational skills are emphasized. From his leadership in Zionist organizations before the war, to his creation of the Workers' Council in Czestochowa in which he organized a successful hunger strike by thousands of starving slave workers against the *Judenrat*. He established contacts with the left-wing Polish National Army, called continuously for armed resistance, and repeatedly refused to save himself. These are, I suggest, the necessary ingredients that logically culminated with Moshe Y. Lubling's leadership of the revolt in Treblinka.

The Last Eyewitness

This conclusion has been recently confirmed again by the publication of Richard Glazer's 1992 testimonial book about the revolt in Treblinka. In his highly acclaimed book *Trap with a Green Fence: Survival in Treblinka,* he identifies a major figure in the organization and execution of the revolt by the name of Lubling (no first name).[24] Not surprisingly, what Mr. Glazer has to say about this person sounds strangely consistent with everything we know about Moshe Y. Lubling's activities, character, and generous spirit. First, Richard Glazer locates Moshe Y. Lubling together with himself and two other conspirators, David Brat and Karl Unger, as they are removing dead bodies after the arrival of a transport.

> The cars have finally been emptied. And now we grab the blankets we'll be using to carry the dead bodies to the 'infirmary.' Karl, David Brad, Lubling, and I carry one blanket together, each of us holding an edge. ... As we lift the blanket, something begins to move. Marshaling every bit of strength she has, a woman, probably middle-aged, sits up. Her undone hair is matted, her entire face smudged and grimy. The expression in her eyes is the worst thing ... 'Mad,' I hear Lubling's strained voice.[25]

Furthermore, Glazer depicts Lubling as a father figure for him and his friend Karl with whom he escaped Treblinka during the uprising. Again, locating Moshe Y. Lubling in the sorting area where prisoners usually obtained (stole) food, he writes:

> 'Well, well.' David's pal, Lubling, walks towards us from his box across the way, a brownish face, sharp features, a little stooped from all the drudgery. 'I don't know this guy. He's probably a real pig. But that boy over there by the stack of pants'— pointing with his hand and raising a single fused clump of eyebrow—'I know him. He's a neighbor, and I know he never saw this much food at home, and out there in life he never stuffed himself as full as he's stuffing himself, here in Treblinka. Not that his family was really poor, but his papa was damned tight, saving up to immigrate, to America, to Palestine. Away from Poland. For this he bought dollars and diamonds ...[26]

After the original plan of resistance failed, Glazer quotes a conversation communicated to him by David Brat. What is most significant about this testimony is that it puts Moshe Y. Lubling together with the other organizers of the revolt, exactly as was testified in 1945 by Mr. Stanislaw Kon and confirmed by members of the Czestochowa resistance organization.

> Yesterday we talked about this [the need to let the world know] in the carpentry shop. Lubling was there, Simcha, people from the machine shop. Then Galewski and Dr. Chronozychi (sic), too. We're going to start over again. Forget Plan H, because we don't know why they sent Zelo 'over there.' All of us here will have to … We know about the three informers, but otherwise every one of us here, every man, must do something …"[27]

David Brat's description of the meeting puts Moshe Y. Lubling in relation to the two or three other major leaders of the uprising, Dr. Chorazycki, Engineer Galewski, and the Forman Zelo Bloch. But not simply in relations to one another, but in relations that involved the conspiracy that led to the uprising.

Now that Mr. Glazer has put Lubling at the center of the "Organizing Committee," he goes on to portray him as the elder and wise leader of the group (he was forty one at the time). Glazer relates a remark my grandfather made regarding the profitability of Treblinka to the Nazis and the Polish residents of the area. "If through some miracle you should ever be able to get out, then you can never let anyone know that you are fleeing Treblinka," Lubling tells us. "They would tear your clothes off your body, piece by piece, they'd kill you, and then they'd probably search you to see if you had money on you."[28] Again, such a remark is consistent with an individual who is in a leadership position, experienced and knowledgeable about the reality of the Holocaust. It also shows the obvious disappointment of the committed socialist at the profitability of the Germans' extermination plan, as well as the low moral character of the Polish peasants living around the camp. He was correct about both; the Nazis used the confiscated property of the Jews to support their military campaign as well as themselves. After the Nazis abandoned the camp, the Polish residents of Malkinia and the surrounding areas dug out dead bodies in the extermination area in search of gold that might have been left on some of the unburned corpses.

Consistent with all accounts of the revolt is the attempt by the organizers to obtain a duplicate key to the camp armory, and according to several testimonies, they were successful. Mr. Glazer was among those prisoners who were in charge of taking out the ammunition door lock in order to make a copy of the key. Again Glazer positions Moshe Y. Lubling at the center of the organization.

> After a while we get the news that the nest has been taken out, Lubling is our contact, and he's working somewhere near the intersection between the ghetto, the SS

barracks, and Ukrainian barracks. Messages and instructions are being carried by whomever Kleinmann sends out, supposedly to go to the latrines.[29]

Locating Moshe Y. Lubling at the area between the barracks and the ghetto, Glazer suggests that Lubling is the contact person for the different working groups in the camp who were involved in the uprising. Everyone reports to him while he passes information to other parts of the organization. Only the most trusted person, the leader and organizer, would have been in control of all the information that passed among the conspirators.

Finally, Glazer takes the reader with him through the hours before the revolt itself, and again he locates Moshe Y. Lubling at the center, communicating with another conspirator, and in a leadership position.

> From way in the front, near the fork in the path, in the direction of the headquarters building, Lubling gives a signal with his raised arm, all the while looking as if he was simply wiping his sweaty face on his sleeve. Kleinmann subtly turns toward Lubling and then returns somewhat more quickly, but still in a very measured gait: 'Listen, from now on we go the moment they make the slightest move to take anyone off to the infirmary or threaten to kill. Not one more man is going to die this way.[30]

This account by Glazer is consistent with others insofar as it correctly describes the unexpected event that started the revolt two hours earlier. As we will see later, two young prisoners were caught in the barracks when they should have been elsewhere. The prisoners were searched and money was found in their possession. They were tortured and were threatened with death if they didn't explain their presence in the barracks with the money. From fear that they will divulge information about the pending revolt, the SS officer present was shot by another prisoner. What Glazer is describing above are the moments prior to the unexpected start of the revolt. It is regarding these two captured prisoners on their way to the *Lazaret* that Glazer quotes Kleinmann saying: "...we go the moment they make the slightest move to take anyone off to the infirmary or threaten to kill. Not one more man is going to die this way." It also unquestionably confirms Moshe Y. Lubling position in the ongoing drama during the minutes leading to the uprising. His post is visible to others at the center of the camp and he is giving signals to the fighting groups. Glazer continues his narrative and Moshe Y. Lubling again emerges not merely as a central figure but as the revolt leader.

> ... 'You,' Kleimann turned towards me, 'go up the barracks with some lumber and other supplies. Act as if you're looking for another saw, and on the way, tell Lubling and the others that things are still under control down here.'
> ...A nod is enough for Lubling to understand that everything's o.k. Rudi must already have emptied the pigeon houses that stand at the fork in the path leading in

one direction to the ghetto, and in the other to the SS barracks. He's probably carrying the hand grenades with him.[31]

Kleinmann, the commander of one of the fighting units, reports to Lubling and "the others" that everything is still under control. Moshe Y. Lubling is the leader for whom "a nod" is enough to understand the situation and communicate with other leaders. The fighting started between 2:45–3:45pm, although it was originally scheduled for 4:45pm on Monday, and Glazer's fate again meets with Moshe Y. Lubling. This time, however, it was Lubling who saves his life and that of his friend Karl Unger. Glazer writes:

> ...We duck and somehow reach the yard in front of the Ukrainian barracks. There are only a few of us. At a loss, Josek is standing there with his empty rifle in his hands. Herschek is nowhere to be seen.
> Lubling is running along the barracks carrying some kind of pole in his hands and chasing people out in front of him like a gooseherd, pointing to the back gate, which leads out onto the field surrounding the camp: 'Outta here, everyone outta here—into the woods!' The gate is broken down. We run out and across the vegetable field.[32]

Moshe Y. Lubling is running across the camp with a wooden pole and breaks down the gate yelling at others to run into the woods, to possible survival. He behaves as a mother goose making sure her young ones follow her instruction to reach safety.

What is more astonishing is Glazer's claim that despite the fact that Moshe Y. Lubling broke down the gate for the prisoners to escape, he himself did not escape the camp together with the prisoners, but rather returned and ran back into the camp to continue the fight. As Glazer and his friend Karl Unger are resting at night after their daring escape, they reflect upon the significance of the uprising and the unusual significance of the man who herded them out to safety. His heroic behavior did not escape their mind.

> 'Well no roll call today. How cautious will they be when they report to their superiors about what happened in Treblinka? Maybe they'll all be punished for having let things come to this.'
> 'Or maybe they'll just try to cover it all up, the whole barbarous mess. And that'll mean that as soon as we get a little farther away from Treblinka, nobody will know a thing about it. There won't be any reports.'
> ...'And who are we anyway, who are we claiming to be?'
> 'I couldn't tell you now. All I know is that tonight we've got a lot of ground to cover, and then maybe we'll think of something.'
> ...'From what I have seen of these things in the movies, I don't think our little uprising was all that exemplary. Sure, we threw a few grenades into the air and set everything on fire. But after that we just fumbled around and let ourselves be shot at like fish in a barrel.'

'Standa Lichtblau probably accomplished the most by blowing up the gas tank.'

'Always said he wouldn't leave his wife and child behind, on the other side. All the older ones who had come with their families said that. *And they organized the whole thing.*'

'I'll tell you, they were so single-minded, they never intended to escape themselves. They just wanted us younger ones to get out. *There's no other way to explain why Lubling herded us out through the fence the way he did ...*'

'And I never saw him after that.'[33]

As the grandchild of Moshe Y. Lubling, Mr. Glazer's account sends shivers down my spine as he brings alive my grandfather's essence through his memories. The "unforgettable" chairman of the Workers' Council in Czestochowa, who twice before refused to save himself, also did not intend to escape from Treblinka. This is why he herded the young prisoners out of the camp only to return and fight the Nazi and Ukrainian guards. The man who preferred to make a mark on history on behalf of his Jewish brethren rather than save himself is, in my view, the definition of heroism. We must also take into account that only 11 months earlier Moshe Y. Lubling lost his wife and twelve year-old daughter to the gas chambers of Treblinka, as well as left a son in the Small Ghetto in Czestochowa who was still alive. As it turns out, Glazer and Karl were on the mark when they concluded that Moshe Y. Lubling was more interested in saving the younger prisoners and avenging the death of his family and the Jewish people, than saving himself. As we will see later, this is precisely what Moshe Y. Lubling wrote to his son Pinchas in a letter from Treblinka only three months before the uprising that ended his life.

It should be pointed out that the Holocaust presented Jews with some impossible moral decisions that today test our moral intuitions and stretch all our philosophical categories. Whatever difficulties ordinary European Jews experienced during the Holocaust, nothing comes close to the cruelty that was involved in breaking down foundational family relations. We know that in most cases when families succeeded to stay together, they also survived together and succeeded in keeping some semblance of continuity with their previous lives. For a father to not have the ability to save his son, and visa-versa, challenges the very foundations of humanity. Of course, this fact didn't escape the Nazis when they designed the killing process. From Pinchas Lubling's perspective, his father preferred to sacrifice his life for others although he could have saved himself and possibly reunite with him. Pinchas spent four and a half years as a slave laborer in Czestochowa and later was imprisoned in three different Nazi camps before he was liberated on May 5, 1945. Witness Elie Wiesel's brilliant descriptions of such a reality between himself and his father and how it challenged his very being. After witnessing his father being brutally beaten and "weeping like a child" while he "looked on and said nothing,"[34] Wiesel writes:

> 'Son, they keep hitting me!'
> 'Who?'
> I thought he was delirious.
> 'Him, the Frenchman ... and the Pole ... they were hitting me.'
> Another wound to the heart, another hate, another reason for living lost. ...
> they could not stand my father any longer, they said, because he was now unable to drag himself outside to relieve himself.[35]

Despite it all, Wiesel acknowledges that his father's presence was the only thing that stopped him from allowing himself to die. "I had no right to let myself die," Wiesel thinks to himself, "what would he do without me? I was his only support."[36] Standing as we are today, over sixty years after the end of WWII, such a total challenge to our basic instincts is still hard, if not impossible, to articulate. How can a child speak of such things or continue to live with such wounds?

THREE

The Son Survives

It is with a sense of fear that I pass through places of human habitation. I have a feeling that all my experiences are etched upon my face. Whenever I look at my reflection in a stream or a pool of water, fear and surprise twist my face into an ugly grimace. Do I look like a human being?

—Jankiel Wiernik, Survivor, "One Year in Treblinka"

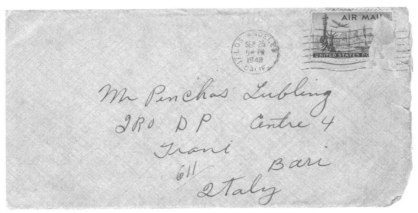

Letter to a Missing Persons' Camp, Bari, Italy

In May of 1949, a twenty-five year old Holocaust survivor arrived in Israel with his wife and their three month old son born in the Trani Missing Persons' Camp in Bari, Italy. The young survivors were Pinchas Lubling and Miriam (Mina) Barmherzig and they named their first born after Pinchas' dead father, Moshe Lubling from Silesia. Pinchas immediately joined the Israeli Defense Forces and later actively fought in the 1956 Sinai War against Egypt. He joined *Harut,* a Labor owned national building company, and started to build the nation his Zionist father dreamed about in Sosnowiec and Czestochowa. Soon after, Pinchas Lubling walked into the offices of Yad-Vashem in Jerusalem and reported the death of his family. His mother Zelda Fisch, his sister Ester, and his father Moshe Y. Lubling, were all murdered in Treblinka. He also reported what he knew about his father's resistance activities in Czestochowa and Treblinka and that he is ready to help the institute in any way possible. Several years later, the Israeli Defense Ministry awarded Moshe Y. Lubling a citation for his active armed resistance to the Nazis in the Treblinka Death Camp.

In his testimony to Yad-Vashem Pinchas described his father's attempt to first escape to the Soviet Union when the war started; his father's activities as the Workers' Council Chairman in the Czestochowa Ghetto; and the last meeting of the Council (by now functioning as the underground resistance group) that took place in Moshe Y. Lubling's kitchen, the night before the liquidation of the Large Ghetto in Czestochowa. He described in detail the liquidation itself, the fate of those who were sent to the trains (including his sister and mother), as well as the work detail that he and his father were assigned to in Czestochowa. A few days later, during a further selection in Czestochowa, his father was taken to Treblinka. The liquidation of the Large Ghetto started on September 22, 1942 (Yom-Kippur), and Moshe Y. Lubling was deported to Treblinka in early October 1942.

Refugees—Mina and Moshe
Lubling, Bari, Italy, May 1949

New Home—Miriam and Pinchas
Israel, August 1949

The Letter

Pinchas Lubling also reported the following event that occurred after his father's deportation to Treblinka: In May 1943, eight months after his separation from his father in Czestochowa, a Polish train driver threw a letter at a group of Jewish slave laborers working on the train's rail-road tracks; the letter was addressed to Pinchas Lubling from his father Moshe Y. Lubling in Treblinka.[1] The letter was written in Yiddish and in the form of a poem so it couldn't be deciphered if it fell into the wrong hands. In the poem Moshe Y. Lubling communicated to his son that he is involved in organizing a prisoner's revolt that will be sure to echo around the world. He assured his son that while he will probably not survive the uprising, the nature of his death, as a fighting Zionist Jew, will be remembered forever within the pages of Jewish history. Pinchas kept the poem in a metal cigarette box sewed into a hidden pocket in his pants where it remained concealed until his 1945 imprisonment in Buchenwald. When the prisoners arrived at the Buchenwald concentration camp they were ordered to strip for delousing. Pinchas was afraid that the letter would be discovered in his trousers and he disposed of it. It was the only thing that was left of his father and the last days of his life. Many individuals in the Czestochowa underground resistance movement were aware of this letter when it arrived at the Small Ghetto in Czestochowa. The letter was delivered to the leadership of the resistance in the Small Ghetto and was read by Tzvi Rozenvayn, Aron Gelberd, and others while Pinchas Lubling was present. Mr. Rozenvayn was a Gordonian Zionist, and as I mentioned earlier, a member of the Jewish underground in Czestochowa, and a former comrade of Moshe Y. Lubling in the Workers' Council. Aron Gelberd was also a member of the underground in Czestochowa who escaped Treblinka after 19 days in October and returned to the Small Ghetto in Czestochowa. According to their testimony, in this letter from Treblinka, Moshe Y. Lubling "urged the people to take up arms against the Nazis."[2] It came as no surprise to Pinchas, then, when in August, 2, 1943, reports arrived to the Small Ghetto in Czestochowa about the uprising in Treblinka and until this day he marks it as his father's official date of death. He was also not surprised to read the testimony of Stanislaw Kon where he describes the Treblinka revolt and names his father Moshe Y. Lubling, among the four original plotters of the revolt.[3] Pinchas, however, was not about to occupy himself with Holocaust politics and instead immersed himself in building the Jewish State. He was the poster-boy for the new nationalist identity movement in Israel and rejected others' over-emphasis on the past. Pinchas was usually skeptical about the attempts by many survivors to paint their Holocaust experience as heroic. From his experience in Czestochowa as a slave laborer, working in place of rich Jews who paid the *Judenrat* to be relieved of hard labor, he had very little trust in survivors' heroic tales. Pinchas saw

Pinchas Lubling during the 1967 Six-Day War

in the survivors' preoccupation with their past an anti-Zionistic and ghetto-like behavior. If other survivors would start speaking Polish or any other Diaspora language in his presence, he would leave the room. Labor Zionism and being an Israeli nationalist stood in total opposition to the behavior and character of many survivors of the Holocaust that didn't resist or share in the hardship of other Jews, and who now engages in creating a heroic past for prosperity. It is, therefore, understandable that Pinchas Lubling was not aware, nor would he have cared, about the 1966 publication of Jean-Francois Steiner's book *Treblinka*, or the controversy it created among survivors of the death camp.

In 1966 Jean-Francois Steiner published his famous account of the Treblinka revolt in France. Using actual participants' names, Steiner failed to mention Moshe Y. Lubling's participation in the planning and execution of the revolt. Steiner, furthermore, by his own admission, relied on eyewitness accounts submitted to Yad-Vashem and the Polish Court of Inquiry. In both cases, the Treblinka Revolt account given by Stanislaw Kon was present and Kon himself was living in Israel. The book *Hurban Czenstochow* in which Moshe Y. Lubling's obituary was published, its authors, and the book's later supplements were all available to read and interview. Pinchas Lubling was living in Israel with direct knowledge of the revolt and other activities, but Steiner did not connect the obvious dots.

Pinchas Lubling never read Steiner's account of the revolt. First, it was in French and second, only a competent account by an Israeli scholar would have meant anything to him. Besides, Pinchas was too busy building the Jewish state, serving in the military, and preparing his two sons to do the same. He was not one to be on top of the activities by various survivors' organizations to document the Holocaust. He wanted nothing to do with those professional Holocaust "handlers" who peddle their stories, who speak their original European languages, and who spent their days living in the past. Despite his father's heroic activities during these horrific days, Pinchas didn't think much of this period as heroic or one that should pre-occupy his new life. The death of his entire family between 1942- 1943 and his continuous attempts to survive alone until his liberation in May 1945, left severe deposits and wounds in this young man's soul. He knew that those who survived did not do so because of their heroism and intellect; it was merely luck, given the enormous set of uncontrolled conditions. He knew very well that those who truly acted heroically, most often, did not survive to tell their story and in most cases had no one else to tell it. It wasn't until the publication of Richard Glazer's book in 1995 that he actually learned that his father "goose herded" the young survivors to safety while returning into the camp himself to continue the fight that eventually killed him.[4]

Pinchas was also aware that his father's activities were directed as much against the *Judenrat* as it was against the Nazis. Despite their common fate, fellow Jews did not always act with kindness towards each other. Pinchas never forgot the long days of slave labor with his father in the Czestochowa Ghetto. They were taking the place of "fat" Jews who paid the *Judenrat* off, instead of sharing the burden with their Jewish brothers and sisters. His father, Moshe Y. Lubling, was not like the others. He never took advantage of his position as the Workers' Council chairman and did not accept the offer to be smuggled out of the Ghetto by the Polish Underground the night before the liquidation. This selfless act was witnessed by others who reported it in *Hurban Czenstochow*. Like the Biblical Moses, Moshe Y. Lubling's selfless act was witnessed by the public and kept as an inspiration through Jewish history. [5]

Bad Faith

Indeed, it is not the place of the researcher to question the morality of activities undertaken under the absurd conditions imposed by the Nazis, but it is surely the right of the survivors to do so. Even under such uncommon circumstances, one can still expect individuals to make choices, moral choices! Like Socrates in the *Apology*, one may die rather then violate the law or disclose secrets that will lead to his friends capture, torture, and death. In this context, one must reflect on the Existentialists' conception of bad-faith—the belief in the absence of choice. The claim by survivors that they had no choice, **if they wanted to live**, but to follow orders and push other Jews into the gas chambers, to burn their bodies, to extract the gold teeth of the dead victims, to become capos, Jewish policemen, or members of a *Judenrat*, is disingenuous. Of course they had a choice, they could have preferred death and many did just so! Socrates put the matter best when he said: "You are wrong my friend, if you think a man with a spark of decency in him ought to calculate life or death; the only thing he ought to consider, if he does anything, is whether he does right or wrong, whether it is what a good man does or a bad man."[6] After the Holocaust we all became aware of the daily acts of suicide by prisoners in concentration camps during the nights, when they were locked inside their barracks without the guards' constant eyes. In a sense, taking one's own life was the only option for Nazi camp inmates to express a free choice. Under conditions in which the only time away from the continuous watching eyes of the camp's guards was a few hours at night, many chose to end it right then and there.

In this context, it was Moshe Y. Lubling that is quoted saying that "the only thing we can lose is our lives," when leading the hunger strike against the *Judenrat* and their exploitation of the working poor in the Czestochowa Ghetto. Like Socrates, he had more than just a spark of decency in him; he did what was right for a decent human being to do, that is, to think of others before himself. As we saw earlier, this sentiment was also expressed through his last words to his son Pinchas before he and his co-plotters burned down Treblinka.

In 1974 the distinguished Holocaust scholar and survivor Reuben Ainsztein, published his comprehensive study, *Jewish resistance in Nazi-*

Occupied Eastern Europe: with a historical survey of the Jew as fighter and soldier in the Diaspora. On p. 916, in the notes sections, he writes the following:

> It was only after completing this book that I came across Stanislaw Kon's account of the Treblinka revolt in *SeferMilkhamot Hagetaot*—an account that clears up a number of crucial points. According to Kon, who arrived in Treblinka on 1 October 1942, the Resistance Committee at first consisted of Dr. Chorazyeki, Zelo Bloch, Kurland of Warsaw and Lubling, a Jew from Polish Silesia. It was enlarged to include Kon; Leon Huberman, a Warsaw artisan; Zalcberg, a hatter from Kielce; the twenty-two-year-old Marek of Warsaw; and the engineer Sudowicz. The Committee at first planned to penetrate inside the armory by digging a tunnel, but gave up the idea because the likelihood of not being discovered by the Germans while digging the tunnel was minute. (The first plan no doubt explain why the participants in the revolt who were taken to Sobibor to be gassed, as well as most of the survivors who provided the first reports on the revolt, believed that the armory had been entered through the tunnel.) The Committee then decided, according to Kon, to create an opportunity for a locksmith to approach the armory door long enough to take an imprint of the lock. ... Kon agrees with the other survivors that only the arrival of large reinforcements of SS and police, as well as of troops from the nearby Luftwaffe airfield, prevented the Jews from over-running Treblinka I and freeing the Polish prisoners, with whose assistance they hoped to create a large partisan detachment. [7]

Ainsztein lists **Lubling** as a **"Treblinka Revolt Leader."**[8] Yet, Pinchas Lubling didn't need to read Ainsztein's conclusion to know about the plan to connect with the freed Polish prisoners. Long before the end of the war, through his communication with his father while he was in Czestochowa, and through the reports that came from his father, he knew about the plans to connect with the Polish prisoners and establish an underground fighting force. Not only did he submit this information to the Yad-Vashem Holocaust Museum, but he always believed that this is why the Israeli Defense Ministry awarded his father the citation for heroically fighting the Nazis.

It is worth pointing out that in a 1980 conference at Yad-Vashem, Yitzhak Arad dismissed the claim that part of the conspirators' plan was to free and connect with the Polish prisoners in order to form a large resistance force. According to Arad, this claim is mere speculation since no evidence existed to support it. [9] Yet, others knew about the plan including Pinchas Lubling who submitted this information to the Museum. Here is a classic example of forcing survivors who lived through the events to accept a conclusion that is contrary to their actual experiences.

In 1979, Isaiah Trunk, another distinguished Holocaust scholar, published his seminal work, *Jewish Responses to Nazi Persecution* which the Jewish Press described as "an indomitable work...required reading for any

A citation for heroism awarded by Israel's Defense Ministry to Moshe Y. Lubling
for his leadership in the Treblinka Revolt, 1967

serious study of the Holocaust." In this work Isaiah Trunk cites an eyewitness account of the revolt in Treblinka given by Ya'akov Miller who was
born in Wlodzimierz-Wolynski, Poland, in 1918 and transported to Treblinka
from the Siedlce Ghetto on August 22, 1942. His account of the revolt was
recorded in 1945 by S. Olitska in Eschwege, Germany, for the Jewish
Historical Commission in Poland. The details are significant since this
account is *the second independent eyewitness account* (the first being
Stanislaw Kon's) that names Moshe Y. Lubling from Silesia as a member of
the original revolt committee. He writes:

> After the hellish experiences of the day, the initiators of the uprising would meet at
> night on their wooden bunks to discuss our plans, with an eye, first of all, to getting
> hold of the right explosives and arms. Among them was Dr. Chorazycki, whom I
> just mentioned, the former Jewish officer of the Czech army, Captain Zela (sic),
> Kurland of Warsaw and Lubling from Silesia.[10]

Being a second independent testimony is significant since such a formal
criterion is used by Holocaust historiographers to determine the authenticity
of a claim or an account. With few additions, Mr. Miller's account is almost
identical to the one given by Mr. Kon during the same year. Trunk also lists
Lubling in the index as a "Treblinka Revolt leader." It should also be pointed
out that in light of these two eyewitness accounts, it is strange for Yitzhak
Arad to insist, both in the above 1980 conference, and in his 1983 book on
Treblinka that "when and within which group the idea of rebellion first
occurred cannot be stated with any certainty." No explanation is given to

why, with all the eyewitness accounts, it was still a mystery to Yitzhak Arad when and who originated the idea of a revolt.[11]

Pinchas Lubling knew nothing of the above accounts and statements by other survivors or Holocaust scholars. The above books were never translated into Hebrew and Pinchas was not actively thinking about his father's role in this drama. However, in 1983 Yitzhak Arad, the then director of the Yad-Vashem Institute, published the much anticipated book on the Treblinka revolt in Hebrew.[12] The book promised to be the most comprehensive account of the revolt using all available sources, even the ones kept in the Jewish Historical Institute in Warsaw, Poland (Poland was still under Communist rule). Yet, the book makes no mention of Moshe Y. Lubling, not even in passing, although all the above information was available. But even more astonishing was the fact that Arad used all the eyewitness accounts submitted in 1945 to the Commission in Poland in which two separate eyewitness accounts named "Lubling from Silesia" as the fourth member of the original revolt committee. He also ignored, or never read, all the information provided by the survivors of the Czestochowa Ghetto, and Pinchas Lubling's account of his father's activities in the archives of Yad-Vashem, the institute under his directorship. He was aware of the existing research that was done so far and should have carefully considered Ainsztein's account and claim that Kon's account clears several important issues about the original plotters of the revolt. Arad did not do any of that and as a result, failed to see the intimate connection between the Treblinka revolt and the Jewish underground organization in Czestochowa.

For the first time in his life (and it was the last as well), Pinchas Lubling decided to speak out about Arad's omission of his father's role in the Treblinka uprising. He contacted Yad-Vashem to meet with Arad and to again submit testimony for the archives. Pinchas brought with him all the above information and asked Arad to explain such a careless omission. But a self-appointed authority on Jewish Resistance was not about to let a Holocaust survivor confuse him with the facts. Arad dismissed Pinchas Lubling as just another survivor who, like many others, is trying to challenge his knowledge of history. History as it really happened, not the one experienced by survivors such as Pinchas. However, in an act of bad-faith, he promised Pinchas that if a second edition of his book is to be published, he will consider adding his father's name to the account. No second edition was ever published and not a single note was recorded in the institute to change the account. Until this day, the exhibition in Jerusalem mentioned only three out of the original four plotters of the revolt. Further contacts with Arad by the author, a philosophy professor who appealed to both former directors of

Yad-Vashem, Yitzhak Arad and Israel Gutman, as fellow scholar and academician, were also dismissed with further empty promises by one of the Institute's employees.[13]

The issue became even more tragic with the newly established Holocaust Memorial Museum in Washington, D.C. Working closely with Yad-Vashem; the Washington Museum continued to omit Moshe Y. Lubling's name and his role in Treblinka and Czestochowa. However, matters seemed encouraging after I wrote a letter to Mr. Miles Lerman, the chairman of the D.C. Holocaust museum, who forwarded the folder with all the evidence to Dr. Michael Berenbaum, the former director of the memorial museum, who responded as follows:

> *Dear Mr. Lubling:*
>
> *Miles Lerman has asked me to respond to your letter of January 22, 1995. I was deeply moved by your letter and touched by the story of Moshe Y. Lubling and the importance of his activity in Resistance.*
>
> *Perhaps the best way to include the record of your grandfather's important work is for you to be in touch with our archivist, Dr. Brewster Chamberlain, and to arrange to present him with the documentary material. We would be able to have the appropriate file as well as the ordinary library collections.*
>
> *Thank you again for your concern, and for the importance of your contribution.*
>
> *Sincerely yours,*
> *Michael Berenbaum*

I contacted Dr. Chamberlain who promised to look at the file and report back. He never did! By the time I started to communicate again with the Memorial Museum, Dr. Chamberlain had retired and there was no sign of Moshe Y. Lubling's file or any of his communication with me. Moshe Y. Lubling's memory was again being overlooked by the paid guardians of the survivors' experiences.

In the meantime, Poland opened its doors for research and very soon a website that lists abandoned Jewish cemeteries in Eastern Europe was created. Very soon, Moshe Y. Lubling's name appeared again. According to the information presented, there stands, in the abandoned and desecrated old Jewish Cemetery in Czestochowa, a symbolic grave for those who died fighting the Nazis. Moshe Y. Lubling's name was the first to appear on the tombstone. My older brother Moshe and I flew to Poland to document this impossible marvel. We discovered that the old Jewish cemetery is now located within a barbwire property owned by a steel factory in Czestochowa. After we negotiated with the guards and tolerated their anti-Semitic looks and smiles, we were escorted to the abandoned cemetery. The latter was a scene to remember. The Holocaust now appeared to us so vivid and explainable. Here stands Jewish property that was once part of the large Jewish Temple in Czestochowa and now it is the property of a state owned steel factory. We found the cemetery desecrated with anti-Semitic graffiti, urine and excrement everywhere; apparently the steel workers used it as their outside toilet. The tombstones were broken and thrown aside; some graves were open with vegetation growing out of them. Although finding one tombstone in this desecrated and destroyed cemetery seemed almost impossible, we did find the tombstone with our grandfather's name. The letters were stone cut and fading. We took some pictures, wrote a few words to leave next to the grave, and sat for awhile to let the place sink-in. As Israelis, we could feel the desperate conditions of the Jews in Poland; even now we felt powerless with regards to the Polish guards watching over us and laughing at our attempt to find evidence of a life lost.

It is not clear to me, however, when this symbolic tombstone was erected and by whom. One thing is clear; Moshe Y. Lubling's family had nothing to do with it since they knew nothing of its existence until the appearance of the website in 2002. Best estimations point to the organization of survivors and former Jewish residents of Czestochowa as the initiators of the symbolic grave; maybe the same individuals who published *Hurban Czenstochow* immediately after the war.[14] They were never aware that Moshe Y. Lubling's son Pinchas survived the war and Pinchas, for his part, never communicated to them of his existence in Israel. However, the more significant point is that again we are faced with the efforts of others who took the time to immortalize Moshe Y. Lubling's heroic life. Again, scholars should have listened to those who spoke on behalf of others, not for their own self-glorification, but for the sake of another who they believed had no one to carry his name and tell his story. They were essentially wrong. No Holocaust scholar paid attention to their efforts and so this symbolic grave continues to stand abandoned, desecrated, and forgotten.

With renewed enthusiasm after the discovery of the grave, I was looking again for a way to communicate my grandfather's life to the Memorial Holocaust Museum in Washington, D.C. and Yad-Vashem in Israel. The opportunity presented itself in 2004 when the Nobel Laureate Professor Elie Wiesel, visited my university as a guest speaker. After a friendly meeting with Professor Wiesel, I decided to write him and ask his help in bringing my grandfather's case to the attention of the Museum in D.C. As I always imagined my meeting with Professor Wiesel, he proved to be an individual of unique sensitivity and generosity. With his personal appeal to the Museum, the director of collection immediately contacted me and promised to look into the matter. I was ecstatic at the news and could finally imagine a

serious effort by the Holocaust institutional establishment to correct the
account of the Treblinka Revolt by including Moshe Y. Lubling's name
among the main plotters.

Although with some hesitation of letting the cat out of the bag, I flew to
Israel to bring the news to my father. I showed him the letter from the
Memorial Museum and shared this moment with him (he is 83 years-old
now). Pinchas, however, was much less optimistic. He had his meeting with
Arad, who dismissed him, and he was not about to put too much faith in
other professional handlers of Holocaust memory. I, on the other hand,
genuinely believed that I broke through the wall of defense erected by the
Holocaust establishment. Sadly, after nearly a year of not hearing from the
new director of collections, I decided to finally contact the Museum. I
received the following short e-mail/letter back:

> *Dear Dr. Lubling:*
>
> *After speaking with several historians in the Museum's Center for Advanced Holo-*
> *caust Studies, as well as contacting a colleague in Warsaw who, in turn, consulted*
> *the director of the Museum at Treblinka, no additional sources have been found*
> *referencing your grandfather's involvement in the Treblinka Uprising. As I wrote in*
> *my letter in May, we must be able to locate at least two primary sources before con-*
> *sidering making a change to the information presented in the Museum. Should addi-*
> *tional research yield more, I will be certain to contact you.*
>
> *Best wishes,*
> *Diane L. Saltzman*
> *Director, Collection Division*

I must admit that after twenty years of communications with Holocaust
institutes in Israel and the U.S., such a response was heartbreaking. When I
communicated the Museum's position to Professor Wiesel he simply
responded, "I am shocked." The key to my grandfather's continuous memory, I now grasped, depends solely on the existence of a ***second primary
source***! It seems that the only testimony they consider to be a primary source
is Mr. Kon's eyewitness account of 1945, and apparently Ya'akov Miller's
account, submitted to the Polish Commission and later cited in Isaiah
Trunk's book does not count! Nor did the publication of Richard Glazer's
book in 1995 (his testimony, however, was available to researchers since the
1950's) count. As one can see above, no explanation was given as to why
not? Nor did the director of collections, or Yitzhak Arad for this matter,
explain why the following do not constitute primary sources: (1) the testimonies by Ya'akov Miller and Aron Gelberd, (2) the references made to Moshe
Y. Lubling leadership in the uprising by Tzvi Rozenvayn, Y. Dorsman,
Moshe Rappaport, and Dr. Benjamin Orenstein from the Czestochowa
Ghetto, (3) the acknowledgment by the historian Reuben Ainsztein that Mr.

Kon's account "clears up" facts about the revolt, (4) the citation awarded to Moshe Y. Lubling by the Defense Ministry in Israel, (5) the testimony provided by Pinchas Lubling in Israel, (6) the symbolic tombstone in the Old Jewish Cemetery in Czestochowa, and (7) Mr. Richard Glazer's new testimonial book in which he identified Moshe Y. Lubling as the "contact person" for the entire fighting force, and the man who "broke down" the east gate through which most survivors of camp I in Treblinka escaped. For the official guardians of Holocaust memory, Moshe Y. Lubling from Silesia simply never existed.

FOUR

Moshe Yehoshua Lubling

Moshe Lubling is an historical, heroic, and a shining example of what the Jewish people and the Socialistic Zionist movement created.
—Dr. Binyamin Orenstein, *Hurban Czenstochow*

Moshe Y. Lubling was born in Wolbrom, Poland, in 1902 to Mendel and Miriam Lubling, the exact date of his birth is unknown. Mendel Lubling's brother was Afraim Lubling whose daughter Sima Lubling-Rappaport, settled in Israel prior to the establishment of the state. To the best of my knowledge, Moshe also had a sister who lived in the town of Czestochowa. She was married to a gentleman by the name of Krakowski who owned a shirt factory and had two children; her name is unknown. The family was deported to Treblinka on September 22, 1942, where they all perished. About Moshe's father I know very little. Mendel Lubling was a wealthy individual dealing with wholesale distribution of grains. It is also known that Mendel Lubling was estranged from his wife (of which we know nothing), and from his son Moshe. The latter defied tradition and married the daughter of a locksmith out of love. From testimonies of Jewish survivors from Wolbrom, Michael Lubling, Mandel's father, was also a respected member of the Jewish community as well as a well to do merchant in the city. The book *Volbrom Irenu*, describes him as follows:

> Michael Lubling was from the oldest members of the Lubling family in Wolbrom. He was the personal assistant of the City's Rabbi, the Righteous Chaim Kaminsky. The latter was fortunate enough to receive a long ivory pipe from Mr. Lubling; he used to smoke it only during holidays. He was an honest man, full of self confidence and at peace with himself.
>
> He was a great wholesale grains merchant, tall and with big shoulders. He was precise about his praying as he was about his food. He was considered by the city as

the "public watch" and he asked everyone who approached him: what is the time? Every Friday he used to fix the clock to the exact time. He was related to the Rabbi Silberberg. In the Synagogue he always made sure that no one spoke during the service, and he encouraged others to respond with Amen. Michael Lubling possessed a unique sense; he could feel the needs and despair of another person and to offer help when the other needed it the most. Unassuming, he used to hide his good deeds and minimize their importance. He was a thoughtful person who never argued or pontificated. He was a man of conscious and of action. He was a man of good deeds who regularly gave loans to other merchants in the nearby villages. During his old age he was considered the town's philanthropist; he died peacefully in the year 1927 at the age of 88.[1]

Raised as a child of refugees with nothing but the clothes on their skinny bodies, it is quite difficult for me to imagine any member of my family as a religious person, a business person, or one with great wealth. However, I can see some amazing similarities between the description of Michael Lubling, my grandfather Moshe Y. Lubling, and my father Pinchas Lubling. I can also see some characteristics that I share with them. My grandfather and father have a unique sense regarding the suffering of others. My grandfather refused to save himself three-times during the Holocaust in order to share in the hardship of others. He organized the Workers' Council for the benefit of the slave workers in Czestochowa, and was described by Richard Glazer as a mother-goose to the young prisoners in Treblinka. My father, despite all the harsh sentiments that many Israelis hold with regards to the Palestinians, he always keeps their pain in his heart. He could never accept some of the consequences of the Israeli occupation, especially with regards to the daily hardship of ordinary Palestinians and the poor morality of some Israeli soldiers. Seeing the efforts made by Palestinians to cross Israeli checkpoints, for example, can bring tears to his eyes. During the famous public trial of John Demjanjuk, Pinchas did not express much satisfaction. His uneasiness with the trial was two-fold: First, he did not think that the nation of Israel had to go through all this again, the Eichmann trial was enough! Second, for Pinchas, Demjanjuk was "an old man" and putting him on trial now will do very little to bring redemption and closure to survivors' lives. He did not forgive or forget, but he found no reason why the survivors, or the state of Israel, had to publicly re-live the period again. Indeed, the majority of Nazi criminals and their collaborators were never brought to justice and went on living freely in many foreign countries, including the United States. There was no good reason to open the wounds of a nation for a Ukrainian thug like John Demjanjuk, whether he was Ivan from Treblinka or just another Ukrainian guard as he himself admitted to be. Finally, Pinchas Lubling never pontificates, he is honest, and you can set your watch by his routines.

As a child, Moshe Y. Lubling was sent to a religious school as was the custom for privileged children of wealthy Jewish parents. However, very soon Moshe became disillusioned with traditional Judaism and in 1916 at the age of fourteen he joined the Zionists Scouts of *Ha-Shomer* (The Guardian). Like many other cultivated intellectual Jews in the 1920s he became fascinated with the ideas of Marxism and Socialism and the power exhibited by the workers in the Bolshevik revolution. Moshe saw in the universal socialist movement an ideology that was not only consistent with Judaism's genuine spirit, but one that can overcome the pathology of anti-Semitism in the European historical mind. He also saw the potential this ideology had with regards to the new Jewish nationalistic movement in Europe and ultimately on the new Jewish community in Palestine. To my father's recollection, however, these ideas were not fully embraced by Moshe's otherwise religious family. However, the personal and collective freedoms allowed under the Austrian occupation of Upper Silesia exposed him to these new ideas; he internalized them and started to envision his future as a Jewish pioneer.

Moshe Y. Lubling (left to right, second row, third person) as a 14 years-old member of *Ha-Shomer* in Wolbrom, Poland, 1916

In 1923 Moshe married Zelda Fisch, also from Wolbrom. They had their first son Pinchas a year later and soon after that Moshe was drafted into the Polish Army. As I mentioned above, the marriage was not the traditional match-making agreement but one of love as befitted a young Jewish revolutionary. The Lubling family also objected to the marriage since at that time the Fisch family was not socially and economically compatible. Although the Fisch family was an established family in Wolbrom, they made their living from a locksmith shop they owned on the town's Main Street. The future, however, was about to change all that and the fates of the two families quickly reversed itself. Zelda's brother, Shlomo Fisch, left Poland after WWI to attend rabbinical studies in Germany and ultimately settled in Leeds, England, where for many years he served as their Chief Rabbi. Unlike Zelda's family that was completely destroyed during the Holocaust, Shlomo's family prospered in England and some immigrated to Israel during the 1950s. In Israel the Fisch family distinguished itself intellectually and politically. Shlomo's son, the late and distinguished Literature Professor Harold Fisch, became the rector of Bar-Ilan University, the only major religious university in Israel. He was also deeply involved in the establishment of *Gosh-Emunim* (Block of the Faithful) that eventually evolved into the modern settlers' movement in Israel. The movement holds the vision of the "Greater Israel" and the return of the Jewish Messiah. In his 1972 book *A Zionist Revolution*, Harold Fisch condemned Labor Zionism which was my grandfather's Zionist ideology and described it as a "pseudo-religious 'return to Nature' movement" that was merely revolting against Ghetto Judaism. It was not work as such that should give meaning to their lives as pioneers, he argued, but the "spiritual revolution" brought about by Zionism itself. "In the aftermath of Auschwitz we have learned that work as such does not necessarily make us free, and that mankind, in descending into its own primitive depths, does not discover the path of salvation."[2]

Considered today, Harold's Fisch's criticism of Labor Zionism (especially Gordonian "return to Nature" ideology) is misplaced and highly misguided. The reality is that the only unique contribution to the new Jewish culture in Israel was created by Labor and Socialist Zionism and indeed, from the rejection of Ghetto Judaism. It is this Ghetto Judaism that, sixty years after the establishment of the State of Israel, continues to split the nation and force the state to immorally engage with its Arab neighbors. In his new edition of *After Auschwitz,* the American theologian Richard L. Rubenstein identifies Harold Fisch's movement in very negative terms. The book examines the various Jewish reactions to the Holocaust and identifies *Gush Emunim's* messianic version of Rabbi Kook's Zionism as one of the most dangerous ideologies that emerged after the Holocaust.[3]

It is heartbreaking to reflect on what an accident of history (Shlomo Fisch's departure from Poland) and twenty years (Zelda Fisch getting caught in Poland during WWII) can accomplish. As a result of the war, the Lubling family became for messianic Zionism, the human "refuse" that were not essential to the revival of the Jewish people in Eretz Israel. Harold Fisch's sons, Menachem, David, and Yosi are all distinguished scholars in Israeli universities with international reputation. David Harel was a recent recipient of the Jerusalem Prize in Israel for his brilliant work on artificial intelligence. Unlike their father, however, the Fisch children found their expression not only in religious imagination, but also in the philosophy of science, artificial intelligence, and sociology, respectfully. While growing together in Israel, the wonderful passion of the Fisch family towards the land of Israel, religion, learning, and their intellectualism was a constant remainder of the family's great potential. Professor Harold Fisch's political ideology, which I will return to later, is still part of the struggle to shape the Jewish character of the State of Israel after the Holocaust. Although I do not share the movement's religious and messianic ideas, I admire the passion that drove Professor Fisch and his tireless work on behalf of his beliefs.

Moshe Y. Lubling possessed no marketable profession but only passionate ideas about a Jewish State in Palestine and workers' rights. He was educated but was never forced by circumstances to work physically and he soon devoted his entire time to the Zionist cause. In 1927 he moved with his family to the near-by town of Katowice, where his daughter Reja (Ester-Shoshanna) was born in 1929, and where Moshe started a more serious involvement in Socialistic and Zionistic activities. His son Pinchas recollects that in 1929, after the notorious Arab riots in Palestine and the massacre of Jews in Hebron, Moshe Y. Lubling was arrested for demonstrating in front of the British Consulate in Katowice.[4] However, Upper Silesia and the town of Katowice were settled by many German nationals and very soon after Hitler's rise to power in 1933, anti-Semitic regulations began to affect the Jewish community. In 1935, according to Pinchas, although physical violence against Jews was limited, the locals organized an economical boycott of all Jewish businesses and there was incitement against buying from Jews. This situation got worse in Poland in the years leading to the war (1937–8); Polish fascist groups were formed with a similar ideology of hatred against Jews as the German's National Socialists. Members of such groups stood in front of Jewish owned businesses in order to intimidate Polish residents and prevent them from buying. Much convincing, however, was not necessary as the majority of middle-class urbanized Poles were already deeply anti-Semitic; their slogan was "Each goes his own way". This situation ultimately forced the Lubling family to leave Katowice in 1935 and move to Sosnowiec, a nearby town under Polish control that was closer to Krakow and its progressive political environment.

In Sosnowiec Moshe Y. Lubling formed and led several Zionist organizations, in particular *Ha-Movil* (The Leader); *Poalai-Zion Yemin* (Workers of Zion - Right); and a movement of professional Jewish workers *Ha-Oved* (The Worker). At that time in Poland such movements were legal but required official registration with the Polish authority. As the chairman of such left-wing Zionist organizations, it was Moshe Y. Lubling's role to register the organizations with the Polish authorities for approval. As a result, his name appeared on all official applications submitted on behalf of the organizations, a fact that will become significant for Moshe's family within a few years. The organizations served as ideological centers for Jewish individuals preparing to immigrate to Palestine. Through the organization, the Lubling family obtained a legal visa to Palestine in 1937 and was ready to make the Aliyah when Zelda Lubling became ill. The organization gave the family's visa to another family that quickly immigrated to Palestine and eventually survived the Holocaust. The only surviving photograph of the Lubling family is the official passport photograph taken for the purpose of immigration to British controlled Palestine.

Moshe Y. Lubling (left to right, first row, first person) as the chairman of the
Zionist group *Ha-Oved* (The Worker) in Sosnowiec, Poland, 1934

Many times I daydream about the above scenario and imagine what Moshe Y. Lubling would have accomplished if the Lubling family came to Palestine in 1937. First, and most significantly, they would have survived the Holocaust which would have given my father a chance to realize his potential? Pinchas is an extraordinarily capable individual who never recovered sufficiently from his childhood trauma and was never able to return to an ordinary way of life and concentration. Also, he was a true Gordonian Zionist who believed in redemption through labor and practiced it daily for 47 years in Israel. Indeed, the Holocaust challenged its survivors in different ways; some attempted to escape the past by adopting seemingly normal lives while for others the Holocaust shaped and informed their every living moment. I remember that some of the survivors were capable of laughing, of telling jokes, of showing great sensitivity to children, of playing cards on Friday night, and even of having a drink and dance once in awhile. But not my father; for him the Holocaust made any ordinary activity seem trivial; only issues that address the reality of such a *Hurban* were worth pursuing. As a philosopher in the classical tradition of American philosophy, I seem to feel the same. After such moral collapse as the Holocaust, most modern philosophical and intellectual concerns seem trivial if not criminally aristocratic. Consider contemporary intellectual preoccupation with the interest and rights of rivers and olive trees while the president of Iran, a man who takes joy in trivializing the Holocaust, is threatening to "wipe" the Jewish state of the map. While there is great need to protect the environment and its rights, we first must address the issues of our inability to protect each other and stop further genocides. The Holocaust delivered a deadly blow to traditional intellectualism and exposes the poverty of their methods to transform the human condition.[5]

Second, the Lubling family would have been the WASPs of the new Israeli society with an established life, rather than the uneducated and penniless refugees other Israelis referred to as "soap"; as those who went "as lambs to the slaughter" without resisting. As pointed out earlier, the Israeli society is unique in its intolerance of any weakness that brings back the memory of Ghetto Judaism. Indeed, there was a visible difference between the native Jews who were educated as Hebrews with roots in the community, and the new Holocaust survivors' families. My personal universe was dominated by stories and memories of childhoods in Wolbrom, Bendzin, Sosnowiec, Czestochowa, and labor camps. Their stories and memories were of the Sea of Galilee, agricultural schools, and the early community of Tel-Aviv with its idealistic poets, painters, actors, and revolutionary philosophers.

Finally, the Lubling family would have been free of the generational transmission of Holocaust wounds; wounds that we carry with us at all times and which shaped our lives and those of our children.[6] As I noted above, the burden of living with the Holocaust and images of one's family's powerless-

The Lubling family passport photograph (left to right), Pinchas, Zelda Fisch, Ester-
Shoshanna, and Moshe Y. Lubling, Poland, 1937

ness, impose unique constraints upon children's imagination. The responsibility to redeem their parents' lost childhood, the lack of roots and family
ties, the need to live with your own executioners, and the absence of justice
is irreducibly existential. The lessons of our parents' experiences during the
Holocaust, as unique and as irrelevant as they might appear today, are still
part of every awakened moment of our lives.

Zelda Lubling was a language teacher and the guiding force in Pinchas'
life. Most of the family's income came from her work and the support she
received from the Fisch family. The Lubling family, on the other hand, did
not support Moshe's "organizing" work or marriage, and no longer provided
him with any economical support. At times, Moshe's family was forced to
live with the Fisch family which explains why Pinchas was born in his
grandfather's house in Wolbrom. Although Pinchas greatly admired his
father's ideological convictions, he never forgave him for not having an
established economical base when the war started. As we become familiar
with the life of the Lubling family during the war, Pinchas' anger will
become more understandable. Pinchas recollects the shape the family found
itself at the eve of the war.

> The reality was very harsh and our condition was desperate. My father's pre-
> occupation with Zionist organizations came at the expense of the family. In his
> youth, my father's family was considered privileged and as such, it was not proper

to teach the child an actual profession. So my father had no profession and he also wasn't a big businessman; he had no economical base ... most of his time he spent on his activities in these organizations. We were mainly supported by my mother's family.[7]

Most of Moshe Y. Lubling's activities took place while the family lived in Sosnowiec and where Pinchas had most of his teenage memories. He can still remember going to the local cinema and watching the 1934 Dzigan and Shumacher Yiddish movie *The Jolly Paupers*. The comedic duo settled in Israel for a short time after the war and provided my parents with some cultural continuation. It was also the only humor that my parents could relate to after the war.[8] The duo also provided me with an introduction to the Yiddish language together with recordings of Shalom Aleichem's *Die Kleine Mentshelech* (The Little People). Pinchas recalls his father working in a separate room in the house with the door always closed due to the secrecy and importance of his work. He was not to be interrupted with his work, which was at times illegal and which landed him in jail several times. But, as Pinchas explains, while it was not like our contemporary life with computers and cell phones yet, it was a "normal life." Pinchas had his grandparents who adored him, his cousins and uncles, the town he grew up in, and a bright future as a pioneer in the new Land of Israel.

Friday, September 1, 1939

The Second World War started on September 1, 1939 and two days later Moshe Y. Lubling and his family fled from the town of Sosnowiec. By that time Pinchas already completed his high-school studies and was an active member of *Gordonia*, a Zionist movement that followed the teachings of A.D. Gordon. In 1937 Pinchas completed his studies and was already participating in the movement's *Maslul Agshama* (realization track) for immigration to Palestine. Pinchas followed his father's ideals and at the end of his school studies he did what no other member of the Lubling family has done before. He chose to acquire a workers' profession that will be useful in building the new Jewish nation; he become a plumber and worked until the war started. The choice of the plumbing profession proved to be the correct one, it saved his life!

The war started on Friday; by Saturday afternoon the Polish government was no longer in the town of Sosnowiec. Pinchas tells of the feeling of powerlessness that came over the Jewish community; nobody talked about what to do since there was very little that could have been done. The town of Sosnowiec was not far from the German border and on Saturday the Germans were already in the town and by Sunday afternoon they were in total control. The Lubling family took whatever they could and started to walk east towards the Soviet border. The family took a train that was still running, but not for long. When the service stopped they joined "a river of refugees" fleeing from the advancing German army. They walked back to Wolbrom and decided to leave Zelda (38) and Reja (12) with the Fisch family; after walking for a week the two were on the verge of collapse. Soon after, Moshe Y. Lubling and his son Pinchas continued their attempt to reach the Soviet boarder. Most on Moshe's mind at that time was not the destruction of the Jews, but his signatures on the applications for Socialist and Zionist organizations in Sosnowiec. Now that the Germans were in control of the records, they could find his name on the applications and arrest him, not for being a Jew but for being a Socialist.

However, the Germans were much too quick for Moshe and his son and after 50 kilometers they were forced to return to Wolbrom by the advancing German forces. They returned to Wolbrom and from there back to their apartment in Sosnowiec. They were trapped! Within two to three weeks, the Germans started to "collect" Jews for forced labor. While they themselves were never "collected," they later found out that forced labor meant deportation to the Soviet Union and a chance to survive the war. Indeed, such confusion regarding the right way to act in order to be saved became a familiar characteristic of the Holocaust.[9] It was also at this time that information got to Moshe that the Germans were sorting through the local Polish offices in search of Communists and Socialists leaders. Very soon the Germans started to arrest people associated with such organizations and for Moshe's family it was time to move again. By now they were penniless, terrified, hungry, and soon to become homeless. They sold whatever was still of any value, gave the rest away, and started their walk to the town of Czestochowa, a 200 kilometer journey through an hostile Polish environment.

They moved to the town of Czestochowa where Moshe had a sister. The Lubling family found a place to live as "secondary tenants" and according to Pinchas, "these were the worst of times." The move to the Jewish Ghetto in Czestochowa was the beginning of the hardest times the Lubling family will experience together during the war. It would also be the last place that the family will be together and alive. The family lived in one room with no heat, no food, no money, and reduced hope. In order to make a few Zlotys, Moshe and Pinchas sold their labor in place of the rich Jews in Czestochowa who paid the *Judenrat* so they will not be chosen for forced labor. The period was crystallized in 16 year-old Pinchas' mind through the following experience:

The winter of 1939/40 was the worst winter in my memory. We had no food or cooking materials and there was no coal to warm the apartment. I remember that the Germans were delivering coal from a train station to their bases with horses and carts. During the journey to their bases, the coal would shake on the cart and every once and awhile a piece of coal fell on the snow. I used to walk after the horse with a bag and pick-up these pieces. In the evening I would bring it home and only then we got to warm the room and cook something. The temperature inside the house was usually -15 to -20 degrees.[10]

The activities of Moshe Y. Lubling became more intense during these years as the Jewish community in Czestochowa was looking for ways to respond to the conditions imposed by the Nazis. The Nazis' demands for Jewish slave labor were communicated to the Jewish community through the *Judenrat* and everyday there were different and more humiliating demands. The *Judenrat* in turn, started to charge Labor Tax from rich Jews who didn't want to work. The money was then used to pay a meager salary to poor Jews who worked in their place. Moshe Y. Lubling and his son were both forced to work. However, the few Zlotys they earned were far from enough to support the family. It is precisely because of this experience in Czestochowa that Pinchas continuously referred to the lack of "economical base" when he described his father.

Regardless of the doomed conditions, Moshe Y. Lubling, who by this time, according to Pinchas "was a type of a person with a very developed social consciousness," started to organize the Jewish slave workers and soon created the Workers' Council to represented their interests. He was elected as the chairman of the council and started to negotiate with the *Judenrat* for better workers' conditions. The *Judenrat* objected to the creation of the Workers' Council, but to their dismay the Council soon became a recognized cultural institution in the ghetto. It should be pointed out that such an organization didn't exist anywhere else under the German occupation. For better or worse, it was the product of a creative soul who was driven by principles of justice under the worse imaginable conditions. It was precisely this drive as Eros, and the ability to maintain clarity of thoughts under abnormal conditions, that made Moshe Y. Lubling a future leader of the Treblinka Revolt. At a time in which most individuals were primarily and naturally concerned with their own basic needs, he acted on behalf of others and a deep sense of justice. The activities on the behalf of the slave workers grew each day and ultimately culminated in a hunger strike against the *Judenrat*. Starving souls were willing to forgo the little they had to protest their conditions, not to the Nazis but to their fellow Jews who made the decisions regarding the distribution of available funds.

11 Katedralne Street in the Large Ghetto in Czestochowa, Poland;
the last residence of the Lubling family (1939 to 1942)

The activities of the Workers' Council, with Moshe as its chairman, soon grew into the Jewish Resistance Organization in Czestochowa as other radicals and intellectuals representing groups such as the Bund, *Gordonia, Garin Dror*, joined the Council. As was documented by Dr. Binyamin Orenstein in *Hurban Czenstochow*, many members of the Council's leadership were frequently arrested by the Jewish police under the orders of the *Judenrat*. The Workers' Council soon started to recruit and prepare Jews for an inevitable immigration to British Palestine. The organization established *Kibbutzim* along ideological lines for the purpose of resistance and for eventual immigration. Pinchas Lubling explains that,

> The groups joined the Workers' Council under the leadership of my father. The Council soon developed its interests and widened its activities, especially as a resistance organization. This was especially true after 1941 when information reached my father that the Germans were murdering entire Jewish communities in Russia. Until this time, no one in Czestochowa thought that the Germans are planning on the total destruction of European Jewry with death-factories; such a scenario was not even a subject of imagination.[11]

Through all of its activities, the Workers' Council became involved with other Jewish resistance organizations such as the one in Warsaw, as well as the left-wing Polish Underground Resistance; the contacts were initiated by the Popular Polish Army headquartered in Russia.

Dr. Binyamin Orenstein, the author of *Hurban Czenstochow* and himself a former slave laborer and resident of Czestochowa, described the Workers' Council in the following terms:

> The Workers' Council was established as a spontaneous movement of the forced laborers. The forced laborers belonged to the poor strata of Czestochowa Jewry. The well to-do Jews ransomed themselves with money, and the poor, not having with what to live, suffering from hunger and want, had, in addition, to toil at forced labor, be vexed, terrorized, tormented and beaten by the masters, foremen, and *kapos* [short for *kameradenpolizei*, the prisoners who served as overseers]. Many times, it occurred that forced laborers fainted from hunger and exhaustion during the hard labor.
>
> On the 12th of May, 1940, the forced laborers came to the premises of the *Judenrat* right from work and held a mass assembly ... After a series of incidents and negotiations, the *Judenrat* partly gave in to the demands of the forced laborers for creating kitchens and the distribution of bread. Later, the forced laborers received wages. The divisions of the Workers' Council were presidium, executive board and advisory committee. The executive board consisted of Moshe Lubling – chairman, Moshe Levenhof—secretary, and Tzvi Rozenvayn—treasurer. The executive board consisted of the following: Moshe Lubling, Tzvi Rozenvayn, Yisroel Shildhoz, Yitzchak Rozenfeld, Mendel Vilinger, Mordechai Openheym, Yitzchak Apatshinski, Chaim Birenholtz, Yisroel Shimanovitsh and Moshe Levenhof. The advisory committee consisted of the following: Dovid Shlezinger, Gershon Frendke, Avrohom Brat, Avrohom Shtshekatsh, and Yankel kofman. Contributing with council and action were influential personalities such as: Yakov Raziner, lawyer Kanarski, lawyer Leib Fogel, the well known writer H.L. Zshitnitzki and many others.
>
> The tasks of the Workers' Council were to carry out political, cultural, and professional activity and to create a whole series of institutions such as the sick fund, mutual help funds, invalid fund, worker kitchens, children's homes, public schools, evening courses, dramatic circles, workers' choirs, and putting out an illegal newspaper.
>
> The Workers' Council conducted multifaceted activities and was the forerunner of the later Jewish Fighting Organization in the Small Ghetto. The Workers' Council existed until the 22nd of September, 1942 when there began mass slaughter, selections, and deportations of Czestochowa Jews to the gas chambers of Treblinka.
>
> The topic of the Workers' Council was treated by a whole series of prominent researchers of the Holocaust literature. Dr. Philip Fridman, the leading scholar and bibliographer of Holocaust literature wrote as follows: 'A rare institution in the era of Nazi tyranny ('Undzer Yortseit [Our Death Anniversary]', Bamberg, 1948, page 10). Another authority in the field, Dr. Rafael Mahler declared: 'Like a light, the description of the activities of the Workers' Council weaved through' (Yidishe Kultur [Jewish Culture]', New York, April, 1949, Number 4, page 9.[12]

If the reader will allow me to indulge philosophically for a moment, I would like to say a few words regarding the above Worker' Council. Looking back at the progress of events during the Holocaust, it seems almost surrealistic to think that individuals like my grandfather and others occupied themselves with such idealistic pursuits and with such formality (president, advisory board, etc.). Even if one acknowledges that workers' right are of central ethical importance, it seems a strange preoccupation at a time in which the entire Ghetto was about to be liquated in a matter of months. Of course, the perspective is inappropriate since neither Moshe Y. Lubling nor others could have grasped Treblinka and Auschwitz. Danger, deportations to work camps, starvation, misery, and daily death, yes, but total destruction, not yet!

What attracted my attention was the attempt by intelligent individuals to still operate in rational and logical manner in a world that was no longer operating within such a framework. Rich Jews exploited their poor brethrens; criminals became favorable with the Gestapo and were appointed to the Jewish Police; and immoral individuals celebrated this Nietzschean paradigm by making money. What intellectuals and persons of logic could not see was the nihilism at the bottom of their condition and the new reality. As an inevitable result, such individuals did not survive for long; they possessed no mental tools to deal with such a reality. A reality that was the precise opposite of rationality, logic, justice, rule of law, and principled life. Although the conditions at the death and concentration camps were genuinely unimaginable, the life in the Ghetto was not far behind and at times even worse. The philosopher and Holocaust survivor Jean Amery wrote the following with regards to intellectuals in the camps. The same logic may apply to some members of the Workers' Council.

> Not only was rational-analytical thinking...of no help, but it led straight into a tragic dialectic of self-destruction. First of all, the intellectual did not so easily acknowledged the unimaginable conditions as a given fact as did the nonintellectual. Long practice in questioning the phenomena of everyday reality prevented him from simply adjusting to the realities of the camps, because they stood in all-too-sharp a contrast to everything that he had regarded until then as possible and humanly accepted.[13]

It goes without saying that the traditional characteristics of the intellectual or the sentimentalist usually involve the confusion between intellectual analysis and ontological facts. This was the confusion that led Plato to argue that the realm of ideas is real in ways that the physical world isn't. Although the realm of ideas is real, it is not subject to space and time; a sort of a self-contained metaphysical reality that is held together by logic and suspension of practical reason. Since the Workers' Council also included militant Zionists and Bundists, one can only imagine the endless disputes among the members as to the correct way to respond to Nazi persecutions. In this regard, one may say that, on the one hand, such preoccupation functioned as an escape from the physical conditions that did not encompass the needed rationality. On the other hand, giving the indescribable condition these individuals lived under, the Council can also be understood, to use Dr. Rafael Mahler's description, "like a light, the description of the activities of the Workers' Council weaved through." As history will soon prove, for Moshe Y. Lubling, organizing the Jews, maintaining civilized conduct, and not losing himself in an intellectualist universe, was a matter of the highest importance, especially if juxtaposed with the conduct of the surrounding Polish population. It is hard not to compare the reaction of the intellectual to the reality of the camps with contemporary intellectuals' reaction to the threat of radical Islam. They simply cannot analytically grasp suicide bombers, beheadings, burning people alive, etc. and as such, still maintain that a rational discourse can resolve the conflict. As with Nazi persecutions, the intellectuals who hope for a rational dialogue with radical Islam would be the first ones to lose their lives. Intellectual analysis should inform actual conditions, not provide an escape from them since the latter will surly prove fatal.

The Last Meeting of the Workers' Council

The first *Aktion* started on September 22, 1942, the day after Yom-Kippur. On the afternoon of the 21st the Council met for the last time in Moshe Y. Lubling's apartment. It is believed that among those who participated in the meeting were the above mentioned Tzvi Rozenvayn, Dr. Binyamin Orenstein, Leib Brener, Aron Gelberd as well as the famous Jewish writer H. L. Zytnicki. The description of the meeting was provided by Dr. Orenstein as follows:

> The last meeting of the Workers' Council came on September 21, 1942 in the residence of Moshe Lubling on 11 Katedralne Street. In this meeting, the writer H. L. Zytnicki declared: "This is the last minute of the existence of the ghetto and of our normal lives."[14]

In a tribute to Moshe Y. Lubling in the same book, Aron Gelberd attests that representatives of the Polish Underground offered to save Moshe Y. Lubling's life by smuggling him out of the ghetto. The offer was not extended to his entire family. Moshe refused to save himself, and according to Gelberd's testimony, declared that he wished his fate to be the same as his people.

In the testimony given by Pinchas Lubling to Yad-Vashem the interviewer asked: "What was the reason given by your father for not leaving the Ghetto?"

"I am uncomfortable speaking in such terms and language," responded Pinchas Lubling.

"No please," the interviewer insisted, what was the reason?"

"...he said that he does not want to save himself since he wishes to share in the fate of his people. I didn't write this, someone else did. Indeed, the *Aktion* started the next day."[15]

The uneasiness that Pinchas felt with regards to his father's statement reflects the reason why he never attempted to peddle his father's story. Such statements belong to another universe of meaning with different type of people, and in situations that after the Holocaust were difficult to share with others since they sounded too idealistic and made-up. But, as Pinchas put it: "I didn't write this, others did." I suggest that the reality in Israel after the Holocaust was such that the memory of the Holocaust was created only by those who survived and promoted their own, and at times, un-documented heroism. To promote and peddle the dignified memory of his father was not in Pinchas' character, he learned such behavior from his father and I learned it from him.

The truth should be pointed out that such altruistic behavior was not the order of the day, not even among other survivors of Treblinka. Without making any moral judgment, one should compare the refusal of Moshe Y. Lubling to save himself (on three different occasions) with Samuel Willenberg's account of his own father. The latter was a high-school art teacher who obtained false identification in order to live on the Aryan side of Warsaw. His son and two daughters were sent to Treblinka and his wife to a work camp. After Samuel successfully escaped from Treblinka during the revolt he returned to find his father in Warsaw, painting portraits of Jesus Christ and the Virgin Mary, and passing himself off as deaf and mute so his heavy Jewish accent will not give him away. Not to risk his father's life, Samuel is forced to leave his father's residence and look for safety.[16] In a world in which physical survival meant everything, Moshe Y. Lubling's idealistic sense of sacrifice for the collective was indeed unique.

The Czestochowa Ghetto had nearly 50,000 Jews living in an area suited for less then half that number. On the 21st of September 1942, the Nazis closed all entrances to the Ghetto and extra units of the SS and special Ukrainian and Polish guards started to arrive. There was no longer a way out! Pinchas recalls the hopelessness of the people and the fact that the Council didn't warn people about the upcoming liquidation.

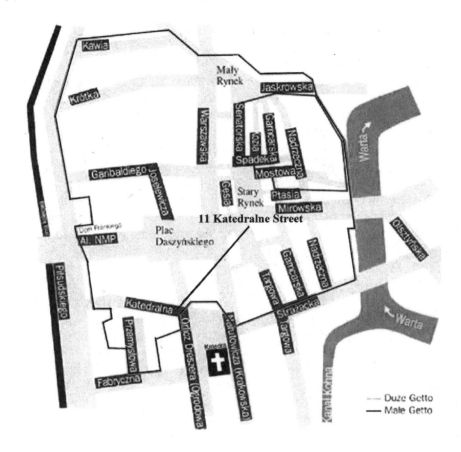

The Large Ghetto in Czestochowa

"I understand from what you are saying that the Workers' Council was aware about the upcoming deportations," the interviewer asked.

"Not just the Council, everybody knew," Pinchas responded sadly.

"Was there any thought or direction as to what to do in this case?" the interviewer inquired.

"There were no thoughts about what to do; there were nearly 50,000 Jews in Czestochowa at that time. The Nazis closed the Ghetto; no one was allowed to enter or leave," Pinchas responds with some anger at the interviewer's insinuation.

But, "did the Council do anything about it?"

Pinchas had enough, "Yes, but don't forget that even among the Jews there were people who were not *Zaddikim* (righteous people), and you had to act very carefully."[17]

Pinchas' point is sadly true. As in all other groups of people, among Jews there were also some who would have been more than willing to warn the Nazis about the Council's activities in return for a piece of bread or for possible freedom. As we know today, one needed to be careful of members of the *Judenrat* and other "privileged" Jews who still believed that their cooperation with the Nazis would save them. However, for those who take delight in the questionable morality of some Jews, a good look in the historical mirror would help. No other group in Europe has been so traumatized and discriminated against; under such conditions, it is inevitable that the morally corrupt will surface to the top. That was clearly true, among others, about the Polish, Romanian, Ukrainian, and French people's conduct during the Nazi occupation. It is not the morality of the persecuted that should be challenged under such conditions, but the morality of the Germans, their morally challenged collaborators, and the indifference of the free world.

On September 22, 1942, during the first *Aktion,* the Lubling family was deported from the Large Ghetto. "It looked like a river of people," recalls Pinchas, "as we marched together towards the town's main Plaza." He further recalls how the Polish residents outside the Ghetto were standing on the rooftops pouring urine on the doomed Jews, yelling anti-Semitic slogans, and ridiculing the frightened victims. "They stopped our family in front of the Commandant of the liquidation. The family was all together for the last time. My mother and sister were sent to the right where the trains to Treblinka stood next to the Church. My father and I went forward towards the parked trucks. I recall looking at them for the last time and seeing the Ukrainian guards and Polish police beating and abusing the Jews ... breaking them into submission."

"Did you have time to say good-by to your mother and sister," asked the interviewer from Yad-Vashem?

"No!" said Pinchas with some expression of surprise at the interviewer's question. "There was a river of people," he repeated, "the selection was so cruel...we didn't have time to say a word!"[18]

Moshe Y. Lubling and his son Pinchas remained in Czestochowa with 5,000 other Jewish prisoners and were housed in *Metalorgja*, a former Jewish owned steel factory. In the meantime, the Germans barb-wired several blocks of abundant Jewish houses and created the Small Ghetto of Czestochowa where all the surviving workers lived; from there the Germans started to organize them for work. Moshe Y. Lubling, now 40 years-old and 17 year-old Pinchas worked at a local steel factory. Back in the Ghetto, the surviving Jewish workers started to "organize," that is, different ideological groups lived together and became families. The underground activities continued and they now established new lines of communication with the underground Jewish organization in the Warsaw Ghetto. Unfortunately, in another *Aktion* in late September or early October, Moshe Y. Lubling was selected for deportation to Treblinka. It will be the last time Pinchas saw his father, but it was not the last time he communicated with him.

In May 1943, eight months after Moshe Y. Lubling was deported to Treblinka, a letter arrived addressed to Pinchas Lubling. The letter was from Moshe Y. Lubling and Pinchas recalls sharing the letter with several friends of his father (Liber Brener, Tzvi Rozenvayn, and Aron Gelberd). Dr. Orenstein writes:

> Until the liquidation of the Small Ghetto 8 letters were sent [to Treblinka], but because of the unusual difficulties in keeping in touch, only three response were received ... the first letter from Treblinka, written by Moshe Lubling, arrived in the small ghetto in Czestochowa on May 1943 to Aron Gelberd. [19]

The event is further described in *Hurban Czenstochow* in the following glorying terms:

> He (Moshe Lubling) sent several letters through train workers to the resistance movement in the Small Ghetto in Czestochowa. In the secret, electrifying, affective, historical letter from the Treblinka Hell to his friends in the Small Ghetto he spoke of resistance and revenge.
>
> After 11 fitly months in Treblinka, situated at the top of the resistance movement, he was killed in the uprising in August 1943.
>
> Moshe Lubling is an historical, heroic, and a shining example of what the Jewish people and the Socialistic Zionist movement created. [20]

In the letter my grandfather is describing what Treblinka is and what is being done there by the Organizing Committee. This letter was sent to the underground organization in Czestochowa three months before the actual uprising which tells us a few important things. First, three months before the revolt Moshe Y. Lubling was still alive and fully knowledgeable about the upcoming uprising. Second, only a well respected individual, by both the Polish Resistance Movement (train driver) and Jewish fighters could send such letters. No one else among the prisoners in Treblinka was capable of communicating with resistance organizations outside of Treblinka; only a leader could! Pinchas proudly remembers that his father was very poetic in the letter and was quoting from a traditional Yiddish song that says in part that, ***"If all woods were pencils and all days were ink, it would not have been possible to describe what is happening in Treblinka."*** Moshe Y. Lubling finished the letter with the following words: "I do not intend to survive the revolt, but I am working on an act of revenge that will forever be remembered in Jewish history." **These are the words of a Treblinka Revolt**

Leader three months before the fateful day on August 2, 1943. It is not surprising, therefore, that many individuals voluntarily wrote in praise of Moshe Y. Lubling's actions during these important years. No words were ever solicited and all of Moshe's comrades who survived believed that his son Pinchas did not survive the Holocaust.[21]

This letter is a truly historical document in the story of Judaism, maybe the only document that can directly attest to the existence of an organizing committee in Treblinka, and Moshe Y. Lubling as one of its leaders, if not its main leader. Pinchas learned about the revolt in Treblinka through underground ties that his Gordonia group kept with other underground Jewish resistance fighters. "For me," says Pinchas, "this was when my connection with my father ended. I consider August 2, 1943 his burial day."[22]

After 64 years of not knowing what happened to my grandfather during the uprising I finally arrived at some clarity. My grandfather was the man my family always knew him to be; he was an idealist, a socialist, a champion of workers' rights, a furious fighter, a leader of men and women, a father to the younger prisoners in Treblinka, and among the most significant members of the Organizing Committee in the Treblinka revolt. He is the "contact person" for the entire uprising because of his work place in between the ghetto and barracks. It is Lubling to whom Kleinmann, the Capo of the Sorting Commando, is reporting to regarding the preparations for the uprising. Why would it be necessary for Lubling "to understand that everything's okay" unless he was coordinating the uprising? Twice in his book Glazer puts him together with the other leaders of the revolt—"Lubling was there, Simcha, people from the machine shop. Then Galewski and Dr. Choronzycki (sic), too." And again after the revolt—"they (the Organizing Committee) were so single minded, they never intended to escape themselves ... There's no other way to explain why Lubling herded us out through the fence the way he did ... So Galewski and the ones around him –Kurland, Sudowicz, Simcha the carpenter—they had no intention of escaping? ... And what about Rudi?" Glazer is practically naming every significant member of the Organizing Committee and puts Lubling in the group's center.

Given all the eyewitness accounts by individuals in Czestochowa, by those who escaped Treblinka, and by three survivors who participated in the revolt, all who put Moshe Y. Lubling at the center of the Organizing Committee, it is almost incomprehensible that the only two serious research books on the revolt in Treblinka did not even mention Moshe Y. Lubling's name. How could scholars such as Alexander Donat and Yitzhak Arad miss all the evidence and reach conclusions that stand in total contradiction to the accounts by all the above survivors? They read the same books, looked at the same evidence, and even had the privilege of speaking to the individuals who wrote all the above accounts. As a fellow academician I can only describe their work as incompetent at best and as criminally misleading at worse.

Alone in the Small Ghetto

Back in Czestochowa Pinchas was still working in the steel factory. In the small ghetto the remaining Jews started to organize into ideological groups they referred to as "kibbutzim." They also formed an underground resistance organization and established contact with the Jewish underground in Warsaw. The latter's representatives, usually women, regularly visited the small ghetto in Czestochowa by mixing with the workers on their way back from work. The underground resistance organization, Pinchas recalls, had a plan to build a tunnel through which individuals could escape into the surrounding woods. They also started to manufacture home-made weapons by stealing materials from their working sites.

After the uprising in the Warsaw Ghetto, the Germans discovered the underground resistance movement in Czestochowa. Apparently, someone disclosed all of their activities to the Germans as well as the ammunition hiding places. One day in May, Pinchas recalls, the workers were waiting to be picked-up by the Nazis at the end of the workday; however, they were not permitted to return and they stayed to sleep in the factory. They quickly learned that the Small Ghetto was being destroyed in reaction to the Warsaw Uprising. With the Small Ghetto gone, Pinchas adds, the underground activities of the remaining Jews virtually stopped. There were no more than 200–300 prisoners in Pinchas' group; the remaining Jewish workers were then concentrated in two different factories. For a while things remained the same and they continued to work and sleep in the factory. They interacted with Polish workers who at times provided food to the starving Jews. Pinchas attests that at this point the condition of the remaining Jews was relatively good. They lived in wooden structures with mattresses on the floor and received a daily portion of soup and bread. However, unlike the Polish workers who worked within a three shift structure, the Jews only had two shifts, from six to six. They had a bathroom and a shower in which the workers disinfected themselves daily. There was a medical clinic with a doctor where several deaths occurred mostly due to sickness and work related accidents. Those who died were offered a simple Jewish service and were buried in the Jewish Cemetery in Czestochowa. Pinchas continued to work in the factory until 1945. As the soviet's Red Army was pushing towards Czestochowa, the Germans evacuated their settlement in the city and

Pinchas was dragged with the Germans and their families as they were fleeing. Many of the other slave workers were left behind and soon were liberated by the Red Army on January 15, 1945. Pinchas' Holocaust journey, however, was far from over.

He kept the letter from his father with him on the fleeing Nazi train into Germany and into the notorious Buchenwald concentration camp; this was at the end of January 1945. In the camp Pinchas was ordered to strip, take a disinfecting shower, and replace his clothes. From fear that they would discover his father's letter and kill him, he disposed of the letter "and this is how a unique historical document of national significance was lost," concluded Pinchas.[23] Pinchas, of course, did not know that Tzvi Rozenvayn and Aron Gelberd would survive the Holocaust and testify to the existence of this letter in *Hurban Czenstochow*. Of course, this letter and the surrounding events were never investigated by any scholar of Treblinka or the Holocaust. The book was never translated from Yiddish and the episode never came to light.

In February 1945, Pinchas was moved to the *Flossenburg* concentration camp in Germany where the Nazis started to build a factory for the manufacture of the weapon known as *Panzerschrek*. He was among thousands of other slave laborers from all over Europe who were brought to do the work; he stayed in the camp until April. Conditions in the camp were especially difficult at the end of the war. Pinchas was a member of a professional group referred to as "the electricians." They were all Jews and were controlled by a Jewish capo nicknamed Narchsis. "He was a helpful man," remembers Pinchas, "who helped the prisoners a great deal, in particularly, he made sure that the group members didn't act like animals when it came to the distribution of food. He made sure they were not reduced to being *musellmen* (Skeletons)."[24] They distributed the food in an organized manner, at times they were even able to have second offerings, and they kept themselves clean. However, it was winter and many of the surviving Jews started to die. The group was dwindling before Pinchas' eyes. "Those who were sick with dysentery were eating pieces of coal to elevate their condition," Pinchas recalls. "There were these Italian prisoners who just couldn't endure the freezing conditions and they literally vanished one by one."[25]

At the end of April 1945 the Germans loaded the remaining "electricians" on trains and for two weeks drove aimlessly through parts of Germany and Czechoslovakia. The prisoners had no food and there was no order. "It got to the point," recalls Pinchas, "that the train would stop for people, including the prisoners, to relieve themselves and find food. After a short time they will all return back to the train, *including the prisoners*." Yes, you

read correctly. As the Germans were fleeing the Allied forces' constant
bombing they would open the trains' cars and allow the prisoners to look for
food in stations along the way. The prisoners did not escape; they felt more
secure with the Germans than on their own. The relations of dependency and
subservience had been created between the victims and their tormentors.[26]

After two weeks, the train arrived at the Mauthausen concentration camp
in Austria. At the beginning the "electricians" were kept in a separate camp
outside the main camp. In the main camp, however, the situation was
desperate as thousands of prisoners were suffering from typhus and other
illnesses. Shortly after his arrival, Pinchas and the other "electricians" went
through a process of disinfection and joined tens of thousands of other
prisoners in the camp. At one point Pinchas arrived at the part of the camp
where famous political prisoners were kept and where the Red Cross was
already providing some assistance. Pinchas still kept his health together. At
the camp the prisoners didn't work and life was aimless and they were idle
all day. The place was crowded and Pinchas recalls the difficulties the
prisoners had organizing themselves for a nights' sleep. They slept on the
floor and organized themselves like sardines. The absurdity of this camp,
Pinchas points out, was that by this time the guards didn't even carry
weapons, yet people didn't escape. Some refugees even smuggled themselves into the camp in order to find food and escape the brutality of the
ordinary citizens.

On May 15, 1945, Pinchas was walking inside the camp when he
suddenly saw what he thought was a soldier with a "different type of hel-
met." It had a white star on it that Pinchas had never seen before. What he
actually saw was the first American soldier climbing over the camp wall.
Within a few minutes more American soldiers' helmets appeared everywhere
and suddenly the noise of a tank breaking through the gates of the camp was
heard. Pinchas Lubling was finally liberated. He was twenty-one years old,
naked, and totally alone in the world. His mother and sister were gassed in
Treblinka and his father was killed during the uprising. There was no family
business to return to, no properties, no monies, and no home—his entire life
vanished. "I had no illusions about going back to Poland, said Pinchas, "I
knew there was nothing there anymore...."

After the liberation Pinchas refused to return to Poland in accordance
with the immediate and official policy of the American liberating force. The
Allies didn't recognize Judaism as a nationality and he had to leave the camp
in order to escape resettlement in Poland. At the beginning of June a representatives of the Jewish Brigades came to the camp and among them was a
person who once headed the Gordonian Zionists Chapter (*gar-in*) in Sos-

nowiec. He recognized Pinchas and arranged for him to move to Italy and join the Gordonian kibbutz *Hulda* that was organizing survivors for immigration to Israel.

In Italy Pinchas met Miriam Barmherzig from Bendzin, a nearby town in Poland and a recent survivor of Grunberg, a slave labor camp for women in Poland. However, members of the *Hulda* kibbutz in Italy later refused to accept Miriam as a member since she was not raised ideologically within the movement's values and goals. Pinchas and Miriam left the kibbutz in Italy and attempted to immigrate illegally to Palestine in 1946 during the second wave of immigration, but they were caught by the British Navy and returned to Italy. They attempted again during the 1948 Israeli War of Independence but the new state did not recruit survivors with families. Pinchas and Miriam spent four years in Italy recovering from their experience. On February 8, 1949 their first son was born in a Missing Persons Camp and Pinchas named him Moshe Maier Lubling (Maier was Miriam's murdered father), and they arrived in Israel on May 15, 1949.

In 1988, after the collapse of the Soviet Union, Pinchas and Miriam went to visit Poland for the first time since the end of the war. It was an attempt to bring closure to a haunting life marked by deep existential trauma, loss of trust in the world, lack of mourning, and a continuously challenging life in Israel. But it did not bring any closure, just more bewilderment.

However, Pinchas never went back to Germany; "my foot will never step on German soil," says Pinchas, "I live my life as if Germany and its culture don't exist. I am one who went through the war from its third day, and I do not believe the stories about the people who didn't know or hear. Everyone knew! Everyone heard! It would have been impossible not to...they are all guilty. The guilt is a collective German guilt, this is my personal conclusion, and this is the experience I had with the Germans."[27]

Pinchas Lubling in Treblinka in front of the rock that represents
the murdered Jewish community of Czestochowa, Treblinka, 1995

FIVE

The Need to Reconstruct the Treblinka Revolt

In writing about the Holocaust, we don't need authors with great imaginations. We need people who can depict the reality as it was. It was so overpowering that the facts speak for themselves.[1]
— Samuel Rajzman, survivor, "The End of Treblinka"

Alexander Donat makes the following observation which I take as a cue for my own reconstruction of the event:

We know very little about the leaders of the Treblinka conspiracy. Extensive research conducted in Warsaw, Israel and in New York to find more biographical data about Dr. Julian Chorazycki has yielded no results whatsoever, not even a photograph... A similar problem arose with other leaders of the uprising who fell in combat, the engineer Galewski. *No one of the survivors seems to know his first name...*Nobody is sure of the first name of Kurland ... some say it was Zev; others, Zvi. *These are, of course, just details but exactly these details make the difference between identification and anonymity, and they are the researcher's biggest problem.*[2]

Donat is correct in describing the work of the researcher as nearly impossible when documenting the events in Treblinka. He is also correct that a small detail, such as a first name, can make the difference between identification and anonymity. Such a difference in the case of Moshe Y. Lubling is of great historical and moral significance. Donat himself, after admonishing other researchers for overlooking details and facts, ignored his own advice. He himself never attempted to ask or to research who "Lubling from Silesia" was, although he anthologized Stanislaw Kon's account in his book—the same account that names Moshe Y. Lubling among the four plotters of the revolt. Neither Donat, nor any other researcher, approached the survivors Stanislaw Kon, Pinchas Lubling, Aaron Gelberd, Y. Dorsman, Moshe

Rappaport, Richard Glazer, Karl Unger, Dr. Orenstein, and Tzvi Rozenvayn who had first-hand information about at least one member of the organizing committee, i.e., Moshe Y. Lubling. In any other professional field, such negligence of existing facts would have constituted a case of malpractice. Having all the above information and personalities available to clarify and support and yet, ignoring their testimonies is an act of assassination—**a second killing**.

Now it is clear that a treasure of Holocaust information was ignored and was forever lost for future researchers. If researched correctly they would have found out that Pinchas Lubling was present in the meetings of the Workers Council in Czestochowa, a council that also functioned as the underground resistance organization until the night before the liquidation of the Ghetto. They would have found out that Pinchas Lubling and others in Czestochowa succeeded in communicating with Moshe Y. Lubling while in Treblinka, and were aware of the preparations for the revolt over a year before the actual uprising. They would have found that all the above information was submitted to Yad-Vashem by Pinchas Lubling and others but was completely ignored. Until this day, regardless of written promises from the Holocaust Museums both in D.C. and Jerusalem, a researcher will not find one reference to Moshe Y. Lubling in their database. The information was submitted countless times to the museums by Pinchas Lubling, the author, and even by Elie Wiesel.

Academically speaking, the institutions and their scholars' research and analytical skills were shameful at times; they simply were unable to put one and one together with regards to the Treblinka revolt and Moshe Y. Lubling. As opposed to researchers in general, it should have been even more prudent for the researchers of the Treblinka uprising to be careful and follow every lead. How else should researchers do their work when their primary sources of information come in the form of eyewitness accounts such as Samuel Willenberg's testimony? The latter, for instance, wasn't aware that Engineer Galewski was one of the organizers from the beginning until his death during the uprising in August 2, 1942. If it was possible for two individuals to exist in the same small camp, organize a revolt, execute it, and yet never know of each others' involvement, then it is infinitely possible that "Lubling from Silesia" was among the first four organizers of the revolt, as Kon, Glazer, Rappaport and Gelberd testified, and for others not to know about it!!! As testified by the survivor Tanhum Grinberg, "our first organizer was Dr. Chorazycki of Warsaw. It was he, too, who set up the committee, but we didn't know who its members were. We only knew the name of the doctor."[3] The fact that most participants in the uprising didn't know who the organizers were is also confirmed by Samuel Rajzman, another Treblinka survivor. He testified that "not one of these 50 [conspirators] knew who the others were. Each one of these 50 knew only one other person on the committee."[4]

By the time Yitzhak Arad wrote his comprehensive account of the revolt in Treblinka all the above information was available, but not necessarily known to him. However, as the ultimate authority on the revolt, he should have known all the limited information available, the limited amount of survivors, and the discrepancies among their accounts. He should have also been aware of the available testimony in his own institution. Even more, when Pinchas Lubling finally appeared in his office and challenged his omission of his father from the account, Arad did not reply: "Thank God we found someone who can shed some light on one person that is mentioned by Mr. Kon's account; an account that was never challenged and was used in many trials against Nazi criminals in Treblinka." Instead of marveling in the new source of information about the uprising, he preferred to ignore Pinchas Lubling's testimony and written support for his father's role in the uprising.

Any individual who was touched by the Holocaust, who visited the scenes of the crimes in Europe, especially Eastern Europe, would have experienced the emptiness and the ordinary-like nature of the place. Millions of Jews perished; their lives and property stolen by locals, their birth places and cemeteries desecrated, and their names vanished from memory. Some acted heroically while others acted cowardly and with disregard to their collective fate with other Jews. Let's not deceive ourselves, even if we do not wish to make judgments about people's behavior during extraordinary times, it is precisely during extraordinary times that some rise to the occasion and act in an extraordinary way. After the war there were numerous cases in which Holocaust survivors were killed by other survivors, most notably the Kastner case in Israel.[5] During his 1955 trial, *Haganah* leader and a member of kibbutz *Meuchad*, Israel Galili wrote:

> We must not allow the *Judenrat* to be rehabilitated; we must not agree with a path that handed over millions and cheated millions—out of the illusion that thus it will be possible to save the selected few. We must not let this enter the people's consciousness, that of the youth ... Such thoughts can destroy the nation's soul.[6]

Moshe Y. Lubling's life and actions are consistent with Mr. Galili's admonition to his fellow Israelis. Every effort should have been made to remember and document those who reflected the opposite spirit of the *Judenrat*. It should have been obvious to the researchers that, if the name of a person keeps on appearing, unsolicited, in different publications by different individuals who do not know each other, it is a good indication that the person acted in a way that people have taken the time to notice! Such individuals, as Moshe Y. Lubling, who were not able to tell their stories, are the true heroes of the Holocaust since they paid the ultimate price without expecting anything in return. By the survivors own admission, many among those who survived Treblinka and participated in the design of the uprising didn't even know who was organizing the uprising. Yitzhak Gruenbaum, a leader of Polish Jewry and a Zionist, correctly wrote that,

> The legend which raised the nation's morals ... which encouraged it in its travails and its bloody road to redemption—this legend laments all the Jews who were murdered, burned and killed ... but it raises the heroes from out of the masses, those who went to their death while resisting. The legend raises the specter of heroism.[7]

It goes without saying that Moshe Y. Lubling's actions during the Holocaust defined the future psychology and character of the modern State of Israel. He was secular, enlightened, a socialist, a fighter, and a leader of men and women. He fought the *Judenrat*'s collaboration and negotiations with the Nazis, the "fat Jews" who enslaved their brothers and sisters, and the various other collaborators who sold their communities in order to save themselves. It is this community of "thick-relationships" that owes its current culture and existence to exceptional individuals like Moshe Y. Lubling. It is also this community that failed ethically to remember his name.

Let's make one thing perfectly clear. The leaders of the uprising, not the 50 or 60 prisoners who participated or even helped organize the uprising, did not intended to save themselves. Those who escaped and those who survived were not among the leaders of the uprising! This was made clear by Richard Glazer and the letter sent by Moshe Y. Lubling to his son and colleagues in Czestochowa. Furthermore, from the original four plotters only engineer Galewski, Capo Kurland, and Lubling from Silesia reached the date of the uprising as leaders. Engineer Galewski, the camp-elder, however, was not among the ideological conspirators from the beginning, the contrary is true. As we recall, according to early testimonies of some survivors, "the first meetings of the Organization Committee was done in complete secrecy because the Jewish 'camp-elder', a corrupt Jewish engineer from Warsaw, who treated Jews brutally ... Later he experienced a 'rebirth' and joined the conspirators."[8] Dr. Chorazycki committed suicide in April 1943, four months before the uprising and in March 1943 Zelo Bloch was sent to Camp II (the extermination area) which was isolated from the rest. In Camp II he later formed a separate Organizing Committee which communicated with the main Committee in Camp I. As such, four months before the uprising the only two individuals who remained from the original plotters were Lubling and Kurland. It is at this point that others joined, including Galewski.

Also, it is obvious why every Treblinka survivor was aware and knowledgeable about some plotters and not others. Dr. Chorazycki was the camp physician who treated the Jewish prisoners and he was there from the time the camp started its construction. Given the health conditions in the camp as well as several epidemics, it is not surprising that many knew him or about him. Engineer Galewski was the camp-elder which makes him visible to all and being the only one who could visit all places on camp. As the camp-elder, it is not surprising that many remember him, but not always as a helpful Jewish soul. Kurland was the Capo of the notorious *Lazaret* that actually led to a pit where scores of prisoners, for a multitude of reasons, were executed. The killing of sick prisoners was often done by Kurland himself. Being a Capo and the person who is in charge of the "pit of death" was a sufficient enough reason to know him or know about him. Finally, Zelo Bloch, a former Czech army officer, was the Forman of the "sorting area" that, other than Camp II, included the largest amount of prisoners. As pointed out earlier, in March 1943, Zelo was punished and sent to camp II to assist in the burning of the bodies, a job that very few could endure and survive for more than a few weeks. Next, Rudolf Masarek, a 28 year-old former lieutenant in the Czech army and the child of a well to do Jewish family in Czechoslovakia; because some survivors spelled his name Masaryk it gave rise to the claim that he was related to Thomas G. Masaryk, the first President of the Czechoslovakia Republic.[9] This apparently was not the case but it made him, nonetheless, memorable to others.

In contrast, Moshe Y. Lubling worked as a *Goldjuden* and in sorting the properties of the victims which would have allowed only a small group of people to know him or communicate with him. This fact, however, made him the perfect person to oversee the entire operation and be the "contact person" for the different fighting units, as described by Richard Glazer. Not being a Capo, a camp-elder, the camp physician, a foreman who was a former Czech army officer, or being supposedly related to the former president of Czechoslovakia, made it harder for prisoners in the camp to know or notice him. But from our previous discussion we learned that Moshe Y. Lubling was an unusual individual who had a long record of resistance and organizational activities long before he arrived in Treblinka. The fact that from the limited Treblinka survivors' accounts, three individuals name him as one of the leaders and three others as *the* leader of the revolt, should tell us something about Moshe Y. Lubling significance. This is especially important when compared with the others who were known by their obvious visible position in the camp and by distinguished origination. One finds in all Treblinka survivors' testimonies a sort of mesmerizing feeling regarding the fact that distinguished Jews found themselves in the same position as ordinary prisoners. The engineer Galewski, according to Richard Glazer's has become "the aristocratic speaker for the slaves of Treblinka."[10] Being a known physician from Warsaw, a known engineer or an agronomist, former military officer, or a non-Polish Jew, obviously made a great impression upon the prisoners. German, Czech, and Austrian Jews usually found common ground with Nazi members who respected their culture and cultivated upbringing. Even among the prisoners themselves such distinctions existed; the Polish Jews were considered the lowest in character.[11]

Polanizing the Revolt in Treblinka

Remembering the life and actions of Moshe Y. Lubling is even more urgent today because of the upcoming Polanization of the Treblinka Uprising in the form of a Polish Memorial Museum at Treblinka. While acknowledging the losses suffered by the Polish nation during WWII, individually and collectively their behavior was shamefully anti-Semitic to the extreme! Indeed, the Polish people hated the Germans but they hated the Jews even more. Andrzej Zbikowski, in the epilogue to Samuel Willenberg's book *Revolt in Treblinka* writes:

> ... there exist a rich collection of memories containing description of events in which Poles adopted a hostile attitude, often a very active one, towards Jews who were hiding ... Despite the suggestions of some Polish researchers, hostility displayed toward Jews was not characteristic solely of a marginal groups of extortionists. 'Grot' Rowecki himself stated in a telegram sent to London already in 1941 that 'the overwhelming majority in the country is anti-Semitic ... on the whole Polish society acted with indifference or downright hostility ... a tone of anti-Semitism and satisfaction that Warsaw had finally become 'Judenfrie'... Moreover, the extermination of the Jews enabled the Polish lower middle class to take over a large part of the Jewish property.[12]

The Holocaust historian Lucy S. Dawidowicz correctly showed that the thesis for Polish historians always "was that the Germans intended 'the biological destruction of the Polish population,' a thesis consciously calculated to downgrade the murder of the Polish Jews, while inflating the Polish losses."[13] The museum in Treblinka is not yet finished but its new director already commented on the Moshe Y. Lubling case. According to Diane L. Saltzman, a former director of the Collection Division at the United State Memorial Holocaust Museum in D.C., after consulting with "the director of the Museum in Treblinka," she reported to me that "no additional sources have been found referencing your grandfather's involvement in the Treblinka Uprising."[14] The director of the Treblinka Museum did not explain what the accepted sources were, by whom, and based on what? Is this the proper response for the director of the new Treblinka Museum to make? Wouldn't such a director, or any scholar of the Treblinka experience, be interested to speak and learn more from the living child and grandchild of an individual who was named as one of the heroes of the Treblinka Revolt? Considering that only a handful of individuals survived and by their own admission they didn't know the leaders of the revolt; **then,** a surviving grandchild of one of the named leaders who is also a respected professor of philosophy and who searched and lived with the story of Treblinka all his life, might be a once in a lifetime opportunity for every existing museum, especially a new Museum in Poland.

Polish-Jewish relations completely evaporated after the Holocaust as Poland was separated from the developing democratic nations by the Soviet Union. Not being an open, cosmopolitan, and enlightened community at the start of the 20th Century, and after losing its Jewish community to the Nazis and its native intellectuals to the Communists, Poland discovered in the 1990s that the world does not recognize their national tragedy and heroism. On the contrary, the six million murdered Jews of Europe, of which half were Polish citizens, were the only recognized victims of Nazi brutality while the Polish nation and its citizens were portrayed as collaborators and anti-Semites. The return of Jewish survivors to Poland in the 1990s, the prospect that they might claim their property back and disclose Polish behavior during the Holocaust, resulted in new expressions of anti-Semitism, denial, revisionism, and as always violence. This time, however, it was literarily against invisible Jews since Poland after the Holocaust was virtu- ally *Judenfrie* (free of Jews). Until this day a visitor to Poland would find anti-Semitic graffiti near former Jewish sites declaring "Poland for the Poles!" while a large number of Poles still believe that the Jews are in control of Poland. I have lived among Holocaust survivors my entire life and without exception they all depicted their former Polish neighbors' behavior as "worse than the Nazis." Furthermore, pointing to the handful of Poles who risked their lives to save Jews does not contradict the general sentiment of the survivors, or the Western world, that Polish attitude towards the Jews was shamefully anti-Semitic and bestial. Until this day, the handful of Poles who saved Jews are still afraid to make their names public for fear of retaliation by their fellow Poles. It shows that for the most part the Polish nation was always deeply anti-Semitic; criminally anti-Semitic.

The debate over Polish-Jewish relations was recently stirred by Jan T. Gross's recent publication of two books, *Neighbors* and *Fear*[15] outlining Polish attitude towards the Jews during and after the Holocaust. In

Neighbors[16] Gross reconstructed a 1941 event in the Polish town of Jedwabne in which 1600 Jewish men, women, and children were brutally murdered by the non-Jewish residents of the town, i.e., "half the town murdered the other half." The book caused harsh reaction from Polish intellectuals that, in my view, only underscored and re-exposed the deep resentment and hatred of the Polish populace towards the Jewish people. The general response by Polish apologists is usually to first, blame the Jews for their own suffering and accuse them of collaboration with the Communists, and second, to eclipse the singularity of the Jewish Holocaust and incorporate their tragedy into a national Polish tragedy, the real Holocaust.

Richard Lukas, the author of *The forgotten Holocaust: The Poles under German Occupation,* reacted immediately to the publication of Gross' book by exposing the above resentment the Polish people feel with regards to having their victimhood stolen by the Jews. First, Lukas noticed the "gigantic enterprise" that is involved in preserving the memory of Jewish victims of the Holocaust. [17] Second, he accused the publishing establishment in America for only publishing Holocaust research that depicts Jews in "pristine terms" and "non-Jewish groups, especially Catholic Poles, as either Nazi collaborators or accomplices or perpetrators of atrocities."[18] Third, he challenged the merits of Gross' book on the ground that the latter "is not a professional historian, but a sociologist" who accepts eyewitness accounts as facts without seeking independent verification. Forth, he accused Polish Jews of "treason in eastern Poland, where Jedwabne is located," and the need of Jews to face their "collaborationist past with Poland's enemies."[19] Finally, according to Lukas, the necessary inference from the above premises is that, "it should not be too surprising that some Poles have sought out Jewish traitors and tried to kill them."[20]

Indeed, Gross is not a professional historian—as if that means much— and Lukas is not a trained philosopher. In his attempt to reject the claim that Poland is anti-Semitic he provided the clearest linguistic expression of anti-Semitism I have seen in a long time. First, Lukas raises the old anti-Semitic sentiments that Jews are only interested in money; that they use Holocaust memory for profit. Second, as most anti-Semites, he accuses the Jews of controlling the media and the publishing industry. This Jewish control, he claims, is at the root of the bad publicity the Poles received in the Western world. Third, he accuses Jews of having a low moral character since Jews lie about the Holocaust and therefore, their testimonies cannot be trusted without resort to "independent verification." Yet, while Lukas rejects Gross' failure to independently verify his eyewitness' varsity, he then goes on to claim that "new documentary evidence has come to light which suggests that the Germans, not the Poles, were primarily responsible for the massacre [in Jedwabne]. According to one report, the Polish role was limited to less than 50 people, who were forced to guard Jews in the town square prior to their execution."[21] The retired professional historian from Tennessee Technological University does not provide any further information about the "new documentary evidence" or what independent verification he conducted to support this un-named report and documentary evidence. Fifth, he charges Jews with being "Poland's enemies." While the Poles were divided among themselves between their official exiled government in England and their newly established Communist leadership in Moscow, when some Polish Jews chose communism they immediately became "Poland's enemies." Finally, he accuses Jews of sensationalizing their victimhood. All anti-Semites find delight in reducing all arguments about crimes against Jews to arguments about the moral equivalency of crimes in general. Lukas' version is that "some" Poles killed Jews and "some" Jews killed Poles. There is nothing anti-Semitic about Poles killing Jews, stealing their property, or desecrating their cemeteries, since some Jews were Poland's enemies. Some Jews (you can count them on your fingers) indeed joined the Communists together with millions of Poles. Later on, the Polish Communist government repressed its citizens, confiscated their private property, killed anti-communists, or converted religious properties into public and social structures. But the Polish Communist government was not a Jewish conspiracy against the Polish people, as some Poles wish to portray it today. The Islamic anti-Semites and their apologists' version of the moral equivalency argument is that there is nothing anti-Jewish about Palestinian terrorism; "some Palestinians kill Israelis and some Israelis kill Palestinians." The intentional goal of a suicide bomber to blow-up a bus full of children on their way to school is morally equivalent to a group of Israeli soldiers' killing of the terrorist group's leader. Besides, Jews are never innocent even at a young age since they will grow up to become Israeli soldiers who kill Palestinians. The apologists for Nazi genocidal intentions also use this argument to show that there was no German plan to exterminate the Jews. There was a war in which Soviets, American, British, and French soldiers killed Germans and Germans killed them; Jews were merely casualties of the war as were millions of other European citizens. In addition, many Jews were communists or liberals and naturally became the enemies of Nazi Germany.

Well, there is nothing equivalent, morally or otherwise, between Jewish intellectuals' attraction to communism and the burning alive of the 1600 Jewish residents of Jedwabne by their Catholic neighbors. There is no equivalency between the Poles' sense of entitlement to Jewish property and the Polish Communist Party that confiscated Polish industrial property or killed its political opponents. There is also no moral equivalency between the acts of Palestinian suicide bombers and the Israeli Defense Forces. One is a criminal organization set on killing as many Israeli civilians as possible; the other is the legitimate defense force of a democratic nation. Finally, there is no moral equivalency between the Allies' killings of German soldiers, or even the bombing of German civilians, and the Germans' unprovoked attack on their European neighbors, the murder of eleven million people in death camps, and causing the death of nearly sixty million people in Europe.

Even more revealing about Poland's apologists is the debate Gross' book inspired between Adam Michnik, a former anti-communist and the current Jewish editor of *Gozeta Wyborcza*, and Leon Wieseltier, the Jewish literary editor of the *New Republic* and the author of *Kaddish*. In a 2001 article in the *New York Times* Michnik attempted to reject the insinuation that the Jedwabne massacre shows a collective Polish guilt. In defense of Polish behavior against Jews during WWII he quoted from Zofia Kossak-Szczucka. In August 1942, the known Polish Catholic writer publicly called the indifference of Poles to Jewish persecution "a disgrace" and encouraged her fellow Poles to show solidarity with their persecuted Jews. We should do so, she encouraged her fellow Poles, despite the fact that "our feelings towards the Jews haven't changed. We still consider them the political, economic and ideological enemies of Poland."[22] Michnik called this an "extraordinary appeal" that shows the painful paradox Poles found themselves under the Nazi occupation. On the one hand "the anti-Semitic tradition compels the Poles to perceive the Jews as aliens while the Polish heroic tradition compels them to save them."[23] Here is a proud Polish Jew who chose to remain in Poland after the war than join his Jewish brothers and sisters with the establishment of an independent homeland. Here is a Polish Jew willing to excuse Polish historical hatred towards him and his faith and instead celebrate a delusional myth about Polish heroism. Michnik correctly referred to his Polish/Jewish condition as schizophrenic by acknowledging that, "I know that if I had been in Jedwabne, I would have been killed as a Jew," but even so, "I assert that ...whoever uses this example [the Jedwabne massacre] to generalize that this is how only the Poles and all the Poles behave, is lying."[24]

In response, Leon Wieseltier calls Michnik's usage of Zofia Kossak-Szczucka's appeal as an example of Polish heroism, "grotesque." He further suggests that, "if these were the philosophical and emotional grounds for 'Polish heroism' on behalf of the Jews in Poland, it is no wonder that such heroism was rare."[25] In a reply to Wieseltier, Michnik continued his defense of Polish behavior during the Holocaust by further arguing that the problem in Polish-Jewish relations is that, while both groups view themselves as victims, Jews haven't been sensitive to the suffering of the Polish people. Expressing the depth of this resentment, he writes:

> For many years after the war the Poles grieved over their Jewish compatriots without acknowledging that the fate of their Jewish neighbors was incomparably more tragic—an utterly exceptional tragedy in the history of humanity ... a triumphalism of pain, as though Jews decided that only the Jewish tragedy was worthy of preservation in the consciousness ... Poles also have a right to the memories of their own pain. And they have a right to expect that Jews will be aware of it as well.[26]

The logic of this response and its expression of self-delusions are quite amazing. Although the Jews were truly the "enemies of Poland," the heroic and exceptional character of the Poles made them "grieve over their Jewish compatriots." It is difficult to understand how the Poles grieved over their Jewish neighbors when all empirical evidence shows the exact opposite. Grieving people do not steal others' property; extort money from hiding Jews, turned them over to the Nazis, and cover-up their crimes. Grieving people attempt to preserve the property of their fallen "compatriots" and they do not desecrate their cemeteries.

What is even more extraordinary is the feeling of resentment by the Poles that the Jews stole the spotlight away from their own tragedy. While the heroic Poles grieved and considered the Jews their "compatriots"; the Jews in turn only thought of themselves as the worthy victims of the war. As such, the Poles who considered the Jews as the "enemies of Poland," who stole their property, and who covered up their crimes against the Jews, now demand that Jews be aware of their compatible pain. It is interesting to observe the way the feeling of inferiority informs the logic of all Jew haters' attack on post-Holocaust Jewry. African-American, especially those influenced by the Nation of Islam, resent the Jews for having a Holocaust Museum in Washington, D.C. while their own "holocaust" is not recognized. The Palestinians resent the Jews for getting the sympathy of the world's consciousness while their own "holocaust" is not recognized. The common thread is the act of projecting onto the Jew all the inadequacies one feels about himself. The African-Americans who resent the Jews do so because of their own failure to overcome their collective tragedy; the Palestinians resent the Israeli-Jews for transforming their own tragedy into a flourishing democratic state, while they are still unable to deliver basic services to their people; and the Poles resent the Jews for getting the sympathy of the world while eclipsing the real holocaust, that of the heroic Polish people. In all cases there is the attempt to deny one's own responsibility for one's moral, spiritual, and collective behavior.

The charge by Michnik that Jews engage in a sort of a "triumphalism of pain" is absurd and shows the depth of Poland's sense of inferiority. As Moshe Y. Lubling's grandson, I would have been more than happy to see that all available pain and suffering goes to someone other than Jews for a change. As an Israeli, I want to be recognized for my independence and ability to overcome my past, not for victimhood. I can care less about the sympathy of the world towards me after the fact. However, as Wieseltier correctly replied to Michnik, "should they [the Jews] forget what they know about the world, so as to be acquitted of a 'triumphalism of pain'?"[27] While I recognize the suffering of the Polish people during WWII, I do not believe that they "grieved" over the Jewish collective destruction in Poland, the contrary is the case. I also agree with Wieseltier that there is no obvious need for a dialogue between Poles and Jews in order to understand each others' perspective. Jewish life in Poland is over and it should never be rehabilitated. Leave Poland to the Poles, they surely deserve it![28]

There is the usual claim by apologists for violence against Jews that there is no other collective responsibility and guilt than the moral one, and therefore, contemporary Poles, Germans, or Ukrainians cannot be held responsible for what "marginal groups of extortionists" did sixty years ago. Indeed, making generalizations about large groups of people is never accurate and should usually be rejected. However, the "you can never generalize" objection can also be used (and usually does) to make it impossible to discuss past guilt and responsibility for acts of injustice. One can easily argue that it wasn't the "collective" Germans who were responsible for the Holocaust; it wasn't the "collective" white man who enslaved the black Africans; or it wasn't the white European colonists who killed 50,000,000 native Indians—you cannot make such generalizations because not every single German or every single white man committed the above crimes. Unless you can show that every single German caused the Holocaust, you are not allowed to generalize about German "collective" responsibility—or anyone else's collective responsibility. If one wishes to continue this line of perverted linguistic game, she can take it one extra step and argue that even if the collective German people were responsible for the crimes committed by the Nazis, the new collective isn't. Well, it is no wonder why John Dewey in 1914 warned against the growing formalism in the modern discourse and quest for knowledge.

The best way to show that it is perverted logic is to point out that for those who use it, the reversal is never true! For most Poles, Jews in general are still responsible for the death of Jesus 2000 years ago, as well as for the few who joined the Polish Communist Party sixty years ago. For most Arabs, young Israelis today are responsible for what their Zionist grandparents did one hundred years ago. It somehow seems natural to generalize and view the Jews as a collective, but not other cultural, religious, or nationalistic groups.

It seems clear that Poland's national interest today is to eclipse their disgraceful behavior towards Jews, as well as the Jews' unique Holocaust tragedy. Such an eclipse is accomplished by intentionally incorporating the Jewish Holocaust into their national narrative as a Polish event, therefore, viewing all extermination sites in Poland as national memorials in which Poles *and other people* have been killed. In the case of Auschwitz, for instance, two-thirds of the estimated 1,700,000 casualties were Jewish and in Treblinka all the murdered victims were Jews. Such historical revisionism will certainly confuse the discussion regarding the sad reality of Poland's extreme culture of anti-Semitism. Their refusal to separate the fate of Poland from the Jewish tragedy was evident in the 1978 speech by the Polish "exterminationist" historian Janusz Wieczorek. Not able to give Jews their moment at the opening of the Jewish Pavilion in Auschwitz he proclaimed that "among those doomed, Jews and Poles rank the first place." This implies, of course, that from the start the German's extermination plan was directed towards the Poles but only started with the extermination of Polish Jews, a view that is factually wrong. The Holocaust historian James E. Young correctly observed "that the death camps were located on Polish soil is viewed by the Poles not as evidence of local anti-Semitism or collaboration but as a sign of the German's ultimate plans for the Polish people. The mass murder of Jews becomes significant in Polish memory only insofar as it is perceived as precursor to the Poles' own, unfulfilled genocide."[29]

In reading the eyewitness accounts of those who survived the Treblinka uprising one sometimes gets the impression that escaping the death camp was the easiest part. Notice Moshe Y. Lubling's advice to Richard Glazer in Treblinka:

> 'If through some miracle you should ever be able to get out, then you can never let anyone know that you are fleeing Treblinka … they [the Poles] would tear your cloths off your body, piece by piece, they'd kill you, and then they'd probably search you to see if you had any money on you …'[30]

Indeed, as we know today, between 200–400 prisoners from Treblinka succeeded in escaping the camp into the surrounding forests but only around 40 made it alive. The majority of the escaped prisoners were either caught and killed or were caught, robbed, and brought by Polish peasants back to the death camp for a cash reward. The prisoners that were brought back were immediately murdered in Treblinka or were sent to Sobibor to be gassed. Samuel Rajzman, a survivor of Treblinka, relates the following event the day after his daring escape:

> We all ran together, twelve people ... by about ten o'clock we were very tired; we lacked food and drink. So we decided that we'd send two people to a peasant's cottage at the edge of the woods to find food and water for us. ... As we were taking the pitcher back, we heard terrific shooting from the place we had just left. ... At twelve o'clock we returned to our friends. We didn't find a single one left alive from the whole group. Nobody was left alive; the only other survivor beside me was Kudlik ...[31]

Samuel Willenberg, also a Treblinka survivor, expressed a similar sentiment when he described his attempt to survive in Warsaw after his escape from Treblinka.

> During the passing weeks and months, the problem of personal security robbed me of sleep and peace of mind. It was a life of emptiness, disorder, endless tension and tremendous fatigue. Like many other Jews, I always had the feeling of being under surveillance; I might be recognized at any moment—by a woman I had known, or by an acquaintance from bygone times who, for any reason, might hand me over to the first German he'd encounter, denounce me to the Polish police, or force me to pay him off—because I had succeeded in living. In the moral world of the Nazis' collaborators, my very survival was a matter of exceptional impudence.[32]

Another survivor, Chiel Rajchman, describes that while he was hiding in a Polish peasant's house "suddenly came in a neighbor and started to hit me in the face shouting, 'Come with me, Jew! Get up! Come with me! To the women, he shouted, 'They are criminals! They burned down Treblinka' ... 'Let me take him to the Germans. I will get a premium for his head.'"[33]

Some readers may object to my strong and negative feelings towards the Polish people and their behavior during the Holocaust. Indeed, there were cases in which Poles assisted and saved Jews with great risk to themselves, but such cases were exceptional when compared with the overall behavior of the Polish nation. As with all victims, executioners, and collaborators in the Holocaust, the Polish people had a choice to make as well! No one forced them to steal Jewish property as if they were entitled to it; to organize anti-Jewish groups that first boycotted Jewish businesses and later killed Jews or handed them over to the Nazis; and to desecrate Jewish cemeteries. In Martin Buber's language, they made their choice and spoke *IT* to their fellow Jewish citizens by objectifying and abandoning them. However, in their delusional view of themselves as heroes, they are now translating Martin Buber's writings into Polish and claiming him as their own; as part of the distinguished and long intellectual heritage of the Polish culture—another delusional tale.

Since the collapse of the Soviet Union I have made several trips to Poland with my family and students. Personally, it was only after I met the Polish people that I could finally understand how the Holocaust happened. It is not the case, as some argued, that it was the largest concentration of Jews that motivated the Nazis to build their extermination camp in Poland. Rather, the Germans constructed all their major extermination camps in Poland because they understood the deep and religiously motivated hatred that the Polish masses held against their Jewish neighbors; neither were the death-camps built in Poland for the purpose of exterminating the Polish nation, as Polish historians want us to believe. None of this, of course, exonerates the German nation, but it also does not excuse other nations' participation in the robbing, raping, and destruction of European Jewry. Witness the following description by Samuel Willenberg of the Polish residents of Czestochowa immediately after the deportations of the Jews started (including my grandfather's family).

> Approaching City Hall, I came upon a crowd. As I moved closer I was engulfed by a mass of enraged men and women, faces red with tension. A kerchief woman turned to me in indignation. Was it right that only the flats on the side streets were being given to people? What of those on the boulevard itself?
>
> 'You see Sir', she went on, 'people with the right connections get the flats on the boulevard.' Then she whispered that there was still some fine furniture inside— although the best had been sent to Germany—and that valuables of other kinds were there for the picking too.[34]

Even more disturbing is the behavior of the Polish residents in the surrounding villages of Treblinka as described by Jan T. Gross.

> Jews were a source of wealth also after they had been killed by the Nazis. Murder sites were dug up after the war in search of valuables … [in Treblinka] the entire area was scattered with holes, several meters deep, with human bones scattered all around … People sifting through the mounds of ashes didn't bother to answer when asked what they were doing … People who enriched themselves with gold dug up from the graves; by night plunder their own neighbors … in a peasant hut … a women was tortured with live fire to reveal the place where she was hiding gold and valuables … Local people came to perceive Jews as a source that could be harvested when the opportune moment arrived. The murderous pogrom in Radzilow in July 1941 was preceded by the arrival of peasants from Wasosz, who had killed and plundered their own Jews two days earlier, but the local chased them away … Evidently, a town's Jews were for the town's people to plunder.[35]

Collective Obligation

Finally, the need to reconstruct the Treblinka Revolt is also necessary in order to maintain, through memory, the identity of the Jewish community that emerged after the Holocaust. As Avishai Margalit pointed out, a community of "thick relations" has the moral obligation to remember those who perished in its name. The Israeli-Jewish community is arguably such a community, especially with regards to those who perished in its name. Not only was Moshe Y. Lubling killed in Treblinka by the Nazis, now Holocaust scholars and institutions around the world are killing him again by omitting his name from history. He is now *twice dead.* The omission will result in the collective forgetting of his name, when in fact, he died in their name. While there are plenty of individuals around the world that wish to deny, trivialize, and minimize the Jewish tragedy, Holocaust scholars should not lend a hand to such travesty by being academically territorial, intellectually elitists, close-minded, and assured in their analytical conclusions about events that the living witness dispute.

While I do not doubt the importance of Holocaust Museums and institutions, there is nothing worse than entrusting academicians with a lived experience and issue. The long history of formalism in the academia with its emphasis on method rather than creativity, oversized egos, detachment from ordinary experience, and it's often dishonesty in research and ideologies, promise to be a sure way to objectify the experiences and issues involved in the Holocaust. Like any other subject-matter that is taken from the stream of ordinary experience, it will not be the intellectual who will shed light and give insights into the phenomena.

Ultimately, what will carry the experience and lessons of the Holocaust into the future will not be the various Holocaust Museums, institutions, or tenure granting manuscripts. It will be the existence of the State of Israel and generations of survivors' children. They are the ones who internalized the experience at home, and they are the only ones who could communicate the lived spirit of the Holocaust. The continuous isolation and rejection of survivors' testimonies by self-appointed Holocaust guardians will surely result in a "plastic Holocaust". Like the existing museums, they will present information and conclusions about an event they only know from afar, and at the end of the exhibition they will sell memorial pins and tee-shirts with "Never Again" printed on them. This is not the way a community ought to honor those who died in its name.

As I argued earlier, my issue with Holocaust research regarding Treblinka is very specific. It does not involve a challenge to the reality of the camp itself or the revolt. Nor does it challenge the eyewitness accounts of the few who survived Treblinka during the uprising, although some accounts involve information that proved later to be incorrect. My argument is specifically aimed at the issue regarding the identification of the original plotters of the revolt and their consequent participation in the revolt itself. Three out of the four original members of the "Organizing Committee" named by the Treblinka survivor Stanislaw Kon had military experience; they were in their forties and fifties with families that perished in Treblinka. However, by the time they arrived in Treblinka they were years removed from their military experience or any other social or political activity. Zelo Bloch was a photographer by profession when he arrived at Treblinka; 57 year-old Dr. Chorazycki was a laryngologist from Warsaw; and Kurland was a middle-aged wood merchant from Warsaw. Only the fourth member, Moshe Y. Lubling, had the experience and proven ability to organize people into action; the most valuable quality in organizing a revolt under impossible conditions. He was the one that organized thousands of starving slave laborers to go on a hunger strike against the policies of the *Judenrat* and Gestapo in Czestochowa. He was the one to turn the Workers' Council in Czestochowa into a resistance organization. And, from the four original plotters he was the only one who could have organized a prisoner's revolt. What was required in Treblinka was not merely to be a noticeable figure in the camp; the contrary was true, such notoriety might have been an impediment. Capos and other camp personalities might have been used for organizational and communication purposes while the actual work was done by less known prisoners. It goes without saying that it took extraordinary men to become leaders of others, especially under the conditions created by the Nazis.

In what follows I will reconstruct the activities of Moshe Y. Lubling in Treblinka based on all available documents, as well as the knowledge I acquired from his son Pinchas. My goal is to create a permanent record of his story so his name and actions would not be forgotten by future generations of Holocaust students and scholars.

SIX

The Treblinka Revolt

"If all forests were pens and all days ink, it would not be possible to write and describe what was happening in Treblinka."

—Moshe Y. Lubling,
From a letter to his son, Treblinka, May 1943

It is time to review the existing information about the Treblinka revolt; the same information that gave assurance to some Holocaust historiographers that Moshe Y. Lubling's participation as one of the revolt leaders cannot be substantiated and does not warrant further inquiry. According to Alexander Donat, 69 individuals survived Treblinka (not necessarily the uprising) and he encountered fifty testimonies by survivors of the camp. Most of the accounts were submitted to the Jewish Historical Institute in Warsaw and the Central Commission for the investigation of German Crimes in Poland.[1] However, Yitzchak Arad's writings and presentations disputed Donat's number of testimonies by survivors of Treblinka. Arad claimed that only 27 such testimonies by Treblinka survivors existed and that, in fact, Donat's account involves several errors.[2]

Regardless of the number of testimonies, there are several facts about the Treblinka revolt that are consistent among all survivors who knew about the organization and preparations for the uprising.

1. Dr. Chorazycki was in Treblinka from the moment the camp started its operations. It is also clear that by being the camp physician who treated the prisoners he was known to everyone whether or not they knew anything about the preparations for an uprising. However, according to several testimonies, "the four plotters of the revolt met at night around his [Dr. Chorazycki] plank bed and discussed the

plans."[3] It is not clear how Dr. Chorazycki attended such discussions since he lived and slept at the clinic while the other three plotters slept in the barracks that were locked at night from the outside. It is also known that the doctor committed suicide in April 1943, three months before the revolt.

2.   We also know that Zelo, the foreman of the labor detail and his as-sistant Adolf Friedman, were punished and sent to the extermination area on March 1943, where Zelo formed another organizing commit-tee. As a foreman and a former captain in the Czech Army, Zelo was known to prisoners regardless of their knowledge of the revolt.

3.   We also know that engineer Galewski was the camp-elder, which made him the most recognized prisoner in the camp by everyone. Kurland was the most controversial Capo in the camp since he was in charge of the "field-hospital" where those prisoners who could not work any longer, or those who were punished, were executed. Every prisoner would have known him.

4.   We also know that after the death of the doctor, other prisoners were added to the Organizing Committee. According to several testimo-nies the new Organizing Committee consisted of 12 members, al-though when adding the names mentioned by different survivors we get over twenty members. Obviously what it meant to be a member of the Organizing Committee was interpreted differently by different individuals. The other often mentioned names are of twenty-eight year-old Rudolf Masarek, and the noted Warsaw agronomist Su-dowicz (Sadovits) who was in charge of the vegetable garden in the camp. The participation of Masarek in the organization was ques-tioned by Yitzchak Arad on the grounds that only "a single testi-mony also places Rudolf Masarek … in the Organizing Committee."[4] This statement is puzzling on two accounts. First, in my research on Treblinka I found an additional three references to Masarek as a member of the committee by the survivors Rajzman, Kohn, and Glazer. Second, if it is appropriate to mention Masarek as a member of the Organizing Committee with the qualification that only one tes-timony exists that attest to his membership, why wasn't it also ap-propriate to mention Moshe Y. Lubling and qualify it by saying that "only" six survivors and scores of historians and residents of Czesto-chowa placed him in the Organizing Committee? The other members of the Organizing Committee, including Moshe Y. Lubling, were not Capos, camp elders, foremen, camp physicians, famous agronomists

from Warsaw, or Czech elite, but they were not just involved in the organizing of the revolt, they were its leaders.

The survivors' testimonial topography can be outlined as follows: First are those who submitted testimony to the Central Commission for Investigation of German Crimes in Poland between 1965 and 1969. However, the testimonies to the Central Commission did not necessarily center around the uprising or the individuals involved but rather on the activities of the German and Ukrainian personnel. Also, some of those who testified also wrote and submitted other testimonies either before or after the Commission concluded its work. The list is based on the work already done by Alexander Donat, Yitzchak Arad, and others. I attempted to provide as much information on each individual as the research warranted.

1. **Brenner, Henoch/Hejnoch**—Settled in the United States after the war.

2. **Czechowicz, Aaron**—Settled in Caracas, Venezuela after the war.

3. **Finkelstein, Leon**—Settled in Paris, France, after the war. In his testimony he described Ivan and Nicholas, the Ukrainian guards as cutting "off the women's breasts with swords," on their way to the gas chambers.

4. **Kon/Kohn, Shalom/Stanislaw/Abe**—Acknowledged by some for being part of the revolt (but not of the four members of the original Organizing Committee) and as such, also submitted eyewitness testimony at the Fort Lauderdale trial. His written testimony was originally published in the Polish-Jewish newspaper *Dos Naye Lebn* on May 10, 1945.[5] In his testimony he named "Lubling from Silesia" as a member of the original committee. **This testimony constitutes the first primary source naming Moshe Y. Lubling among the four original members of the Organizing Committee.** His honesty and the authenticity of his account have never been challenged. His testimony was used by virtually every scholar of the Treblinka revolt. And since the other three names he cited were accepted by everyone ... why was there a need to doubt the fourth name, i.e., Lubling of Silesia? In fact, Mr. Kon's account of the revolt in Treblinka is still the most anthologized account of the revolt and is required reading in many classes on the Holocaust. Finally, since Mr. Kon only died several years ago in Israel, he was always available to scholars who researched the revolt, including Yizhak Arad. Yet, no attempt was made to inquire further into the fourth name.

Interestingly, however, Mr. Kon's account does not mention anything about the fate of the *Goldjuden* after the suicide of Dr. Chorazycki. This is a significant point since, until I read Richard Glazer's account in 1995, I believed that the incident provides an insight into the nature of Moshe Y. Lubling's possible death. Kon writes that after the death of Dr. Chorazycki in April 1943, only three month before the uprising, new members joined the committee, among them were Dr. Leichert and Rudolf Masarek.

5. **Kudlik/Kudik, Arie/Alexander**—In Treblinka he worked at the zoo as a woodworker and craftsman. After the war he designed a map of the camp (together with Marian Platkiewicz and Mojrsz/Mietek Laks) which was submitted to the Central Jewish Historical Committee. In his testimony he reiterates what most survivors acknowledged, that "through the entire period people in the camp did not know a thing [about the uprising] since the matter could have dripped out and fallen into undesired hands."[6] The significance of Kudlik's statement is that if most people in the camp did not know about the plan, they certainly did not know the identity of the leaders. This fact must be taken into account when considering the omission of Moshe Y. Lubling from Yitzhak Arad's account of the uprising. The fact that "only" three survivors placed Moshe Y. Lubling as an original member of the "Organizing Committee" is amazing given the absolute need to keep the plan secret. Even the few who joined the Organizing Committee after Dr. Chorazycki's death, were not aware of all the leaders' names.[7]

In his testimony Kudlik relates an event that inspired the uprising. It involved a Jew from Czestochowa by the name of Langer who was caught with money in his cloths. After being beaten and then hanged by his feet, he cried out to the Jews not to look at the food, money, and possessions that were flowing into Treblinka, but instead think of taking arms against the Nazis. Arie Kudlik settled in Israel after the war.[8]

6. **Poswolski/Pazovalski, Heryk**—Originally from Warsaw, settled in Rio de Janeiro after the war.

7. **Rajzman Samuel**—Arrived in Treblinka on September 21, 1942 (Yom-Kippur - the Jewish Day of Atonement). Yet, while Kon suggests that Masarek joined the committee after the death of Dr. Chorazycki, Rajzman contends that Masarek and Dr. Chorazycki were the first to "come up with the idea of a revolt."[9] He also re-

ports that "afterwards there were more people who joined, but the strict Organizing Committee consisted of 12 people. We had organized it from the first minute to the last."[10] It should be pointed out that while Rajzman mentions Zev Kurland, he doesn't mention either Mr. Kon nor Mr. Grinberg or Mr.Willenberg who also claimed to have joined the new Committee. During the uprising he was working in the lumberyard. As all researchers have noted, selective knowledge about the underground committee seems to have been purposely imposed, as well as being the product of the conditions in the camp. Rajzman settled in Montreal, Canada after the war and served as a witness in the Düsseldorf trials, and with Mr. Kon in the Fort Lauderdale trial.[11]

8. **Reichman, Yechiel/Henryk**—Born in 1914 in Poland. For a while he worked as a barber in Treblinka and later was sent to work in the extermination camp. Alexander Donat commented that it is not clear if he is the same person as Henryk Reichman who submitted the testimony to the Central Commission for investigation of German crimes in Poland. By now we know that it is the same person. He was living in Montevideo, Uruguay in 1988 when he submitted testimony to the United States Holocaust Memorial Museum. Reichman provided testimony at the John Demjanjuk proceedings in the United States and Israel. In his testimony he suggested that "the uprising was planned by Camp I. The clothes sorting camp with 700 inmates. They organized the uprising ... They send to us some people ... among them were two officers of the Czechoslovakian army ... they brought the information ... and they stayed in contact with the first camp. ... Originally, the uprising was planned for May 1943 ..."[12] Reichman testified that he escaped together with Rudolf Masarek and that when the latter "saw the Germans coming near the field, he cut his veins. He did not want the Germans to take him alive ... I bandaged his arm ... I don't know if he survived."[13] This testimony contradicts Richard Glazer's and Karl Unger's suggestion that Masarek never had any intention of escaping the camp during the uprising. It should also be noticed that in this interview in 1988 Reichman still maintained that Masarek was related to the former president of Czechoslovakia. Obviously, Mr. Reichman knew very little about the members of the Organizing Committee. He returned to Poland after the war and served in its post-war administration as a factory manager. He left Poland in 1946.[14]

9. **Strawczynski/Strawaczynski, Oscar**—Arrived at Treblinka on October 5, 1942 and worked together with Capo Yourk in the unloading and disposing of dead bodies that remained in the carts of the arriving transports. He participated in the revolt. He settled in Canada after the war and testified against the Nazis in Düsseldorf in 1964–5. His testimony was used heavily by Yitzhak Arad since Strawczynski seems to have been familiar with many individuals who arrived or survived the camp. To say, however, that an individual participated in the uprising is somehow misleading. The uprising was imposed on all the inmates whether they were involved in the uprising or had any prior knowledge of the revolt. In this sense, many participated in the uprising, and some even survived as a result of the chaos caused by the fighting. However, they were not the plotters of the revolt or among its leaders and fighters.[15]

10. **Turowski, Eugen /Eugeniusz (Genek)**—Arrived at Treblinka on October 5, 1942 from the Czestochowa Ghetto. In Treblinka he worked at the mechanic's shop. He claimed to have been the individual who made a duplicate key to the camp's armory. He settled in Israel.[16] Although the duplication of the key marked a central event in the development of the revolt, Mr. Turowski's testimony provides very little information as to the identity of the Organizing Committee. It must be pointed out that Mr. Turowski was not the only survivor to claim that he was the one to duplicate the key to the armory. According to the survivor Marian Platkiewicz, it was Budnik who duplicated the key.

11. **Warszawski, Szyja**—According to Alexander Donate she arrived in Treblinka on July 23, 1942 and worked in the extermination area burning the bodies of the victims.[17] I have found no further information about this individual.

12. **Wiernik, Jacob ("Yankl" / "Jankiel")**—Arrived in Treblinka on August 23, 1942 from Warsaw where he worked as a building contractor. In Treblinka he worked as a carpenter and was instrumental in communicating between the two camps' organizing committees. He participated in the revolt and successfully escaped and survived the war. In his account of Treblinka he acknowledged that the Organizing Committee was a "secret organization" and agreed with Kon that the plotters of the revolt used to meet at night in the barracks. It should be noted that although he was aware of Samuel Willenberg's presence in Treblinka, he was not aware of Willenberg's involve-

ment with the uprising. He died in Israel in 1972.[18] The fact that the
organizing committee was a secret organization, and that many were
not allowed to know the organizers names, seems obvious for simple
reasons. If caught by the Nazis, a person could not have given any
names even under torture. Also, many prisoners were not trustwor-
thy![19] Under the physical and mental conditions in Treblinka, many
prisoners would have done almost anything for a piece of bread or to
escape torture and death. It is logical to infer, then, that Moshe Y.
Lubling's name as one of the main conspirators of the revolt would
not have been known to Mr. Wiernik, or others. Wiernik's agreement
with Mr. Kon regarding the meeting place and time of the committee
gives further credibility to Kon's account and the fact that "Lubling
from Silesia" was among the initiators of the uprising. Nothing in
Wiernik's account is inconsistent with the role of Moshe Y. Lubling
in the revolt as claimed by Kon and others. In fact, as I pointed out
earlier, the credibility of Kon's account of the revolt was never contradicted by anyone. In his written testimony, Wiernik acknowledges
that he "sacrificed all those nearest and dearest to me. I myself took
them to the execution site. I built their death chambers for them. ...
Perhaps some day I shall know how to laugh again."[20] Elsewhere in
his testimony Wiernik writes that "it was our task to carry the
corpses to the ditches. We were dead tired from working all day at
the construction site, but we had no recourse and had no choice but
to obey. We could have refused, but that would have meant a whip-
ping or death in the same manner or even worse; so we obeyed without grumbling."[21] This acknowledgment seems to support Jean-
Francois Steiner's 1966 insinuation that the Treblinka prisoners were
partially responsible for the death of nearly one million Jews.[22]

The following is a list of survivors of Treblinka who also submitted testimony about the events in the camp.

1. **Bomba, Avraham/Abraham**—Deported to Treblinka from Czestochowa, Poland. In Treblinka he mainly worked as a barber before he
   escaped in January 1943. In his testimony he described the chaos
   that was involved in the deportations from Czestochowa as follows:
   "People were running around crazy, starting to get a paper from the
   Judenrat and also from the Germans that ... all kind of paper: red,
   green, with a stamp, without a stamp and everybody tried to do the
   best even with money to get the right paper. But nobody knew what

the right paper was."[23] Mr. Bomba was not part of the conspiracy and his testimony sheds no new light on its members or its activities.

2. **Gelberd, Aron/Aaron**—Deported from Czestochowa to Treblinka together with Moshe Y. Lubling on October 2, 1942. He was kept alive as a *Goldjuden* but succeeded to escape after 19 days and returned to Czestochowa. Dr. Orenstein in *Hurban Czenstochow* reported that this escape was arranged by the first underground cell in Treblinka which included Moshe Y. Lubling and Gershon Frendke. He also named Moshe Y. Lubling as the leader of the revolt, as well as confirmed the fact that Moshe Y. Lubling was kept alive in Treblinka as a *Goldjuden*. Finally, the book also suggested that it was Mr. Gelberd that received the letter sent by Moshe Y. Lubling from Treblinka to the underground organization in Czestochowa.[24] His 1948 collaboration and testimony in the book *Hurban Czenstochow* regarding Moshe Y. Lubling was never used by any researcher. Yet, since he was in Treblinka together with Moshe Y. Lubling, worked together with him as a *Goldjuden,* escaped Treblinka and reported this information to Yad-Vashem as well as other institutions and publications, *his testimony counts as a second primary source.* It seems to me that his testimony could have served well those who were really interested in knowing who was Moshe Y. Lubling. However, in his written testimony in the 1967 *Sefer Tshenstokhov,* Mr. Gelberd does not mention Moshe. Y. Lubling or the letter he received from him in May 1943.[25] It is not clear why such forgetfulness occurred after 20 years since the original collaboration on *Hurban Czenstochow.* His passing away made it impossible for me to interview him.

3. **Glazer, Richard**—Born in Prague and was deported to Treblinka on October 1942 from Theresienstadt with his friend Karl Unger. Until his death in 1997 he lived in Switzerland where he worked as an engineer. In his testimonial book *Trap with a Green Fence* he placed Moshe Y. Lubling among the leaders of the uprising, the contact person for all the fighting units, the person who blew-up the back gate from which the majority of prisoners escaped, and the leader who went back to the camp after he opened the gate for others to escape. **This testimony constitutes the third primary source naming Moshe Y. Lubling among the leaders of the uprising.**

4. **Goldfarb, Abraham**—Arrived in Treblinka on August 25, 1942 at the age of 37 with a wife and four children from Bialystok, Poland.

A shoemaker by profession; in Treblinka he worked inside the pits at Camp II as well as with the construction crew led by Jankiel Wiernik. In his testimony he insisted that the initiation of the revolt, at least in Camp II, started from the "simple and ordinary workers." The latter needed to find a way to get the Capo in on the conspiracy; at the time it was a prisoner named Yoel. "We put them as the organizers—the big shots—to make it seem as if it came from them."[26] Almost everyone in Camp II knew about the coming uprising, except Capo Singer who was asleep on the day of the revolt. He further emphasized the difficulties involved in the planning due to the existence of snitches and the need for total secrecy. He recalled a case in which a Jew from Czestochowa gave away 30 prisoners who were involved in the conspiracy. Contradicting Sonia Lewkowicz's assertions that prisoners in Camp II never heard about the Warsaw Ghetto uprising, Goldfarb insisted that they were inspired by the Uprising. In Camp II about 30 prisoners were involved in the conspiracy, among them Zelo and Adolf who arrived in March 1943. As the uprising started Mr. Goldfarb was working with the body burners. He took a bucket and ran yelling: "It's burning, we need water!" The Ukrainian guard at the water well was then killed. Zelo took the rifle off the dead Ukrainian, and since he was a "sharpshooter," he started to "clean" the surrounding area of German and Ukrainians during the uprising. Mr. Goldfarb ran north when the uprising started and "broke through the north gate" and climbed on a tree in the woods. From other prisoners he learned that Zelo Bloch and Adolf Freidman fled the camp into the woods and that's where they were killed. This contradicts other testimonies suggesting that Zelo was killed in the camp during the revolt.[27]

He settled in Israel after the war where he worked for the Israeli National Railways. In his testimony he identified several central figures of the revolt and the Organizing Committee such as engineer Galewski and Zelo Bloch as well as other fighters. He insisted, however, that Dr. Chorazycki was the leader of the revolt until his suicide on April 1943. Strangely enough, in his testimony Mr. Goldfarb suggested that a group of prisoners from Camp II "killed Ivan Grozny" otherwise known as the Ukrainian guard "Ivan the Terrible."[28]

5. **Grinberg/Greenberg, Tanhum**—He was deported to Treblinka from Warsaw; was active in the camp's underground and participated in the uprising. On the day of the revolt he worked at the

workshop in the ghetto. He was sadly killed in a car accident in Israel in 1976. In his testimony he asserts that, "our first organizer was Dr. Chorazycki of Warsaw. It was he, too, who set up the committee, *but we didn't know who its members were. We only knew the name of the doctor...*The doctor was able to bring the group of *Goldjuden* under his command and even to get needed funds from them."[29] Mr. Grinberg describes the incident that led to the death of Dr. Chorazycki although he suggests that the *Goldjuden* were tortured "and the men were finally released."[30] Grinberg identifies himself as the individual who discovered that the stolen grenades had no detonators.[31] Again, three important points come to mind: First, that there existed more than one Organizing Committee since, as was the case with Dr. Chorazycki, some were killed long before the final revolt.[32] Second, and most significantly, it acknowledges the fact that the organizing committee was a "secret organization" and that even those who participated in the uprising did not know the members' names. Again, it is consistent with Kon's account and with the fact that while no one from the Organizing Committee survived, those who did were purposely prevented from knowing the names of the organizers.

Third, from all available accounts by those who knew my grandfather in Czestochowa, including Pinchas Lubling's testimony, Moshe Y. Lubling, upon arrival in Treblinka, was selected as a *Goldjuden*.[33] He was probably "chosen" by others in the underground that either recognized him or knew about his arrival. This also explains Moshe Y. Lubling's ability to communicate with his son and the remaining resistance organization in Czestochowa, i.e., Tzvi Rozenvayn, Aron Gelberd, and others. Even more telling and consistent with the above information is that according to Grinberg, one of the *Goldjuden* was a member of the organizing committee. The logic is as clear as two plus two equals four. Moshe Y. Lubling was a *Goldjuden* and Gelberd's as well as Glazer's accounts confirm it; the plan started in earnest only when Dr. Chorazycki recruited a member of the *Goldjuden* in order to raise money to bribe guards for weapons; Mr. Kon names "Lubling from Silesia" as a member of the original committee; Mr. Grinberg's account supports the fact that a *Goldjuden* was a member of the original committee, therefore, there is a good chance this person was Moshe Y. Lubling from Silesia.

6. **Hellman, Shlomo**—Arrived at Treblinka from Warsaw in September 1942. In Treblinka he worked both in the construction of the gas chambers and later in burying the dead in Camp II. He escaped Treb-

linka during the uprising. In his testimony he described Himmler's visit to Treblinka in 1943 for inspection; Dr. Chorazycki, as well as the uprising. His testimony does not contain any detailed information about the Organizing Committee or its activity. As usual, prisoners from Camp II were not knowledgeable about the Organizing Committee that operated only in Camp I.[34]

7. **Helfing, Isadore**—Arrived in Treblinka and without others' notice, joined a group of prisoners that carried the dead bodies out of the arriving transports. According to Mr. Helfing: "I was the one who knew we're going to have the uprising because they came to the stable and they told me, 'Listen, there is going to be an uprising.'"[35] He escaped during the uprising. He identified the leader of the revolt as "the commander at the camp ... with the Capos ... whoever was in Treblinka knows him."[36] Although he could not recall the name, it seems that he was referring to Galewski who was the "camp elder".

8. **Kolski, Abraham**—Deported to Treblinka on October 2, 1942 from the Czestochowa Ghetto. In his 1990 testimony he confirmed several assumed facts. First, that Dr. Chorazycki committed suicide by taking poison; second, that there were numerous dates for the uprising (April and May 1943); and third, that the uprising did not start as planed. His testimony, however, sheds no new light on the Organizing Committee or its members. He was a witness in the Düsseldorf trials, 1965–69.[37]

9. **Klajman/Kleinmann, Moshe**—Mr. Kleinmann was in Treblinka for 10 months. It is not clear if he was the same person mentioned by Richard Glazer as a central member of the fighting force during the Treblinka uprising.[38] He was a former soldier in the Polish army and a Zionist. In his 1947 testimony to the Jewish Historical Institute in Poland he described the existing conditions for Jews before his deportation, the nature of the camp, and the mission to acquire a duplicate key to the armory in Treblinka.[39] He does not shed much light on the Organizing Committee which indicates to me that he might not be the same Kleinmann described by Richard Glazer.

10. **Krzepicki, Abraham**—Deported to Treblinka from Warsaw on August 25, 1942 and succeeded to escape after eighteen days. In his testimony he describes his experience starting from the deportation site in Warsaw, the transport to Treblinka and the killing process, his escape from Treblinka, and joined the Jewish Fighting Organization in

Ghetto Warsaw. While his testimony is extremely comprehensive it obviously cannot shed much light on the resistance activities in Treblinka.[40]

11. **Lewkowicz, Sonia**—The sole survivor among the women who worked in Treblinka. She settled in Israel after the war. She arrived in Treblinka on December 1942 and on March 5, 1943 was sent to work at the extermination camp. Her testimony is revealing and makes some significant and surprising points. 1) That the Germans did not want the camp's work to be finished for fear that they will be sent to the Eastern front. Similarly, the prisoners could live only as long as there was work to be done; a reality which created a sort of symbiotic relationship between the two groups. 2) She reported on the unusual relationship between the Jewish Capo Singer and Franz Stangl, the second commandant of Treblinka, since they were both Austrians. The conspirators succeeded in keeping the uprising plan secret from Capo Singer. 3) The prisoners from Camp II didn't escape by running towards Camp I, or visa-versa, but escaped directly through the fences surrounding the respective camps. 4) Zelo Bloch was seen firing his rifle while kneeling and that he was later killed. 5) That after her escape she witnessed the cruelty of the Polish peasants toward the Jews. She said that "The Poles are the worst and biggest anti-Semites. They alone caused the death of many Jews who were captured by them. They murdered people on the roads and in the forests."[41] 6) That the prisoners in Camp II wanted to revolt as early as possible since the "work" was dwindling which meant that the prisoners would soon be killed as well. She contended that the leaders of the Organizing Committee in Camp I were not aware of this danger. This testimony is consistent with Mr. Rosenberg's testimony below as well as Jean-Francois Steiner's insinuation that the prisoners revolted only after they concluded that they will not survive. It seems to me that such a view was indeed consistent with the testimony of many survivors of Camp II and other marginal figures in the uprising. Factually, we know that the leaders of the revolt were planning the uprising from the first moment the camp started its operations and many of them did not revolt in order to escape. 7) She suggested in her 1979 interview that the Ukrainian guard Ivan "the terrible" Grozny was caught alive and he is in prison awaiting trial. It is not clear why she thought the above only several years before the John Demjanjuk trial in Israel. 8) That the news about the Warsaw

Ghetto Uprising didn't reach Camp II nor was the uprising the catalyst for the Treblinka uprising.[42]

12. **Lieberman, David**—Deported to Treblinka from Czestochowa.
Succeeded to escape Treblinka shortly after his arrival and returned
to the small ghetto in Czestochowa. His testimony provides no information regarding the Organizing Committee or the uprising.[43]

13. **Miller, Ya'akov/Jacob**—Born in Wlodzimierz-Wolynski, Poland in
1918; Mr. Miller was deported to Treblinka from the Siedlce Ghetto
on August 22, 1942. He submitted testimony in 1945 to S. Olitska in
Eschwege, Germany (American Zone), for the Jewish Historical
Commission in Poland.[44] Mr. Miller was identified by Stanislaw Kon
as a participant in the uprising.[45] In his testimony Mr. Miller claimed
that "the number of Jews exterminated in Treblinka before the uprising and the destruction of the death camp is over 3 million."[46] It
should be noted, however, that while the official estimate is around
800,000 Jews killed, the Central Commission for Investigation of
German Crimes in Poland acknowledged that the number is "clearly
far higher."[47] Regarding the Organizing Committee, Mr. Miller ech-
oed Stanislaw Kon's assertion that "the initiators of the uprising
would meet at night on their wooden bunks to discuss our plans.
Among them was Dr. Chorazycki ... the former Jewish officer of the
Czech army, Captain Zela (sic), Kurland of Warsaw, and Lubling
from Silesia."[48] **This is the fourth primary source naming Moshe
Y. Lubling among the original four members of the Organizing
Committee.**

14. **Perelsztajn/Perelstein, Leon**—In Treblinka he managed the tool-
store for the construction commando. In his testimony he described
engineer Galewski as a "respectable man" who knew about the conspiracy, but did not take an active part in the planning although provided help to the underground. He claimed that the idea of the
uprising was first developed among the prisoners who worked in the
tool-store/warehouse (his place of work). According to Perelsztajn,
together with Kurland, 18 year- old Capo Moniek from the barrack,
an unknown 40 years old seamaster, and others devised a plan to
make a duplicate key and take over the armory. The uprising was
originally planned for July 12, 1943 but was postponed. A few days
later, 14 individuals involved in the conspiracy were taken out of
line at roll call, sent to Camp II, and shot. He confirms the fact that
the organizers of the revolt worked in total secrecy and the rest were

not involved in the planning, but were only waiting for orders. The fighting force was picked up from among prisoners who possessed military background and knew how to use weapons. Perelsztajn's assignment, together with eight other prisoners, was to destroy the telephone lines in the camp headquarters and neutralize the SS secretary. After the duplicate key was made, two boys entered the armory and removed the weapons. Members of the construction commando then took the weapons in carts and hid them with other groups in the camp. Many arms were hidden in the garage which had a "huge basement." The revolt was supposed to start at 4:15pm and at 1:15 Jacek, one of the cleaning boys, entered the armory and started to hand out the weapons to the construction workers. Starting at 2:30, the weapons for the revolt were handed out. The plan, according to Perelsztajn, was to stop the train from Treblinka II and have the passengers join the uprising. At 3:35pm two workers were discovered by Kuba, the Jewish informer, in the barracks. Kuba sent for SS Küttner who, after finding money in the prisoners' possession, began to beat them. According to Perelsztajn, *it was he who then gave the signal for the revolt to start.* Salzberg then shot SS Küttner and the latter retreated to his barrack. This is how the revolt started. His group then cut through the barbed wire in order to reach the back entrance of the camp. Also according to Perelsztajn, the biggest task belonged to Rudolf Masarek. Together with another prisoner they took a machinegun to the main area of the camp and went on top of a little tower (presumably the zoo) and started shooting at the camp headquarters and guard stations; the Germans or Ukrainians were unable to reach his position. The barracks were set on fire and the German and Ukrainian staff killed. The camp burned from all sides and SS Suchomel was shot at through the windows of the prisoners' barracks. The uprising happened very quickly and by 6:30 everyone was freed. Finally, according to Perelsztajn, Engineer Galewski succeeded in escaping the camp during the revolt but after running for a few Kilometers "his nerves failed him." He took poison and died.[49]

Perelsztajn's testimony in most cases is consistent with the majority of survivors' testimonies except his own involvement. There are no collaborating testimonies supporting his claim that it was his order to shoot SS Küttner that started the revolt, or that it was among the tool-store/warehouse prisoners that the idea of the revolt developed.

15. **Platkiewicz, Marian**—Served in the Polish army from 1938 and
    was taken prisoner by the Germans in 1939 before returning to the
    Warsaw Ghetto. He was deported to Treblinka from the Warsaw
    Ghetto in July 1942. In Treblinka he first worked at the sorting area
    (*Lumpenkommando*) and later with the "potato cleaning" commando.
    In 1970 Mr. Platkiewicz was invited as a witness to testify at the trial
    of Kurt Franz in Düsseldorf, Germany. As with all other testimonies,
    Platkiewicz's testimony about Treblinka and the uprising reveals
    contradictions with other testimonies, falsities, as well as some new
    insights. First, Mr. Platkiewicz was among a few survivors who
    claimed that engineer Galewski become the sole leader of the Orga-
    nizing Committee after the suicide of Dr. Chorazycki. At the same
    time, however, Platkiewicz contended that what was discovered at
    the hands of the Doctor that led to his suicide were weapons not
    money.[50] This claim contradicts all other testimonies regarding this
    event. In fact, Samuel Willenberg has identified himself as the indi-
    vidual who delivered the money to Dr. Chorazycki and witnessed the
    suicide immediately afterwards.[51] Platkiewicz also contended that it
    was Galewski, stationed in the sorting area, who was supposed to
    give the signal for the revolt by firing from his machine gun.[52] The
    rounds were never fired by Galewski and there are no details known
    about the whereabouts of Galewski and Kurland during the uprising
    since it actually started in the Ghetto area. According to Platkiewicz
    the revolt started when he and his comrades attacked the German
    personnel with grenades as the latter were gathering in the Camp's
    Headquarters. The attack came as a result of another sign given by
    the shoeshine boy who took his hat off to indicate that the Germans
    are inside the Headquarters. It is not clear why the group didn't wait
    for Galewski's signal or how does this attack corresponded to Leon
    Perelsztajn above reported attack on the SS Küttner that started the
    revolt one hour earlier than planned.[53] In his account Platkiewicz
    claimed that after his group launched the attack, all other groups in
    the camp went into action. One group attacked the Ukrainian bar-
    racks with grenades while another group, led by Rudek Lubrenitski,
    knocked out three or four Garman tanks stationed in the camp as
    well as the gasoline tank. After attacking the headquarters his group
    ran immediately towards the Ghetto (where Glazer placed Moshe Y.
    Lubling) to join the others. Finally, Platkiewicz reported that the bar-
    racks had been turned into a fortified position with the addition of
    loopholes for firing rifles. He incorrectly asserts that in the aftermath

of his group's attack "not less than 40 [Ukrainian guards] were killed by us," and that "at this stage prisoners arrived from the other two parts of the camp: from the extermination area and even the Polish labor camp."[54] From Sonia Lewkowicz's testimony above, as well as what scholars learned afterwards, it was physically impossible and logically absurd for Camp II prisoners to escape to Camp I where Platkiewicz was; nor is it correct that Polish prisoners joined the re-volting Jews. Also, contrary to his claims, only a handful of Ukrain-ian guards were killed or wounded during the uprising, and the prisoner who made the duplicate key to the armory was not Budnik but Eugen Turowski who testified to that effect.[55] Finally, as an in-sight, Platkiewicz provides collaboration to others' claim that the *Goldjuden,* of which Moshe Y. Lubling was possibly a member, "was the foundation from which the organization of the uprising started in Treblinka."[56]

16. **Rappaport, Moshe**—Also from Czestochowa, Poland, and also an eyewitness to Moshe Y. Lubling's activities in Treblinka. For a while he worked together with Moshe Y. Lubling in the sorting-commando team. He escaped Treblinka together with Jacob Eisner (also from Czestochowa) in January 1943 and returned to the small ghetto. His testimony and collaboration with Dr. Orenstein's 1948 book *Hurban Czestochowa* also named Moshe Y. Lubling as the leader of the revolt. He settled in the United States after the war. As with Aron Gelberd's testimony, Rappaport's account was also ig-nored by all researchers of the Treblinka uprising. **This constitutes the fifth primary source to name Moshe Y. Lubling among the leaders of the revolt.**

17. **Rosenberg, Eliyahu**—On August 20th 1942, at the age of eighteen, Mr. Rosenberg was deported to Treblinka from the Warsaw Ghetto. He worked in the extermination camp from the start. In his testimony he describes in detail the violence towards the prisoners, the gassing process, and the impossible task of burning the bodies. He recalls that in October 1942 "all the gas chambers worked; the 10 big chambers and the three small ones. This was a large transport, 11,000 people, and within one hour only nothing remained of them."[57] He also describes the Ukrainian guard Ivan and "how he stood with his long knife and cut pieces of flesh from us and also from the people who went into the gas chambers."[58] Although never mentioned by any other account or survivor of the Treblinka revolt,

Mr. Rosenberg was an active advocate of his own participation in the uprising. By his own admission he was brought into the "secret" about the revolt in July 1943, only a few weeks before the event. He reported that at the day of the revolt members of the body burning detail volunteered to work in the afternoon in order to carry out the uprising. This fact was collaborated by others.[59] He escaped through the fence during the fighting. At the 1987 John Demjanjuk trial in Israel the defense showed that in two signed testimonies, once in 1945 in Poland, and again in 1947 in Vienna, Mr. Rosenberg claimed that he witnessed the killing of the notorious Ukrainian guard "Ivan the Terrible" during the revolt in Treblinka. However, in the 1987 trial, Mr. Rosenberg also identified John Demjanjuk, a Ukrainian auto worker from Cleveland as the notorious guard in Treblinka; the same guard he previously testified was killed during the uprising.[60] He later corrected his testimony to say that he heard from others that Ivan was killed during the uprising. Based on this testimony, Jean-Francois Steiner described in his 1966 book *Treblinka* the killing of the notorious Ivan. Needless to say, the issue became an embarrassment to both Steiner and the prosecution.

I personally have no doubt that Mr. Rosenberg was in Treblinka and that he survived the prisoners' uprising. However, he was a young man at that time and very impressionable. Incorrect testimonies are an insult and embarrassment to many survivors, their children, and for the genuine attempt by many scholars to document the Holocaust. What is even more disturbing is the sad fact that, by his own admission, much of Yitzhak Arad's basis for understanding the Treblinka revolt came from Mr. Rosenberg's testimonies and self-promoting activities.[61]

18. **Taigman, Kalman**—In his 1959 testimony, Mr. Taigman provides many details that seem to support other's claim that the uprising started an hour earlier due to an incident involving SS Küttner. According to Taigman, two prisoners were discovered in the barracks by a Jewish informer, caught, beaten and interrogated by SS Küttner. A grenade was thrown at SS Küttner which by default started the uprising between 2:00pm and 3:00pm. He confirms the production of a duplicate key to the armory by the prisoners; that it was the p*utzer* (cleaners) boys (Salzberg among them) that removed the weapons and hid them in the trash cart as well as with the potato commando, garage, and construction detail; and that the prisoner who normally disinfected the rags replaced the disinfectant with gasoline and

sprayed down everything he could.[62] With regards to the Organizing Committee, Taigman suggests that Dr. Chorazycki was "one of the first leaders of the underground" which is consistent with all other testimonies. However, with regards to engineer Galewski, he contradicts Marian Platkiewicz's claim that Galewski was the leader of the uprising. Although he acknowledged that Galewski was part of the secondary Committee, he was not the leader of the uprising or the main impetus behind the conspiracy. In fact, he describes Galewski as "overly cautious" and "full of uncertainty"[63] which is consistent with others' claim regarding Galewski's original negative attitude regarding the revolt and his later "rebirth". He also identifies Rudolf Masarek during the revolt shooting an automatic weapon at the Ukrainians on the watch towers; as well as Rudek Lubrenitski and Standa Lichtblau as the ones who blew-up the main gasoline tank and the garage. What I found surprising about Taigman's testimony is his description of a power struggle among the leaders of the uprising. He suggests that Moniek, the Capo of the "Court Jews" refused to collaborate with the conspirators unless he was made the leader of the uprising. Apparently, some agreement was made and he became a member of the secondary committee and later was instrumental in making the removal of arms from the armory possible. Finally, Taigman's testimony ought to be taken as more than just his own memories or personal knowledge. By his own admission, he was "very young then and only repeat what other people told me."[64] Therefore, his testimony reflects common knowledge among the prisoners regarding engineer Galewski, the reason for the early start of the revolt, and even some embarrassing information about a power struggle among the conspirators.

19. **Schneidmann, Wolf**—He was deported to Treblinka in 1942 and worked as a "Court Jew". In his testimony he erroneously claimed that the Organizing Committee came together a few weeks before the uprising and planned everything. He also claimed, contrary to other testimonies, that only 30 people were involved in the conspiracy—others put the number anywhere from 60–100. However, he also reported correctly that the first plan for a revolt scheduled for May 1943 was abandoned because the grenades had no detonators and only one gun was acquired. He also reported that on the day of the revolt, the prisoner who disinfected the rags put gasoline in his sprayers which he then sprayed all over the German barracks and prisoners' bunks. In his testimony he agrees with others regarding

the reason for the early and premature start of the revolt. According to Schneidmann, the revolt was supposed to start at 4:30 but started earlier since Kuba (the informer) notified SS Küttner that some prisoners are in the bunks when they weren't supposed to be there. Salzberg, a member of the Secondary Organizing Committee and the commander in charge of the Ghetto area during the revolt, ordered the killing of Küttner an hour earlier so the prisoners will not reveal anything about the upcoming uprising. He claimed that Küttner was then killed on the spot although later it was discovered that he was only injured.[65] This testimony contradicts Leon Perelsztajn's above testimony that it was he, not Salzberg that ordered the killing of SS Küttner which in fact started the revolt.

20. **Willenberg, Samuel**—As I write this book, Mr. Willenberg is the last remaining survivor of the Treblinka Revolt and currently lives in Israel. He arrived at Treblinka in 1942 from Czestochowa at the age of nineteen and actively participated in the revolt on August 2, 1943. In his account he acknowledges that although he arrived late in 1942, the "underground activity began in camp almost as soon as the camp had been set up. These were monomaniacs whose plans were the fruits of imaginings and visions completely divorced from reality. It is truly unbelievable, but the group decided to purchase arms from the Ukrainian guards and even made contact with them for this purpose."[66] It is not clear how Willenberg, who became aware of the Organizing Committee only in April during the incident in which Dr, Chorazycki took his life, would know first hand when the organization started. By his own admission the Organizing Committee "had only a few members; only a few of these knew of the plan, and no one knew it in its entirety."[67] What I find a bit distasteful is Willenberg's critical and demeaning comments about the original plotters of the uprising. He was a nineteen year-old man with no organizational or military experience who only became aware of the plans for the revolt three months before the actual event. To describe the original plotters as "monomaniacs" whose plans were "divorced from reality" is a bit presumptuous. His actual military experience was acquired after the uprising when he joined the underground organization in Warsaw. The reality is that he was a marginal figure in the organization and execution of the uprising. This is evident in the fact that he was not aware of engineer Galewski's involvement in either the planning or the execution of the revolt. In fact he reflects in his written testimony that "Galewski could not have been ignorant"

of the existence of an underground movement, but chose not to join.[68] This is three months before the uprising! Giving that the majority of the survivors and researchers support the claim that Galewski was part of the enlarged Organizing Committee, Willenberg's lack of knowledge about Galewski is clear proof that he was not among the leaders of the uprising and therefore, could only provide information on one level of the underground activity. He writes that "in every block and barrack, groups were organized which constituted cells of the underground. Each group numbered from five to ten members; the total number of cells was ten. Nearly everyone in the *Kommandos* [labor details] belonged to the underground, and each group comprised from 15 to 25 men."[69] It is clear that no matter how one understands and calculates these numbers, the total will be larger then the accepted number of 60 conspirators. After news arrived of the Jewish revolt in the Warsaw Ghetto the "leaders" of the Organizing Committee met at the carpentry—"I was one of those initiated. This is why I was admitted to the deliberations. Altogether about 15 persons were present ... for various reasons some of the conspirators could not be present. I remember some of those who attended: Zygmunt Strawczynski ... his brother Oscar ... and many others.[70]

First, if Mr. Willenberg was "initiated" into the Organizing Committee it was only three months before the uprising since it corresponds to the time the uprising in the Warsaw Ghetto was taking place (April 19 to May 16, 1943). It is clear today that the Organizing Committee started its activities in earnest after the transports from Czestochowa arrived in late September and early October 1942. After the suicide of Dr. Chorazycki and the removal of Zelo Bloch to Camp II, other prisoners joined a "secondary" Organizing Committee. Other survivors testified that the new Organizing Committee numbered 12 individuals, but according to Willenberg there were 15 leaders in the room and some could not be present. I suggest that this was not a meeting of the Organizing Committee but of a secondary and new group of prisoners that was included later. This is why Willenberg cannot name one member of the Organizing Committee except Zygmunt and his brother Oscar Strawczynski, neither of which were among the "leaders" of the uprising or the Organizing Committee.

Mr. Willenberg's testimony gives the impression that the Warsaw Ghetto Uprising was the catalyst for the uprising in Treblinka which is factually wrong. In fact, Sonia Lewkowicz, a prisoner from Camp II strongly denies that the news about the Warsaw Ghetto Uprising ever reached Treblinka or that the news had anything to do with the plans for the Treblinka uprising which started much earlier.[71] It also explains why in the interviews for his book, Yitzhak Arad insisted on questioning survivors about the influence the Ghetto Warsaw Uprising had on the uprising in Treblinka. Following Willenberg's testimony, one would certainly get such an impression.[72]

The impression that the entire operation took three months to plan, and was planed by nineteen year-old men such as Willenberg, simply makes no logical sense. What is important about his account, however, is that it confirms that there were at least two generations and levels of the Organizing Committees, one before Dr, Chorazycki's suicide and one after his death, and that this claim agrees with Stanislaw Kon's account.

According to his testimony the chronology of events planned for August 2, 1943 was as follows: The servant boys unlocked and emptied the armory while the weapons were quickly distributed first to the potato commando. A prisoner by the name of Malpa had access to wire-cutting tools in the storage area and the prisoners went to obtain these tools during an afternoon break. The servant boys, after removing the weapons, were to hurl grenades into the German's living quarters. At the same time, the construction commando would have to cross the fence along the German huts to an armored vehicle which was permanently parked there. The prisoners would then seize the car and open the gate. Most participating prisoners did not receive rifles since their task only involved setting fires around the camp. The revolt was set to start at 4:30pm. A potato commando member brought two rifles to the men at the lumberyard. An explosion from the German huts was the first indication that the uprising started. The Ukrainians at the gate to the vegetable field let loose a burst of gunfire. One of the prisoners returned fire and killed the Ukrainians. Willenberg seized a rifle and ran towards the German compound. He observed rifles protruding from the windows of the Ukrainians' huts firing towards the southern part of the forested area. His friend, a Christian Reverend stood behind a tree firing at the Ukrainians. A group of prisoners, including many Court Jews, ran towards the gate leading into the vegetable field. Members of the potato commando joined Willenberg in running towards the gate (the gate broken down by Moshe Y. Lubling per Richard Glazer's testimony). Thunderous explosions came from the garage ... the fuel depot ignited a "pillar of fire." Willenberg's friend Alfred is killed. The Reverend is wounded and Willenberg kills him in an act of mercy. As he escaped he observed a mass of human corpses scattered all over the tank traps and barbed wire fences. Machine gun fire rains relentlessly from the guard towers. Willenberg is shot in the foot.[73]

Time-Line

The following is a time-line that supports Moshe Y. Lubling's participation and leadership in the uprising:

1. From its start in late July to September 1942, Treblinka was involved in the extermination of the Jewish population of Warsaw. At the end of the killings of Warsaw Jewry, the prisoners who were kept alive to process the extermination were killed.

2. Transports from Czestochowa started on September 22, 1943. The majority of prisoners that were kept for permanent work in the camp were selected from among the Jews from Czestochowa. This is supported by the unusual large number of survivors who came from Czestochowa and who participated in the uprising.

3. Stanislaw Kon arrives in Treblinka on October 1, 1942. He claimed that "Lubling from Silesia" was among the original four plotters of the revolt. Moshe Y. Lubling participated in the uprising on August 2, 1943 and there is no reason to believe that he did not remain one of the leaders throughout the eleven months leading to the revolt.

4. Moshe Y. Lubling arrives in Treblinka between September 28 and October 3, 1943. He is kept alive and later becomes a *Goldjuden* or a member of the clothes commando.

5. In his 1945 testimony Kon names "Lubling from Silesia" as one of the original four members of the Organizing Committee; the others were Dr. Chorazycki, Kurland, and Zelo. His testimony was confirmed at the same time by Ya'akov Miller, another survivor of Treblinka.

6. In October 1942 Aron Gelberd and Moshe Rappaport are deported to Treblinka from Czestochowa. Gelberd escaped after 19 days and Rappaport in January 1943. Both successfully returned to the small ghetto in Czestochowa and reported their meetings with Moshe Y.

Lubling in Treblinka. Both testify that Moshe Y. Lubling was the organizer and leader of the resistance movement in the camp and that he was planning a prisoners' revolt.

7. In May 1943, a letter from Moshe Y. Lubling arrived in the small ghetto in Czestochowa and was received by Aron Gelberd. It was read by many including Tzvi Rozenvayn and Dr. Orenstein. The existence of the letter and its contents are documented in *Hurban Czenstochow*. This fact conclusively shows that three months before the revolt, Moshe Y. Lubling is still alive and in the leadership of the revolt. He has been the only Treblinka prisoner that succeeded in communicating through letters with the outside world.

8. May 10, 1945, Mr. Stanislaw Kon publishes an article, "The Treblinka Revolt" in *Dos Naye Lebn* in Poland naming Moshe Y. Lubling among the original four plotters of the Treblinka uprising.

9. Also in 1945, Ya'akov Miller submits testimony to S. Olitska for the Jewish Historical Commission in Poland, naming Moshe Y. Lubling among the four original plotters of the Treblinka revolt.

10. In September 1945 Mr. Kon's account is translated into Dutch and published in Amsterdam under the title *Opstand in Treblinka*. Again, naming Moshe Y. Lubling among the four plotters of the revolt.[74]

11. In 1947 the book *Kiddush Ha-Shem* is published in New York. A. Dorshman identifies Moshe Y. Lubling as one of the leaders of the Treblinka revolt.

12. In 1948 the book *Hurban Czenstochow* is published in West-Germany. Four different individuals (Orenstein, Gelberd, Rappaport, and Rozenvayn) identify Moshe Y. Lubling as the leader of the Treblinka revolt. The book also contained an obituary for Moshe Y. Lubling in which his son Pinchas was assumed dead. All the information was provided by Moshe Y. Lubling's colleagues and friends.

13. In 1956 the book *Sefer Milkhamot Hagetaot* is published in Israel. Mr. Kon's account is translated into Hebrew, still naming "Lubling from Silesia" among the original four members of the Organizing Committee.

14. Also in 1956, an article by the Holocaust scholar and partisan M. Bakalczuk is published in the Polish magazine *Reviews*. In the article Mr. Bakalczuk names Moshe Y. Lubling as a Treblinka revolt leader.

15. In 1958 the supplement to the *Czenstochower Yidn* book is published in New York. Moshe Y. Lubling is identified by Tzvi Rozenvayn, a former member of the Czestochowa Resistance Organization, as the "unforgettable" chairman of the Workers' Council in Czestochowa. Again, he confirms Lubling's leadership in the Treblinka uprising.

16. In 1967, the Ministry of Defense in Israel awards Moshe Y. Lubling a citation honoring his resistance to the Nazis in Treblinka.

17. In 1967 a two-volume book *Sefer Czestochowa* is published in Israel. An obituary for Moshe Y. Lubling is printed naming him the leader of the Treblinka revolt.

18. The same year another book is published in Israel *Volbrom Irenu* and it contained another obituary for Moshe Y. Lubling, again naming him among the leaders of the revolt in Treblinka.

19. Stanislaw Kon's account of the revolt is translated into English and published in *Anthology of Holocaust Literature*; still naming "Lubling from Silesia" among the original four plotters of the revolt.[75]

20. In 1974 Reuben Ainsztein publishes *Jewish Resistance in Nazi-Occupied Europe*. Although in his analysis of Treblinka he does not mention Moshe Y. Lubling, he acknowledges in a long footnote that only after he completed the book did he discover Mr. Kon's account of the revolt. He acknowledges that Kon's account clarifies many points about the revolt, including the makeup of the original four members of the Organizing Committee which includes "Lubling from Silesia."

21. In 1979 Alexander Donat publishes his comprehensive study of Treblinka *The Death Camp Treblinka - A Documentary*. Although in his own analysis of the uprising Donat fails to acknowledge Moshe Y. Lubling's participation in the uprising, he prints Mr. Kon's account of the Treblinka Revolt in which Kon names "Lubling from Silesia" among the four original leaders of the revolt.

22. In 1983 Yitzchak Arad publishes *Treblinka: Hell and Revolt* in Israel. He does not mention Moshe Y. Lubling, not even a respectable footnote!

23. In 1992 Richard Glazer, a Treblinka survivor and uprising fighter, finally succeeds in publishing his memories of Treblinka under the title *Trap with a Green Fence* (his previous testimony was available since the 1950s). In his account he identifies Moshe Y. Lubling as a

central member of the Organizing Committee and the man who broke down the gate leading to the vegetable field through which the majority of survivors escaped. He also reports that Moshe Y. Lubling saved his life (and that of Karl Unger) during the uprising and that Moshe Y. Lubling declined the opportunity to escape and returned to the camp to fight.

The following are among those who participated in organizing the revolt in a leadership role but did not survive:

Sadovicz/Sudowicz—An agronomist from Warsaw, Poland. His first name is still unknown. According to several testimonies he worked in the vegetable garden and was among the early members of the Treblinka underground.

Engineer Galewski—According to the Austrian version his name was Marceli Galewski. In Treblinka he served as Camp-Elder—*Lagerälteste*. He was 42 years old when deported to Treblinka from Lodz, Poland. According to Alexander Donat, "he was involved in the Treblinka inmate conspiracy from the beginning, *but was able to keep his role so secret that not even Samuel Willenberg was aware of it.*"[76] This is a very significant point since Willenberg's account was heavily used by researchers although he did not have knowledge of the Organizing Committee members' names or identity. Alternatively, one might say that Willenberg was not aware of Galewski's role in the revolt because he was not a member of the Organizing Committee as such! Following Donat's logic, Moshe Y. Lubling also succeeded in keeping his role in the uprising secret from Willenberg, Rajzman, Grinberg, and others. According to one eyewitness account Galewski escaped during the uprising but could not continue afterwards. He committed suicide in the woods according to Platkiewicz testimony and the claim is confirmed by Gitta Sereni.[77] His leadership and participation in the revolt is confirmed by many, including Richard Glazer, Willenberg, and Kon. Finally, it should be noted that Galewski's involvement in the conspiracy started only four months before the revolt. This is what Donat means when he writes above that Galewski was involved in the conspiracy "from the beginning." It should also be noted that Marian Platkiewicz is the only survivor who claimed that Galewski was the revolt leader. According to other testimonies he opposed the conspiracy at the beginning and only joined later after experiencing a re-birth.

Rudolf Masarek—He was 28 years old when arrived in Treblinka and a former Lieutenant in the Czech Army. According to Yitzhak Arad, his membership in the Organizing Committee is supported by only one eye-witness account! However, both Glazer and Kon identify him as part of the Organizing Committee and Kon puts him in the revolt itself. His membership and participation in the revolt is confirmed by the survivors, Richard Glazer, Stanislaw Kon, Ya'akov Miller, and Samuel Rajzman. Also, according to the testimonies of Kalman Taigman and Yechiel Reichman, Masarek survived the revolt but committed suicide soon after.

Salzberg—A father and son, Kielce furriers, both were involved in the uprising. The father was in charge of the ghetto and workshops area while the son was a Court Jew. According to testimonies his son was instrumental in breaking into the armory and obtaining weapons on the day of the uprising. The father, according to the testimony of Wolf Schneidmann, gave the order to kill SS Küttner after two young prisoners were caught by the informer Kuba. It was this attack that in fact constituted the unplanned signal for the revolt and resulted in an early start.

The Original Members of the Organizing Committee

Dr. Julian Ilya Chorazycki—Camp physician—A 57 year-old known laryngologist from Warsaw and a former Captain in the Polish army. According to Alexander Donat, his room/office was opposite the *Gold-juden*[78] which is how he originally collected money to buy weapons for the revolt. However, not much else is known about him. Donat writes that "the exact details of Chorazycki's death are not known. ***The extant testimonies of survivors show a number of discrepancies.*** The most likely account seems to be that of Samuel Willenberg."[79] It is believed that in April 1943 (four months before the revolt) he was caught with money obtained by Moshe. Y. Lubling for the purpose of buying weapons from the Ukrainian guards. When caught he swallowed poison and immediately died. Mr. Willenberg claimed that the money obtained by the *Goldjuden* was given to him by Alfred Boehm and that he transferred it personally to Dr. Chorazycki. According to the testimony by Tanhum Grinberg, the organization started in earnest only after Dr. Chorazycki recruited a member of the *Goldjuden* into the Organizing Committee. This recruitment took place in early October per Kon's and Gelberd's testimonies. It is assumed by many survivors that he was the initiator of the underground in Treblinka although such claims have been challenged by Dr. Orenstein who claimed that it was Gershon Frendke and Moshe

Y. Lubling who initiated the first underground cell in Treblinka. His participation and leadership in the Organizing Committee are confirmed by the survivors Kon, Glazer, Willenberg, Miller, Grinberg, Rajzman, and others.

Zev (Zvi) Kurland—The Capo in charge of the *Lazaret,* where those who were punished or couldn't work were put to death. Although there were some claims that he was involved in the killings of inmates, other survivors categorically deny that charge.[80] None of the survivors were sure about his first name. His whereabouts during the uprising are still unclear since the fighting started in the Ghetto area, where Moshe Y. Lubling was situated, and not in the sorting area near the "field-hospital" where he worked. It is believed that he was killed immediately during the uprising. His leadership is confirmed by the testimonies of Glazer, Willenberg, Kon, Miller, and Rajzman.

Zhelomir /Zelo/ Zialo Bloch—A former lieutenant in the Czech army and a photographer by profession. In Treblinka he was appointed Forman of the labor detail. According to testimonies, in March 1943, after money was discovered on prisoners under his authority, he was punished and moved to the extermination area together with his foreman Adolf Freidman. In Camp II he organized a new committee that worked together with the Organizing Committee in Camp I. According to several testimonies (Willenberg, Goldfarb, Lewkowicz) he was seen shooting his rifle at Ukrainian guards during the uprising. His leadership and participation in the revolt are confirmed by the survivors Glazer, Willenberg, Greenberg, Kon, Miller, Rajzman, and others.

Moshe Y. Lubling—Born in Wolbrom (Upper Silesia), Poland, in 1902. He served in the Polish army between 1926 and 1928. Before arriving in Treblinka he was the chairman of *Ha-Oved,* and other Zionist organizations in Sosnowiec, Poland, and during the war he was the chairman of the Workers' Council in the Czestochowa Ghetto. The Council evolved into the Resistance Organization in Czestochowa and established relations with the left-wing Polish Resistance Movement. He was deported to Treblinka with his wife and 12 year-old daughter between September 28 and October 3, 1943. In Treblinka he was selected as a *Goldjuden* although he had no previous knowledge of valuables or currencies. It is believed that he was picked-up by prisoners who recognized him from his resistance activities in Czestochowa. Indeed, at the time of his arrival in Treblinka, the majority of the prisoners were from Czestochowa. He met with Aron Gelberd and Moshe Rappaport in Treblinka in October of

1943 and reported the preparations for the uprising. They reported their meetings with him in the 1948 book *Hurban Czenstochow*. Moshe Y. Lubling also dispatched a letter to the resistance organization in Czestochowa in May 1943, three months before the uprising; the only known communication between the organizers of the Treblinka uprising with the outside world. The letter confirms the preparations for the revolt and encouraged the Czestochowa Resistance Organization to do the same. The existence of this letter is confirmed by the testimonies of Aron Gelberd, Tzvi Rozenvayn, Moshe Rappaport, Pinchas Lubling, and Dr. Binyamin Orenstein. According to Richard Glazer's testimony, Moshe Y. Lubling was among the leaders of the revolt and was seen during the uprising. In fact, according to Glazer, it was Moshe Y. Lubling who forced the east gate open, pushed the young prisoners to safety, and returned to the camp to finish the fight. He was killed during the uprising. His leadership and participation in the revolt is confirmed by three survivors - Richard Glazer, Stanislaw Kon, and Ya'akov Miller; by two Treblinka escapees, Aron Gelberd and Moshe Rappaport; and by two members of the Resistance Organization in Czestochowa, Dr. Binyamin Orenstein and Tzvi Rozenvayn.

Secondary Committee

After the death of Dr. Chorazycki and the removal of Zelo to the extermination camp the committee added new members. According to some accounts up to 12 new people were added. It is my position that these new individuals were not full members of the Organizing Committee but a "Secondary Committee." This explains why some eyewitness suggested that the Organizing Committee was put together around May 1943, when in fact, such a committee was operating from October 1942 and the arrival of Moshe Y. Lubling to Treblinka. By the survivors' own testimonies, not a single "member" of the new Committee was capable of naming the other 12 members of the Secondary Organizing Committee, let alone the original leaders of the revolt. I suggest that in May 1943 the main Organizing Committee contained only Lubling and Kurland; two of the original plotters. As the Capo of the "field-clinic" Kurland's movement in the camp, although freer than most prisoners, was also closely scrutinized. In fact, other privileged prisoners in Treblinka like *Lagerälteste* Rakowski, who replaced Galewski as camp-elder for a short period, was executed for bribing a Ukrainian guard, and Zelo was sent to Camp II because money was found in the clothes of members of his commando. Indeed, other than the description of Kurland as reciting the Kaddish (mourners' pray) every night in the barracks, there is virtually no information on the extent and the ways in which Kurland was directly involved in the organization or the execution of the uprising. The only person who remained to coordinate the entire process and recruit new members was Moshe Y. Lubling as partially confirmed by Richard Glazer—"Lubling is our contact." At this point, only four months before the uprising, new individuals were added, some to the Organizing Committee, most to the secondary committee. The following are members of the Secondary Committee.

1. **Rudolf/Rudi Masarek**

2. **Engineer Galewski**

3. **Samuel Willenberg**—According to Willenberg the following were among the underground movement in Treblinka: Klein, Klin, Gustav Boraks, Brojer, Kleinmann (who Glazer suggests reported to Lubling), Kon, and others.

4. **Samuel Rajzman**—He was 40 years old when he arrived in Treblinka on September 21, 1943. According to his testimony he was a member of the Organizing Committee from the beginning! However, such a claim is not confirmed by anyone else. Given his age, it can be assumed that he was privileged to information from the beginning, but he was not a member of the original four plotters of the uprising.

5. **Stanislaw Kon**—Acknowledged that "Lubling from Silesia" was among the original four plotters and that he himself was added to the committee after the death of the doctor. His participation is acknowledged by Willenberg but by no one else.

6. **Tanhum Grinberg**—Participated in the preparation for the uprising. By his own admission he had no knowledge about the members of the Organizing Committee other than Dr. Chorazycki. Later he became aware of Zelo's part in the conspiracy. In his testimony he acknowledged that the preparations for the revolt started in earnest only after the doctor recruited "someone" from the *Goldjuden* to the Organizing Committee, probably Moshe Y. Lubling.

7. **Dr. Leichert**—According to some testimonies he replaced Dr. Chorazycki after the latter's suicide. The available information, however, does not place him in the uprising.

8. **David Brat**—Identified by Richard Glazer as Moshe Y. Lubling's pal in Treblinka. He puts him in conversations with other members of the organizing committee. Unfortunately, although his participation was central, his name does not appear in any account of the Treblinka revolt other than Glazer's. However, Glazer may be actually referring to Abraham/Avrohom Brat from Czestochowa. The latter was a member of the Workers' Council of which Moshe Y. Lubling was the chairman, and he arrived in Treblinka together with Moshe Lubling, Gershon Frendke, and Aaron Gelberd. It is probably this previous relationship with Lubling that led Glazer to refer to him as "Lubling's pal."

9. **Markus/Marcus**—According to Stanislaw Kohn he was 14 years old and the son of a furrier from Warsaw. He was instrumental in obtaining a copy of a key to the camp armory. According to Arad, he was the leader of the "*putzers*" who were assigned the task of removing the weapons from the storeroom. This fact is collaborated by several testimonies. However, the fact that a 14 years-old "*putzer*" was included in the new organizing committee shows that it was not the "Organizing Committee." Under no circumstances can it be believed that a young man with no education, military experience, or organizational skills was among the planners of the revolt. Again, my point is that the "secondary committee" was not a replacement for the original Organizing Committee but an addition. The planning was still done by Lubling and Kurland, and later on with the addition of Galewski and Masarek.

10. **Kleinmann**—His participation is confirmed by Willenberg and Richard Glazer. Glazer's testimony claims that he was a member of Kleinmann's fighting unit. The testimony also puts him in conversations with Lubling, or reporting to Lubling, on the day of the uprising. He did not survive the uprising.

11. **Salzberg** —According to Kohn he joined the committee after the Dr. Chorazycki's death.

12. **Sadowicz**—According to Kohn he joined the committee after the death of the doctor.

13. **Haberman**—According to Kohn he joined the committee after the death of the doctor.

Without distinguishing between the Organizing Committee and the Secondary Committee; if we list the names of those who have been mentioned as first, possessing knowledge about the uprising in advance, second, those who were named by survivors as members of the organizing committee that was formed after the death of Dr. Chorazycki, third, individuals who were identified in conversations with other members, and fourth, those who testified on their behalf, we get the following:

1. Samuel Willenberg	20. Rudolf Masarek
2. Klein	21. Yankiel Wiernik
3. Klin	22. David Brat
4. Gustav Boraks	23. Alexander Kudlik
5. Brojer	24. Yechiel Reichman
6. Kleinmann	25. Oscar Strawczynski
7. Stanislaw Kon	26. Sygmunt Strawczynski
8. Samuel Rajzman	27. Eugen Turowski
9. Tanhum Grinberg	28. Abraham Kolski
10. Dr. Leichert	29. Leon Perelsztajn
11. Markus	30. Alfred Boehm
12. Salzberg (father)	31. Marian Platkiewicz
13. Wladek Salzberg (son)	32. Moniek
14. Haberman	33. Wolf Schneidmann
15. Sudowicz	34. Standa Lichtblau
16. Moshe Y. Lubling	35. Rudek Lubrenitski
17. Zvi Kurland	
18. Zelo Bloch	
19. Galewski	

This is by no means a comprehensive list but it nonetheless makes my point. It is obvious, and not surprising, that the above names do not add to 12 members as was testified by several survivors. The majority of survivors that claimed to have been members of the Organizing Committee came from the second phase of the uprising organization. The majority of these individuals came from the ranks of the fighters (Platkiewicz) and sometimes served as local unit commanders (Kleinmann). The above list would be more consistent with testimony if we distinguish between two organizational units—Organizing Committee (OC) with six members: Dr. Chorazycki, Zvi Kurland, Zelo Bloch, Moshe Y. Lubling, and later on Engineer Galewski and Rudolf Masarek. Secondary Committee (SC) with 12–13 individuals including, Kon, Rajzman, Grinberg, Monick, Sudowicz, Willenberg, Wiernik, Salzberg, Markus, and Kleinmann. However, if one adds all the names mentioned by survivors of individuals who knew or had a role in the uprising you will reach many more than the usual figure of 60 conspirators. For example, according to Samuel Rajzman, there were four fighting units with 12 people each. Each fighting group had a commander and only the latter was in contact with one person from the Organizing Committee. He writes:

> ...the strict organizing committee consisted of 12 people. We had organized it from the first minute to the last. We had four companies, 12 people in each company, so we had about 50 fellows who could do the job. But not one of these 50 knew who the others were. Each one of these 50 knew only one other person on the committee. [The idea was that if] the Germans should catch one of those 50, even if they should torture him to death, he wouldn't be able to put the finger on more than one person. So that's how we organized it. It's evident that everybody tried in every way not to talk about the uprising. Even among ourselves, we didn't want to talk about it. ... They took me into the committee a few weeks after I arrived in Treblinka, after I had reproached Galewski for saving my life. So the organization effort took about one year.[81]

Rajzman's account, however, reveals several puzzling claims. The claim that "we had organized it from the first minute to the last," is not consistent with the claim that "they took me into the committee a few weeks after I arrived in Treblinka." Logically speaking, he could not have been among those who initiated the planning if he was taken into an already existing committee. If Rajzman arrived in Treblinka on September 21, 1943, and was only taken into confidence after a few weeks (the end of October), then he was far from being there from the beginning since by that time Dr. Chorazycki had already been in Treblinka since July 1942. Moshe Y. Lubling already met with Aron Gelberd in Treblinka, and the latter already escaped and reported to his colleagues in Czestochowa about the underground organization. Rajzman seems to mark the beginning of the Organizing Committee from the time he arrived in Treblinka. However, the organization obviously started earlier since Zelo and Kurland were from earlier Warsaw transports. Finally, by talking only about the 12 member committee, Rajzman was obviously not aware of the original members and only became knowledgeable of some names later on. His description of the structure of the conspirators (all 50 of them) is correct and explains why most survivors who participated in the uprising had only partial knowledge of the organization. In his own account, Rajzman does not mention Zelo, Kohn, Willenberg, Kleinmann, Glazer, Wiernik, or Grinberg, etc. etc., and others do not mention him as a member of the Organizing Committee or even among its secondary leaders. The lack of precise knowledge about the make-up and activities of the Organizing Committee until May 1943 support the assumption I made above. That is, that *those who survived were not members of the Organizing Committee nor did they have direct knowledge of its members or their activities.*

The Fighters

I attempted to locate as many names of individuals who participated in the preparations and execution of the uprising, as well as their working duties. It should be recognized that some survivors worked in more than just one area of the camp, and that some individuals who were part of the preparations for the uprising were killed earlier and were replaced by new prisoners. Again, the list is by no means comprehensive and I am sure I omitted some names; I apologize in advance for such careless overlooking.

Lumpenkommando
1. David Brat
2. "Little" Abraham
3. Adasch (foreman)
4. Alfred Boehm
5. Gershonowitz
6. Dzialoszynski
7. Langer
8. Wolff (foreman)
9. Oskar Strawczynski
10. Turowski
11. Glazer
12. Wallabanczik—The person who shot SS Küttner.
13. One prisoner in charge of the store—no name is provided.

Yellows
1. Simcha
2. Standa Lichtblau
3. Oskar Strawczynski
4. Zygmunt Strawczynski
5. Rudek Lubrenitski
6. Dr. Leichert
7. Irena Levkovski (according to Arad, she replaced Dr. Chorazycki)
8. Prisoner who regularly disin infected the camp

Reds
No individuals in this group have been identified.

Blues
No individuals in this group have been identified.

Extermination Camp

1. Wolff
2. Zelo
3. Eliyahu Rosenberg
4. Abraham Goldfarb
5. Sonia Lewkowicz
6. Yechiel (Henryk) Rajchman
7. Jerzy Rajgrodski
8. Adolf Friedman (foreman)
9. Moshe the Tailor
10. Pinchas Epstein

Goldjuden

1. Alexander Kudlik (Capo)
2. Moshe Y. Lubling
3. Willy
4. Salo

Camo Commando

1. Karl Unger
2. Moshe Kleinmann
3. Jurek
4. Herschek
5. Kleinbaum (may be the same as Kleinmann)
6. Malpa
7. Willenberg
8. Leiteisen
9. Richard Glazer

Court Jews

1. Sadowicz
2. Mietek Laks (Was ironically appointed "shit-Capo" of the camp)
3. Arthur Gold
4. Schutzer
5. Moniek
6. Saltzberg
7. Jakob/Ya'akov Miller
8. Wolff Shneidmann
9. Marian Platkiewicz
10. Kalman Tajgman
11. Ya'akov Domb
12. Yossef Czarny

Survivors (Prisoners, fighters, and escapees)

1. Augustyniak, Czeslaw
2. Berger, Oskar—Escaped in 1942 by hiding in a train.
3. Bomba, Abraham—Barbar at Treblinka. Escaped by train.
4. Boraks, Gostav—Barbar in Treblinka.
5. Brener, Henoch
6. Ciechanowski, Chaim
7. Ciechanoewski, Leizer
8. Czarny, Josef
9. Czechowicz, Aaron

10. Domb, Ya'akove
11. Eisner, Jacob—Escaped with
    Moshe Rappaport in January,
    1943. (Rappaport identified
    Moshe Y. Lubling)
12. Epstein, Pinchas—Worked in
    the extermination area when he
    was 18 years old.
13. Finkelstein, Leon
14. Gelberd, Aron—Escaped after
    19 days in October 1942. Re-
    turned to the small ghetto in
    Czestochowa where he re-
    mained until the liquidation.
    (Identifies Moshe Y. Lubling).
15. Glazer, Richard—Member of
    the fighting underground. (Not
    identified by anyone but
    identifies others including
    Moshe Y. Lubling).
16. Goldberg, Szymon
17. Goldfarb, Abraham
18. Gostynski, Zygmunt
19. Grabinski, Sonia
20. Grinberg, Tanhum—Member of
    the fighting underground. (Not
    identified by anyone but
    identifies others.)
21. Grinsbach, Eliahu
22. Gross, Yosef
23. Helman, Shlomo
24. Horn, Otto
25. Jakubowski, Jacob
26. Jankowski, Kalman
27. Kelin, Judah
28. Kohn, Shlomo (Stanislaw
    Kon)— Member of the under-
    ground. (Identified by Willen-
    berg and identify others
    including Moshe Y. Lubling).

29. Koszycki, Jacob
30. Kudlik, Arie Alexander—Capo.
    A member of the underground.
    (Identified by Glazer)
31. Lachman
32. Laks, Moszek (mietek)—
    Identified by Richard Glazer.
33. Miller, Ya'akov—Identified by
    Stanislaw Kon. In his testimony
    Mr. Miller identified "Lubling
    from Silesia" among the
    original four plotters of the
    revolt.
34. Lewi, Leon
35. Lewkowicz, Sonia—Member of
    the underground in the extermi-
    nation camp. Escaped during
    the revolt.
36. Lindwasser, Abraham—A
    "dentist" at Treblinka Camp II.
37. Luck, Moshe
38. Markus—Court Jew. A young
    member of the underground.
39. Mitelberg, M
40. Pacanowski, Moshe
41. Platkiewicz, Marian
42. Poliakiewicz, Symcha (escaped
    after one day).
43. Porzecki, Moshe
44. Poswolski (Pazovalski), Henryk
45. Rajchman, Henryk (Yechiel M.
    Reichman)—Worked in the
    extermination area (camp II)
    burning corpses.
46. Rajgrodski, Jerzy (george)—
    Worked in the extermination
    area (camp II) burning corpses.
    Participated in the revolt.
47. Rajzman, Samuel—Worked in
    the sorting area. Member of the

underground. Participated in the uprising. (Not identified by anyone but identifies others).

48. Rak, Meir
49. Rappaport, Moshe—Escaped Treblinka in January 1943. Met Moshe Y. Lubling and identified him as the revolt leader.
50. Rojtman
51. Rojzman, Berek—Not part of the underground, but fought in the uprising.
52. Rosenberg, Eliahu—Worked in The extermination area. Fought during the uprising. Not identified by anyone as a member of the underground.
53. Shneiderman, Wolf
54. Siedlecki, Joseph—Participated in the revolt.
55. Strawczynski, Oscar—Member of the underground. Identified by Willenberg.
56. Strawczynski, Sygmunt—Oscar's brother and a member of the underground. identified by Willenberg.
57. Sperling, Henryk—From Czestochowa. Arrived around the same time as Lubling.

58. Sukno, Bronka
59. Szejnberg, Wolf
60. Szmulowiczm Jacob
61. Steir, Chaim (Haim Sztajer)—Worked in the extermination camp.
62. Taigman, Kalman
63. Tobias, Mieczslaw
64. Turowski, Eugen
65. Unger, Karl (Charles)—Member of the Underground. Identified by Glazer.
66. Warszawski, Szyja—Worked in the extermination camp.
67. Wasser
68. Weinstein Eddie—Arrived in Treblinka on August 24, 1942 and escaped on September 9, 1942. He designed a blue print of the camp.[82]
69 Wiernik, Jankiel—Worked as a builder in the extermination camp. Member of the underground. Identified by Willenberg.
70. Willenberg, Samuel—Worked in the sorting area. Member of the underground. Not identified by anyone but identifies others

---

One can clearly see from the above records that only a handful of individuals who survived Treblinka had any direct knowledge of the Organizing Committee (13 individuals)—they are Glazer; Grinberg; Kon; Kudlik; 14 year old Marcus; Platkiewicz; Rajzman; Oscar and Zygmunt Strawczynski; Unger; Taigman, Wiernik; and Willenberg. From among the 13 only three knew of each other's involvement—Willenberg identified Kon and Wiernik, they in turn did not identify him. Glazer identified Unger and visa-versa, Glazer also identified Kudlik. Willenberg identified Oscar and Zygmunt Strawczynski but he was not identified by anyone.

Again, it is important to notice that according to Richard Glazer's testimony, the leaders of the revolt did not plan to save themselves, but only to make sure that the younger prisoners survived! With the exception of Samuel Rajzman who was 40 years old during the uprising, the rest of the fighting survivors were between 14–22 years old. All the leaders of the revolt were married and had children with whom they came to Treblinka. In the majority of cases they had no desire to live after the destruction of their families, but only to revenge their deaths! We should also remember that Moshe Y. Lubling called for an armed revolt already in Czestochowa and in his letter from Treblinka in May 1943. Aside from one eyewitness account by Marian Platkiewicz claiming that Galewski escaped the camp but committed suicide later in the woods, there are no further claims that any of the other central figures attempted to escape. It also suggests that Galewski was not a central member of the Organizing Committee, especially its ideological leader since originally he was opposed to the underground. I suggest that his participation came from a different personal source than the one that motivated Moshe Y. Lubling. Regardless of Galewski's possible escape, I want to push this line of thought further. In the letter that was sent by Moshe Y. Lubling to the small ghetto in Czestochowa he expressed the exact same sentiment. According to the testimony of his son Pinchas, Moshe Y. Lubling wrote that he does not plan to escape during the uprising; that he wants the revolt and his eventual death to sound around the world. His purpose was ideological and greater than himself. It is also consistent with Tzvi Rozenvayn testimony in "The Hunger Strike in the Czestochowa Ghetto," where Moshe Y. Lubling declared in front of thousands of slave laborers that "*the only thing we can lose is our lives.*" It was also Moshe Y. Lubling who refused three separate times (recorded accounts) to save himself and went on to express his wish to share in the fate of his people.

My argument is that those who survived the uprising in Treblinka were *not* among the members of the original Organizing Committee but of the Secondary Committee and fighters at best. They were mostly younger individuals with very little organizational experience, knowledge of weaponry, or idealistic passion that existed prior to Treblinka. The only individual among all the above mentioned that was logically capable, experienced, idealistic, Zionist organizer, former soldier, chairman of the Workers' Council in Czestochowa, the one that established contact with the Polish Underground, the one who called for armed resistance in Czestochowa before the liquidation, and the only individual that dispatched letters from

Treblinka to the Czestochowa's resistance organization reporting on the plan for the revolt was Moshe Y. Lubling.

Summary

Moshe Y. Lubling arrived in Treblinka between September 28 and October 3, 1942. He was 40 years-old and was picked-up to work as a *Goldjuden* although he had no experience with money, gold, or precious stones. The fact that he was kept alive at his age in such a position clearly indicates that matters had been manipulated by the existing prisoners in order to keep him in Treblinka. As was testified by Willenberg, most prisoners working during this period were individuals from Czestochowa. He was recognized as an active member of the underground in Czestochowa and was intentionally kept alive by the prisoners in order to assist in the organization of the uprising. The original members of the Organizing Committee first attempted to build a tunnel, not to escape, but to reach the armory where they could obtain weapons to rise against the SS and Ukrainian guards. They also attempted to bribe Ukrainian guards in order to obtain weapons for the uprising. It is also clear that Aron Gelberd's escape after 19 days was planned and had the goal of making contact with outside resistance forces in order to smuggle weapons into Treblinka. Furthermore, Moshe Y. Lubling was the one who obtained the money and gave it to Alfred Boehm who supposedly gave it to Willenberg, who finally gave it to Dr. Chorazycki (Willenberg did not know that it was money he was delivering to the doctor). After the death of the doctor and the departure of Zelo, other individuals were recruited into the underground group. At the same time (May 1943), he dispatched a letter to Czestochowa reporting on the upcoming revolt. Also, on the day of the revolt, Lubling is identified by Richard Glazer as the person who broke down the east gate and orders the younger prisoners to escape into the woods. Moshe Y. Lubling, instead of escaping together with Glazer and Unger, returned to the camp to fight until death. He is never seen or heard from after the revolt. He fell in Treblinka as a leader and hero who sacrificed himself so that others can live! Some returned the favor by remembering him, others promoted themselves.

Finally, although several survivors and fighters were young Zionists and settled in Israel after the war, many were not motivated by such ideological backgrounds or served as leaders in militant Zionist organizations as Moshe Y. Lubling. There is no evidence that Dr. Chorazycki, Kurland, Zelo, Galewski, and Masarek had any background in Zionist movements or any other political or militant groups. The only leader of the Treblinka revolt that shared in Israel's upcoming National paradigm of Identity was Moshe Y. Lubling. The Israeli community that constitutes and represents this paradigm of identity today has the obligation to make sure that his name is not forgotten. They miserably failed to do so! Instead, the celebrated heroes of the Treblinka uprising were those who chose to reside in France, Canada, America, Switzerland, and Argentina, etc. They obviously did not revolt for Jewish honor if they freely preferred to live with former Nazis and their collaborators in foreign countries while the State of Israel was forming and could use their help. Regardless, these survivors and fighters are heroes and post-Holocaust generations have the obligation to remember their names, no matter where they chose to settle after the Holocaust. But, the case is categorically different when it comes to the community of the early Labor Zionists; their ethical obligations are different from the ethical obligations of post-Holocaust generations in general. Labor Zionists, unlike other Jewish communities, owe their very identity to the actions and character of individuals like Moshe Y. Lubling. He saved others; he was secular; he redeemed himself through labor; he worked tirelessly for the new Jewish identity; he engaged in armed resistance; and he sacrificed himself for the new Jewish nation. Forgetting his existence and contributions to the new and emerging State of Israel is an ethical failure that forms a hole in the heart of the Israeli society today.

SEVEN

Monday—August 2, 1943

Across the brush and dry grass she sees dark, wriggling specks, and as her eyes adjusted to the distance, the forms of running men materialize rising from the silvery mirage, liquefied in the shimmering heat. Three, four of them, no, a dozen. More than a dozen. Then it appears to be sixty or seventy, a line of shapes enlarging in a molten undulation. They are not wearing uniforms ... The men coming are not soldiers—they are Jews, and they have apparently broken out of the camp. What had the farmers and villagers called them? The evil ones, the devils, the blood drinkers? That is not possible—no one leaves the camp unless the Germans let them leave.[1]
—Ian Macmillan, Village of a Million Spirits

In his work on Treblinka Yitzhak Arad provided a general outline of the revolt plan that, in my judgment, is sound and follows the general information provided by the survivors. Of course, one needs to take into consideration that the plan was unexpectedly interrupted and the prisoners were forced to begin the uprising about two hours earlier. As a result, weapons were still in their hiding places, fighters were not in their positions, and there were very few rifles available. It is conceivable that if the plan was implemented successfully many more prisoners would have escaped. Arad envisioned the following outline:

Stage A: From 14:00 to 16:30—Acquisition of Arms and Deployment

1. Removal of the arms from the arms store and their transfer to the combat groups' assembly points.

2. Deployment of the combat groups near the targets of attack—the camp headquarters, the quarters of the SS and of the Ukrainians, the guard towers.

3. Quiet elimination of Germans entering workshops and work sites.

Indeed, the plan was to use the *putzer* boys to enter the armory with the duplicate key acquired earlier and hand out grenades and rifles to other prisoners waiting outside. With working carts the prisoners outside were to distribute the weapons to specific stations to be concealed until 4:45pm, the agreed upon start of the uprising. At the same time prisoners sprayed the barracks, headquarters, and other wooden structures so they would quickly be engulfed in fire at the start of the revolt. According to Arad's outline, however, the prisoners were to engage in a quiet killing of Germans for two and a half hours. This seems illogical for a revolt since a score of missing Germans would have been noticed and the plan would have been discovered hours before the assigned time. On the one hand, strategically, it seems proper to suggest that on the day of the uprising one would want to take out as many possible obstacles as possible. On the other hand, the only way an uprising could have been successful in Treblinka was if the element of surprise was used. In reality, the prisoners succeeded in taking out the weapons from the armory and successfully distributed them to the designated stations.

Stage B: Beginning at 16:30—Seizing Control and destroying the Camp

1. Attack the camp headquarters and SS people in various places.

2. Cut telephone lines and open fire on the guard towers, forcing the guards to abandon their positions.

3. Break into Ukrainians' quarters, seize their weapons and lock them up under guard in the barracks.

4. Set the camp afire and destroy it.

5. Arm with additional weapons taken from the SS and Ukrainians.

6. Link up with the extermination area people.

Arad is correct in suggesting that the signal for the uprising was supposed to be the sound of grenades exploding and not the sound of rounds from a machine gun. However, this conclusion contradicts the testimony of Marian Platkiewicz. The latter claimed that engineer Galewski was supposed to give the signal by firing several rounds from his machine gun. Platkiewicz's group did not wait for Galewski's signal but followed another signal and attacked the headquarters with grenades. This scenario, of course, contradicts the other account in which SS Küttner was attacked after the prisoners concluded that the tortured prisoners would divulge the plan for the upcoming attack. This event is described by Richard Glazer and it clearly involved

Moshe Y. Lubling. On the day of the revolt Glazer turned to his commander, who was allowed to have a watch, and asked:

"Kleinmann, what time is it?"

"Almost two."

"Is your watch right?"

Glazer then describes Moshe Y. Lubling standing "near the fork in the path" signaling with his arm to the fighting units. Kleinmann, the unit's commander, is concerned about the capture of the two prisoners and with determination he tells Glazer: "Listen, from now on we go the moment they make   the slightest move to take anyone off to the infirmary or threaten to kill. Not one more man is going to die that way."[2]

This scenario seems to be supported by the majority of survivors while Platkiewicz's testimony seems to be the only one that contradicts it. It should be noted that this event took place at two o'clock which supports the testimonies that the revolt started two hours earlier because of the incidence involving SS Küttner. While weapons were distributed and stored the above event occurred. Within a few minutes SS Küttner was shot and the revolt started. It is also clear that the revolt started under the watching eye of Moshe Y. Lubling who observed the events and signaled to Kleinmann to wait. Apparently, matters got out of hand and Salzberg shoots Küttner, the latter survives and retreats into the headquarters, the revolt started and all hell breaks out. The prisoners who waited for the grenade explosion signal did not necessarily know that the revolt started. However, very quickly some grenades were thrown into the Nazi headquarters and that allowed others to join the uprising, many unprepared and without their hidden weapons. Despite all that, the prisoners succeeded in attacking the headquarters, they cut the phone line but failed to cut the electricity. As a result, scores of prisoners died when attempting to escape through the electric fence that surrounded the camp. They succeeded in setting fire to most structures but failed to force the guards to abandon all of their positions or lock the other Ukrainian guards in their barracks. Finally, Arad insists that there was a plan to link up with the extermination area people despite the fact that Sonia Lewkowicz insisted in her testimony that such an idea would have been illogical. For the prisoners from Camp II to escape by crossing into Camp I where all the Ukrainian and Nazi personnel were stationed would have guaranteed their death. It was much easier for prisoners from Camp II to escape directly through the fences surrounding their immediate area. Indeed, if the sole purpose of the uprising was to escape, then it doesn't make much sense that prisoners from Camp II should risk running to Camp I rather than escape directly from their area. However, it is completely possible that in the original plan the aim was to neutralize the Ukrainian and Nazi personnel and then, open a clear passage between the two camps. In fact, Arad remarked that, although no evidence exists to support such a claim, some survivors suggested that originally the leaders planned to link up with the nearby camp of Polish military prisoners. Together, all freed prisoners would form a partisan force that will fight the Germans. However, Pinchas Lubling insists that this information was contained in the letter that was dispatched by his father from Treblinka in May 1943. This might explain why such information is contained in Moshe Y. Lubling's obituary, that is, because Aron Gelberd and Tzvi Rozenvayn read it in the letter sent by Moshe Y. Lubling to the resistance organization in Czestochowa. Arad's assumption, then, might be correct after all since I do not believe that my grandfather's sole reason for organizing the revolt was merely to survive. For a man who repeatedly refused to save himself, and who wrote to his son that the revolt in Treblinka will be remembered in Jewish history as the Jewish revolt in Masada, is not about to do all this so he can live another day. I still hold that the ideological leaders of the Treblinka revolt had no intention of escaping and in fact none survived. However, if the revolt would have been successful and my grandfather would have survived, there is no doubt in my mind that he would have formed a partisan force against the Nazis. Unfortunately, only a handful of young prisoners escaped during the uprising and they never attempted to organize themselves into a partisan group.

Finally, according to Arad, the plan for the prisoners at the extermination area contained the following stages:

1. Prisoners leave the barracks where they were kept in the afternoon hours after work.

2. Attack the SS men and Ukrainian guards near the barracks and seize their weapons.

3. Prisoners burst into the guardroom and seize the guards' weapon.

4. Take over the guard tower where a Ukrainian guard armed with a machine gun was stationed.

5. Take control of the entire extermination area, destroy it and link up with the people of the lower camp for a joint escape.

Stage C: Organized Departure to the forests by All Prisoners[3]

It is clear that Arad had to make some difficult decisions regarding the facts provided by survivors' testimony. But in essence his general plan can be imaginatively teased-out from the available testimonies. What is missing from Arad's account of the Organizing Committee and the revolt itself is the *Czestochowa-Connection* that underscored the entire operation from beginning to end. The reason for this omission is surely grounded in the fact that he never attempted to find out who Moshe Y. Lubling was, despite the fact that his name kept appearing in survivors testimonies. Basing his analysis on what young survivors with obvious ignorance of who organized the revolt testified to, and without searching into the origin and background of the leaders, seriously compromised his account.

The following is an interpretation of the event on August 2, 1943, based on my understanding of survivors' testimonies, as well as knowledge about Moshe Y. Lubling that was ignored by Arad's analysis. I believe that it provides a better and more warranted outline of the uprising itself based on all available information.

"Moshe Y. Lubling: Escape from Treblinka"—
A drawing by Anne Simpkins

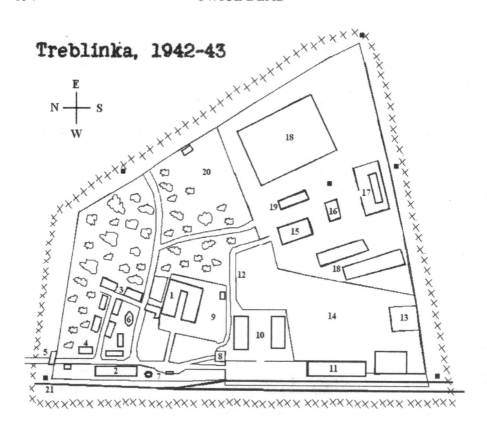

Treblinka, 1942-43

1. Prisoner barracks and workshops
2. SS barracks
3. Ukrainian barracks and potato mound
4. Camp headquarters
5. Main gate
6. The "Zoo"
7. Fuel depot
8. The garage
9. Roll-call square
10. Undressing area
11. The "Train station"
12. The "Road to Heaven"
13. The *Lazaret*
14. Sorting area
15. Gas chambers
16. Old gas chambers
17. Camp II barracks
18. Mass graves
19. The "Roasts"
20. Lumberyard
21. Treblinka rail spur [a]

---

[a] A special gratitude to Aron Tyson Smith for designing the maps of Treblinka, and for his help in creating the following chronology of the uprising.

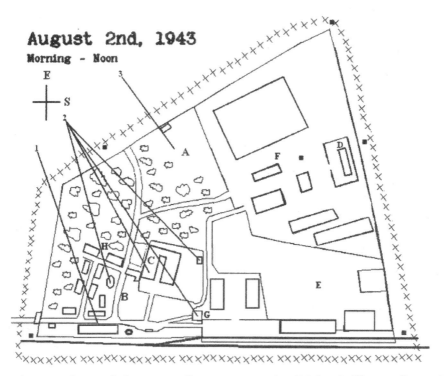

August 2nd, 1943

Morning - Noon

A. The members of the camouflage commando. Richard Glazer, Samuel Willenberg, Samuel Rajzman, and their foreman, Kleinmann, are stationed at the lumberyard on the day of the uprising. Glazer writes the following:

> After morning roll call Küttner sends the camouflage commando to the lumberyard. We were supposed to take over the work of the woodcutter … Kleinmann uses the return to work as an opportunity to pass on information. From the outside it looks as if he's giving instructions for work: 'Things start at precisely four o'clock. We are responsible for our guard here, for the one along the fence, and the one at the gate, and of course for any SS man who might happen along this way. Rifles and anything else that shoots are to be handed over immediately to Josek and Herschek … The camouflage commando gets back to work in the lumberyard, cutting branches, chopping and splitting logs , Karl and I pick up our saw again. [4]

B. Moshe Y. Lubling "is our contact, and he is working somewhere near the intersection between the ghetto, the SS barracks, and Ukrainian barracks." His role on the day of the uprising was to act as contact between the various work groups in the camp and direct activities in the northern end of the camp. Nearby, at the "Zoo," is Rudolf Masarek. He is tasked with hiding rifles and grenades. Also working at the "Zoo" is Alexander Kudlik.[5]

C. Kalman Taigman, Oskar Strawczynski, Zygmunt Strawczynski, David Brat, Eugeniusz Turowski, Leon Perelsztajn, and Tanhum Grinberg are located in the ghetto. Salzberg is in charge of the fighters there.[6]

D. Jankiel Wiernik and Sonia Lewkowicz are located in the Camp II barracks. Zelo Bloch, the leader of the underground in Camp II is part of a group of prisoners tasked with carrying water from the well to the camp kitchen.[7]

E. Galewski and Kurland are located in the sorting square. Kurland is in command of the fighters there.[8]

F. Zelo's lieutenant, Adolf Friedman, is out burning bodies with 30 other prisoners. The men are armed with the picks and shovels they use to dig up bodies for burning.[9]

G. Standa Lichtblau and Rudek Lubrenitski are stationed in the garage. They are tasked with sabotaging the fuel depot and armored car.[10]

H. The agronomist Sudowicz, head of the potato and vegetable details, is tasked with overseeing the removal of the weapons from the munitions depot. His objective is to lead the fighters under his command against the Ukrainian barracks and the camp headquarters. Marian Platkiewicz is in this group.[11]

   1. Early afternoon—Sudowicz lures SS Müller away from the munitions depot, which enables the trash detail led by Markus to collect rifles and grenades. The key to the armory had previously been copied by Turowski. The weapons are passed by Markus and young Salzberg (named Wladek) to Ya'akov Miller, who then hides them in the trash cart.[12] Miller later identified "Lubling from Silesia" among the original four members of the Organizing Committee.

   2. Lunchtime—Grenades and weapons taken from the munitions depot are hidden in the workshops, latrines, pigeon house and garage. The construction commando distributes weapons to other groups of fighters throughout the camp by hiding them in carts carrying construction materials. Several grenades are also distributed to the potato commando near the Ukrainian barracks. These are added to several petrol bombs the potato commando men have already hidden. The prisoner who disinfects the clothes and possessions of the new arrivals replaces the disinfectant in his sprayer with petrol, which he then sprays all over the buildings in Camp I.[13]

3. After lunch, Richard Glazer is sent by Kleinmann to communicate "all is well" to the other groups of fighters in the ghetto/workshops and disrobing area. Along the way he nods to Moshe Y. Lubling, signaling that all is well.[14]

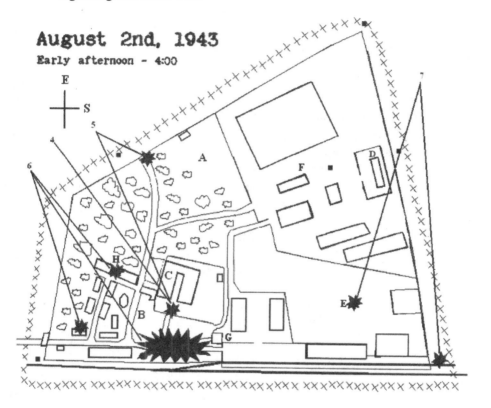

August 2nd, 1943
Early afternoon - 4:00

4. The informer Kuba discovers two men in the barracks when they aren't supposed to be there. Kuba summons SS guard Küttner into the ghetto to report the matter. Salzberg, afraid that Kuba may have knowledge about the uprising, sends for an armed man to kill him. While interrogating the two men he discovers that one is carrying money; he begins to beat the men and threatens to shoot them if they don't talk. The underground members fear that the men will break under torture and reveal the plans for the uprising.[15] It is in this context that Kleinmann, after his communication with Lubling, returns to his group and says: "Listen, from now on we go the moment they make the slightest move to take anyone off to the infirmary or threaten to kill. Not one more man is going to die that way."[16] This event must have taken place between 2:00pm - 3:00pm.

5. 4:00 PM. A prisoner named Wallabanczik shoots Küttner, sparking the uprising (according to Perelsztajn, Salzberg shoots Küttner). Küttner is only wounded by the shot; he retreats from the ghetto area to the SS barracks. Kuba the informer, however, is shot and killed. Prisoners in the ghetto workshops open fire on another SS guard by the name of Suchomel who is riding his bike along the East-West path that runs from the SS barracks to the lumberyard, but miss. Hearing the commotion from the ghetto, the Ukrainian on duty at the east gate opens fire on the prisoners at the lumberyard; one of the camouflage commando returns fire and kills him.[17]

6. Members of the potato commando attack camp headquarters with grenades. The attack is timed so that many of the SS men will be gathered together in the building. The headquarters building takes some damage from the grenades, but there are no casualties. Another group attacks the Ukrainian barracks with grenades and Molotov cocktails; the buildings are set on fire but casualties amongst the Ukrainians are light. The Ukrainians inside the barracks exchange fire with prisoners in the ghetto, the potato commando, and members of the camouflage commando. Ukrainian guards pursue members of the potato commando in the direction of the ghetto; covering fire from the prisoners in the ghetto kills or wounds several Ukrainian guards. Rudek Lubrenitski and his partner Standa Lichtblau set off the fuel depot, creating a massive fireball which sets nearby buildings alight, including the SS barracks. The two are shot and killed by machine gun fire from the guard tower immediately afterward.[18]

7. Prisoners in the sorting area open fire on nearby Ukrainians and watch towers.[19]

8. The original signal, according to Platkiewicz, was supposed to be given by Galewski by firing several rounds from a machine gun while in the sorting area. This was supposed to signal to one of the fighting units to begin attacking the headquarters with grenades, which in turn was to provide the signal for the rest of the fighting units. However, Galewski never fired his machine gun and the members of the potato commando acted on their own following a signal one of the "*putzer*" boys that the SS were gathered in the camp headquarters. Hearing the grenade blasts in Camp I, Zelo Bloch and

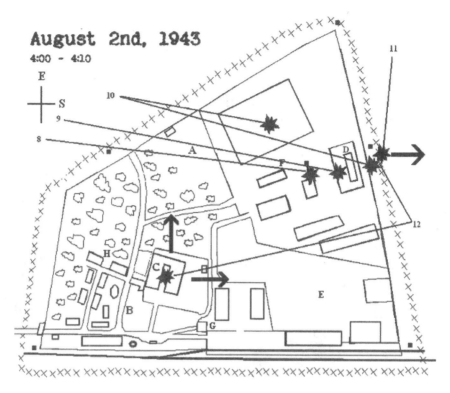

August 2nd, 1943
4:00 - 4:10

from other prisoners within Camp II kill the Ukrainian guard at the well and take his weapon. Zelo Bloch then opens fire on the guard tower, injuring the Ukrainian guard on duty there. In reality, the revolt began when Küttner was shot (refer to No. 5 above).[20]

9. The prisoners in the barracks, including Jankiel Wiernik, use shovels and pitchforks to break through the barracks gate. They kill the guards on duty at the barracks and guard stations.[21]

10. Adolf Friedman and the prisoners in the cremating site kill the Ukrainian guard overseeing their work. Camp II is now under the control of the prisoners. The prisoners begin to make their way for the fence behind the Camp II barracks. They use pitchforks and shovels to cut through the fencing.[22]

11. The fence is breached, but many of the fleeing prisoners are cut down by machine gun fire from the guard towers as they attempt to cross the tank traps.[23]

12. The prisoners in the ghetto set fire to the workshops. Prisoners in the ghetto make their way south and east towards the camp fence. Those

fleeing south join the Camp II prisoners in escaping through the breached southern fence.[24]

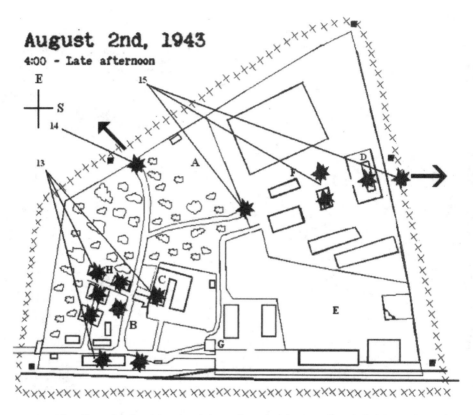

13. The fires ignited by Rudek Lubrenitski, Standa Lichtblau, the prisoners in the ghetto, and members of the potato commando spread over the north end of the camp. Rudolf Masarek and another prisoner hoist a heavy machine gun atop the "Zoo" pigeon house and open fire on the Germans and Ukrainians.[25]

14. Moshe Y. Lubling leads the prisoners in Camp I towards the east gate; he uses a pole to force open the gate, enabling prisoners to escape. Richard Glazer and his friend Karl Unger escape through the breached gate. Samuel Rajzman and Samuel Willenberg, who were both stationed nearby at the lumberyard, escape through the gate. Alexander Kudlik also escapes through the east gate. In all probability, Moshe Y. Lubling was killed soon after by machine gun fire from the watch tower.[26]

15. Zelo Bloch is seen moving from Camp I to Camp II, rifle in hand. He continued to fight while others fled the camp. In Camp II, fires are ignited in several buildings, but the gas chambers are not destroyed.

Silence of Treblinka, 1995

"Night fell. The battle had already been going on for six hours. The Germans were getting reinforcements, and our ranks had become thinner. Our ammunition was running out. We had been ordered to make for the nearby woods. Most of our fighters fell but there were many German casualties. Very few of us survived."[27] This is how Stanislaw Kon in 1945 described the end of the uprising.

Heroism

The issue of heroism, as any other human activity, is subject to different interpretation and competing ideologies. It is not surprising, then, that my grandfather's actions in Treblinka have been questioned by various thinkers of diverse significance and intellectual competency. In a recent book, the historian Samuel Moyn has recreated the intellectual storm in France that was caused by the 1966 publication of Steiner's famous book *Treblinka*.[28]

The controversy drew many known French intellectuals such as Pierre Vital-
Naquest, Emmanuel Levinas, David Rousset, Simone de Beauvoir, Claude
Lanzmann, as well as the philosopher Hannah Arendt, the Holocaust scholar
Rachel Auerbach, and the Treblinka survivors Richard Glazer and Eliyahu
Rosenberg, to only name a few. The controversy centered on Steiner's
insinuation in the book and in his interview of March 1966 in *Le Nouveau
Candide*—"The Jews: What No One Ever Dared to Say"—that the Jewish
prisoners in Treblinka were partially responsible for the murder of nearly
1,000,000 Jewish men, women, and children. More specifically, that the
prisoners in their passivity enabled the murder of Jews and in fact carried out
the work of extermination for over a year. Finally, only when the prisoners
realized that they were not going to survive, did they actually take desperate
actions and revolted! In other words, the accusation is that if the organizers
had believed that they might still be able to survive themselves, they would
have continued to facilitate the Nazis' plan to exterminate the Jews. Steiner
writes:

> Physically weakened and morally broken, the Jews had let themselves be led to
> death like a flock of animals to the slaughterhouse, had let themselves be trans-
> formed into accomplices in the extermination of their people. And these accom-
> plices were not criminals but good Jews, sometimes even great Jews. And then,
> suddenly, came the miracle. Just when their abdication was total, when all values
> had ceased to exist, when their humanity had almost left them, the Jews, rousing
> themselves at the bottom of the abyss, began a slow ascent which death alone would
> stop.[29]

Quite a charge in 1966 while most Nazi criminals were still alive and
enjoying the warm weather in Brazil, Syria, Egypt, or Argentina.

After the publication of the book in France, some of the survivors whose
names Steiner used protested the book's insinuations and he was forced to
omit and replace their names. The survivors, represented by Rachel Auerbach, also lunched a lawsuit in order to prevent the publication of the book in
America, and as we can clearly understand, the book was never published in
Israel. The controversy in general is not new and has raged in Israel since the
famous Jewish Partisan, Abba Kovner, coined the phrase "going like lambs
to the slaughter" to describe the general passivity of the Jewish population in
Europe during the Holocaust; a phrase he latter regretted.[30]

On one side of the controversy are those who find the very idea of
blaming the victims of Nazism with criminal culpability, at the time in which
most Nazi criminals have never been brought to justice, to be criminal.[31] No
one has the right to judge individuals under conditions in which all normal
categories of understanding have been put on their head. The Holocaust saw
the complete failure of the modernist notion of the social contract in which

the authorities are supposed to guarantee the safety of their citizens, not hunt them down like animals. When such reversal in the actual conditions under which ordinary individuals' lives occur, it is not the place of armchair intellectuals to question the morality of the victims. Such intellectual detachment from the experience of ordinary men and women is what usually makes intellectual analysis irrelevant to our understanding of historical events.

On the other hand, there is Steiner and those who argue that passivity was a uniquely Jewish quality during the Holocaust that, in part, contributed to the massive losses among European Jewry; a view that in part is shared by the native Israeli community. The Jews have no one else to blame but themselves. One can also argue that it is precisely under conditions like the ones created during the Holocaust, that one can see the difference between those who succeeded in maintaining their ethical integrity and those who sank to the bottom of bestiality. The latter were willing to assist in the process of extermination just for the chance that they may survive. In essence this position is anti-Semitic since it also suggests that Jews, more than any other group of people, will sell their own families for mere survival. The Diaspora Jew, this position implies, is of a low moral character, if at all, which both explains why such a great number of Jews perished, and contra-dictorily it also explains why Jews would lie about the Holocaust.

As a "vicarious witness," I frequently reflected on that period and imagined myself in my family's shoes during the Holocaust (a reflective exercise I do not recommend to others). I too share Amos Oz's sentiment that all Jews who were affected by the Holocaust carry within themselves a numb feeling of pain because they did not kill Hitler with their own hands and save their families.[32] But these are merely the nightmares of a "vicari-ous witness" and not the press of experience that faced the Jews of Eastern Europe during the Holocaust. As a philosophical naturalist I am astutely aware of the practical difference between intellectualism and pragmatism, as well as the "vicious" nature of the former. As such, I know better than to judge survivors who had to make decisions under dramatic conditions that cannot be reduced to intellectual qualities. Those who transgress against their brothers and sisters should be forgiven (or forgotten) and those who acted in an exemplary fashion should be commended and remembered as role models. Nothing more should be said or be done in this regard. Jews were not acting any differently than any other group that found itself under such conditions—no one did!

I must also point out that such self-doubt and sense of moral shame seems to be a uniquely Jewish quality, not shared by many other cultural groups. What other group of victims will question their own moral conduct during the Holocaust before they question German's moral behavior? What sort of people will be more ashamed of their own temporary loss of humanity as victims, than the victimizers are ashamed of theirs? What sort of victims will be more concerned with the displacement of 400,000 Palestinians, than the obliteration of two-thirds of their European brothers and sisters (with the personal encouragement and support of Amin El Husseini, the Grand Mufti of Jerusalem and the Palestinians' spiritual leader)? Do not misunderstand me; I am not suggesting that the displacement of the Palestinians was necessary or proper. What I am suggesting is that giving the moral collapse of Western and Eastern civilizations during the Holocaust, Jews should allow themselves a moral break! In a context that involves the mindfully con-structed plan for the "Final-Solution of the Jewish Problem" with the silence of the free world, the Jews and the "criminal Zionists" are still the steady light of morality in a world full of flitting and evil shadows.

As a related issue, the controversy about the prisoners' revolt in Treb-linka also raises the question about the Jewish view of Heroism. While some saw in the Treblinka armed revolt the spirit of a new Jewish generation, others saw in the passivity of Diaspora Jews a traditional virtue unique among peoples.[33] Taking arms and engaging in the killing of your own executioners is the easiest way out of a problematic situation and would be sure to pull one to their enemy's amoral universe. The Jewish hero, like Christ himself, ought to hold eternal moral values while the rest of creation sinks into the depths of immorality. As such, in his response to Steiner's accusation, the French and Jewish philosopher Immanuel Levinas wrote that "the highest duty, when 'everything is permitted' consists in feeling oneself responsible with regards to values of peace … in not concluding, in a universe at war, that warlike virtues are the only sure ones; in not taking pleasure, during the tragic situation, in the virile virtues of death and desper-ate murder; in not living dangerously only in order to remove dangers and to return to the shade of one's own vine and fig tree."[34]

Furthermore, Levinas' position that Jewish uniqueness is grounded in the desire to maintain virtues of peace rather than join the "virtues of war" follows a similar philosophical view by Martin Buber and Yeshayahu Leibowitz, both former members of the philosophy department at the Hebrew University in Jerusalem. The late Professor Leibowitz was a furious critic of the military culture that developed in Israel, especially after the occupation of Arab territories in 1967. True Jewish heroism, Leibowitz argued, is always linked with the struggle between a man's choices of values. On the one hand, there is the person's conscious act of decision-making, and on the other hand, there is an urge arising from a person's nature. The latter operates within him without his knowledge and mostly against his will. "If in such a struggle the individual stands his ground in keeping with his decision and against the prompting of his nature, that is heroism: it is the meaning of the sage's words: 'What is a hero? He who overcome his urges' (M. Avot 4:1)."[35]

One of those urges is for physical existence which, according to Leibowitz, is greater then the urges for possessions, honors, power, or even sexual pleasure. Values are established in relation to what one is willing to pay for his fear of death and urge to cling to life. Those who are willing to pay the highest price reflect the heroism of *Kiddush Ha-Shem*, the giving of one's life for the sake of others—the heroism I wish to attribute to my grandfather. However, to my disappointment, according to Leibowitz,

> ... it can be determined that military heroism is the least worthy kind of heroism. For it is the only one that is to be found among the masses and in every people and culture in every period in history regardless of the spiritual, moral, or social level of those who possess it. This is certainly not the case with regards to the heroism of controlling the natural urges."[36]

The position is obviously heavily Platonic, Religious, and Kantian in its emphasis on overcoming instinctual urges in order for the free will to capture the eternal virtues of insights and reason. However, as most philosophers would have to acknowledge, such a view of ethics is practically unworkable since it contradicts the experiences of most ordinary men and women, Jews or not. The position that taking arms to defend oneself in a morally corrupt universe reflects a moral failure is analogues to Kant's conclusion in the *Categorical Imperative* that one should never tell a lie even if doing so would save his or other lives. Such experiential absurdities, in my view, reflect the last stage of philosophical and intellectual demoralization. As John Dewey correctly observed in his debate with the pacifist, any theory "which will have nothing to do with power on the ground that all power is force and all force brutal and non-moral is obviously condemned to a purely sentimental, dreamy morals. ... Not to depend upon and utilize force is simply to be without a foothold in the real world.[37]

The ethical issue that should concern us is not whether or not to use force, this choice is taken away from us by the very nature of reality, but rather who is going to use it and how.[38] As Albert Einstein correctly remarked on the "pacifist problem" during the Holocaust, "such people are not to be relied on in our time of crises ... In my opinion, the best method in this case is the violent one."[39] Or in Woody Allen's terms, "true physical force is always better with Nazis, because it's hard to satirize a guy with

black boots on."[40]   The existence of force is endemic to the human condition
and to suppose that one can escape its demands reflects the reason why
religious beliefs cannot inform ordinary life. Making God's ethical demands
inaccessible to plain men and women, Nietzsche correctly observed, declares
the death of God. The Holocaust revealed that life cannot be judged from the
position of "dreamy morals" without insulting and marginalizing the lives of
its victims. To suggest that the Jew must behave in a way that contradicts the
very nature of the physical world and the process of history is to make
Judaism an irrelevant "myth' by which to live our lives.

Martin Buber, the originator of this contemporary Jewish perspective,
was also heavily criticized for condemning the use of force by Jews after the
Holocaust and during their attempt to secure a homeland. While for most
Jews, in particular the survivors, the 1948 Israeli War of Independence was
not only morally permissible but historically and existentially justified, for
Buber it was "the most grievous of the three" wars (the other two being the
two World Wars). Given Buber's prophetic view of Zionism, we can
sympathize with such a claim. Nevertheless, since WWII included the
Holocaust, this statement constitutes, according to Emil L. Fackenheim, "a
lapse in judgment."[41]   Richard L. Rubenstein, the Death of God theologian,
also argued that Buber's failure to understand the nature of political sover-
eignty reflects his "larger inability to deal realistically with the world of
concrete actuality."[42]

As an Israeli that was educated by the anti-religious and national
paradigm of the early pioneers, I can only relate to the above pacifist
tradition in Judaism in historical terms, not existentially. My understanding
is that early Jewish thoughts usually involved a deep concern for the common and ordinary experience of plain men and women. As such, it recognized the irreducible empirical, contingent, and relational character of human
existence. The Bible, for example, reflects such a realistic view of the
relationship between power and dignity and a naturalistic need for self-
preservation, i.e., of war. Power relations were viewed as a necessary
character of the imperfect physical world in which we act and have our
being. The participation in a war was at times an obligatory and noble
activity in which God himself participated, i.e., God as "A Man of War."[43] It
is no coincidence that in Hebrew the words *Le-chem* (bread) and *Mel-chama*
(war) share the same linguistic root.

However, the Jewish experience in the Diaspora transformed this
participatory view of existence for nearly two thousands years. The Jewish
community of the Diaspora lost any sense of political power or of the
realistic dimensions associated with a sovereign nation. More specifically,

after the Judaeo-Roman war and the fall of Jerusalem, all the "Zealots" among the Jews were defeated, and the pacifist wing of the Pharisees under the leadership of Yohanan ben Zakkai agreed to live under the domination of the Romans in exchange for some religious freedoms. Thus, Rubenstein correctly suggests that, "every aspect of Diaspora Judaism for the next two thousand years was decisively affected by the political bargain made between the Romans and the Pharisees in the aftermath of 70 A.D." [44] In the two thousand years of exile, Jewish thought was transformed from a normative involvement in the practical flow of experience into one which was highly spiritualistic and voyeuristic. The realistic and naturalistic participation in the "power-dignity" relations was now the estate of other nations. The Jewish community was now an ideational and powerless group of believers replacing real conflicts of power with verbal disputes over the Torah.

The Holocaust then, was an inevitable result of these two thousand years of dependency upon other sovereign nations with their own particular interests, whims, and versions of anti-Semitism. In contemporary history, Germany became the Rome of the Pharisees and exercised total domination over the lives of the Jews. One can argue then, that Buber's, Levinas', and Leibowitz's celebration of Jewish passivity and their "leaps of judgments" about what is heroic, belong to the spiritualistic tradition of the Pharisees and its later manifestation in European history. The revolt in Treblinka, the Zionist spirit of Moshe Y. Lubling, and the establishment of the state of Israel marks the end of this voyeuristic tradition in Jewish history, although its remnants will always be around.[45]

Finally, with regards to the charge that those who revolted in Treblinka did so only after the realization that they will not survive, it is simply factually wrong. Plans for armed resistance were on Moshe Y. Lubling's mind from the moment information was received in Czestochowa that the Germans started a process of systematic killings in 1941. From Treblinka he communicated to his comrades in Czestochowa, encouraging them to take-up arms, and revealing the preparations in Treblinka for the uprising a year before it actually took place. The real issue, I suggest, is not whether or not the Jews should have refused to assist in the process of extermination. This is a non-issue since there were only 600–700 Jewish prisoners in Treblinka and they could have been easily replaced by Ukrainians, Lithuanians, Croatians, Polish, or any other group of anti-Semitic thugs. The real question was - what would be the most efficient way to take the camp out of commission, save as many young prisoners, and make the uprising count as a transformative event in the life of the Jewish people. It accomplished all three goals. As records show, there were many cases of individual acts of revenge in all camps and during most deportations. But such spontaneous acts did nothing other than increase the amount of violence that afterwards was imposed on the collective. Only an organized act of revenge could have made any difference to the overall German operation. This is precisely what the plotters in Treblinka planned from the start, and in the case of Moshe Y. Lubling, long before he arrived in Treblinka.

EIGHT

The Ethics of Memory

My family was all born in the same town, Wolbrom. My father was born in 1902 and so did my mother; I do not know the exact dates of their birth.
—Pinchas Lubling, Yad-Vashem Testimony

I told him that I do not know my mother's maiden name or her precise place of birth; the policeman looked at me with suspicious little eyes. How is it possible for a person not to know his mother's name and place of birth? [1]
—Dahn Ben Amotz, *To Remember and Forget*

Recently, as I was describing my frustrations and pain over the treatment of my grandfather's memory by Holocaust institutions and writers, I was asked by an Israeli friend: "Why do you care if they remember your grandfather and his actions? Isn't it enough that you remember him?"

The question took me by surprise since I always took it for granted that the Israeli-Jewish community "owes" people like my grandfather a place of honor in their collective memory. It's their ethical duty!

"Is it possible that the reason I want others to acknowledge my grandfather's name and significant contributions is for self-promotion?" I was wondering for a minute but then responded angrily.

"Because he fought and died for Jewish honor and his actions are the stuff that our national inspirations are made of, besides, what sort of a community forgets those who sacrificed their lives so others can live? What sort of a community celebrates the heroic acts of some and forgets others, especially when most of those who truly acted heroically did not survive? To further take credit for other peoples' genuine heroism and sacrifices is morally shameful. It sometimes makes you want to wash your hands of the entire ..."

As I was arguing my case to my friend, I could feel the regular philosophical uneasiness creeping into my mind about the limits of ethics, in particular practical ethics. "What gives epistemic force to our claims about individual or collective ethical obligations?" I thought to myself. "After all, religious education about loving one another and rational ethical thinking has been around for thousands of years, yet it didn't stop the burning of millions of people in the middle of Europe only 64 years ago."

The challenge by my friend to the claim that the Israeli-Jewish community *ought* to remember those who died in its name sets the framework for the present chapter. As the previous chapters demonstrated, my grandfather's name, Moshe Y. Lubling, was omitted from the "official" accounts of the prisoners' revolt in the death camp Treblinka. I refer to those accounts that are recorded and displayed in state sponsored Holocaust institutions, and in publications they the latter supported, although the ultimate responsibility rests with the historiographer.[2] As I demonstrated, this oversight is the result of incomplete research, narrow-mindedness, and straight-out disregard for existing documents. If allowed to go uncorrected, my grandfather's name will soon be forgotten; it will never become part of Israel's collective consciousness. By neglecting to realize and record Moshe Y. Lubling's heroic leadership, the Holocaust establishment engaged in a second act of killing; *an assassination by unimaginative narratives.* It is the claim of this chapter that such negligence constitutes an ethical failure on the part of the Israeli collective.

More specifically, I want to argue that a man who planned and executed the prisoners' revolt in Treblinka in order to stop the killing operations of the camp and was killed as a result, *ought* to be remembered by those who survived! And, if the spirit of this person's actions and death led to the rebirth of a new collective, then this collective has an obligation to remember his name and actions. Even more, it is an ethical failure on the part of the Israeli collective to forget the name of a Zionist who devoted his days during WWII to his fellow Jews, who on three different occasions refused to save himself so he could fight with his comrades for Jewish honor, and who paid the ultimate price for his actions.

A similar case was recently argued for by the philosopher Avishai Margalit[3] by citing a recent incident in which, during a public appearance, a commander in the Israeli army failed to remember the name of a soldier that was killed under his command.[4] The commander was immediately condemned by the Israeli public, the military establishment, and the press. We should note, furthermore, that the officer in question did not forget the soldier himself, but only his name. Why, asks Margalit, does a community such as the Israeli community hold the act of remembering or forgetting names as "a proper subject of moral praise and blame?" Why does forgetting the name of a comrade-at-arms constitute an ethical failure on the part of the surviving commander? The reason rests in our belief that names are not merely tags or hooks on which personhood is hung but rather that they stand for "the essence of human beings in a way nothing else does," and as long as the name survives "the essence somehow survives as well."[5] Indeed, as Alexander Donat correctly suggested, when it comes to the Treblinka revolt, knowing and remembering the correct names marks "the difference between identification and anonymity."[6]

An ethical obligation to remember, however, is not universal but only applies to individuals and/or collectives that stand in what Margalit calls "*thick* relations" to one another. Thick relations involve the elements of care and commitment that individuals or a group has for one another and it manifests itself through a mutual commitment to respect, honor, protect, help, nourish, and have awareness of the other's unique existence. Remembering the names of others is a clear expression of care which is analogous to the relationship of friendship and responsibility; both recognize the unique essence of the other.[7] Indeed, Margalit is correct to argue that when one remembers the names of friends, colleagues, or family members who passed away, "one induces them with a sort of continuous existence in one's conscious life." The same ought to be the case with regards to a group's collective memory. By forgetting the name of a person with whom the collective shares in the category of care will erase that person's essence from the group's collective memory forever; an act of total negation of the other's existence. Finally, the relational modality of care, Margalit argues, is already a legitimate category of contemporary ethical discourse and therefore, if care entails memory and care is part of ethics, then the question of memory (as care) is a legitimate subject for ethics. Therefore, when a collective that stands in *thick* relations to each other forget someone's name it provides empirical evidence that it does not care about the other person.

The Israeli public, then, is justified in condemning the officer for not remembering the name of the soldier who was killed under his command. By implication, the military that represents the soul of the Israeli nation may also be condemned for producing officers with such low moral character. The opposite, however, is also true. When such a collective forgets the name of a person who died under their historical watch and on their behalf, it is the duty of its members to admonish the collective's low moral character. To put it differently, unlike relations in general, *thick* relations involve a more expansive sense of selection and preferences. Similar to the modality of romantic love, the act of caring/memory involves an abnormal amount of attention devoted to one person over others.[8] Also, memories of another's life and actions capture the essence of the person and further bestow upon her a sort of immortality. As observed by Plato, all persons innately seek immortality, and consequently, they are all pregnant either in body or in soul. For many, immortality is achieved by physical propagation (the body) and the continuous existence of the name through blood. For the few, however, immortality is achieved by the production of works of art, heroic actions, and other gifts of the spirit. For those whose offspring are of the spirit, it is our memory of their names and works that creates their immortality. Plato's and Socrates' names are a case in point. We remember their names as a result of the spiritual offspring they gave birth to and which kept their essence alive for over twenty-five hundred years.

What accounts for *thick* relations and shared memory in the Israeli community is not difficult to ascertain. The tragedy of the Holocaust and persistent anti-Semitism in their exiled countries brought their respective fates together. They all share a commitment of care to each other that comes from being a part of something larger than their own individual loss. Such a community of memory does not only dwell in the past through memories, but uses them to design and shape the future. Hence, Margalit is correct when he argues that the power "to bring to life by collective memory ... strongly indicates that a community of memory is a community based not only on actual thick relations to the living but also thick relations to the dead. It is a community that deals with life and death, where the element of commemoration verging on revivification is stronger than in a community based merely on communications. It is a community that is concerned with the issue of survival through memory."[9] The distinction between communities based on communications and those based on revivification is very significant. The latter is a community with a living center that uses memory to create new life and identity for itself. In the case of the Israeli community, the violent course European history took in the 20th century and the memories associated with such history constitute its force of revivification today. Without such collective memories to assist in the future survival of the Israeli community, it will dissolve into a community based on the impersonal and non-committal nature of communications alone. In other words, it will cease to exist. Compare the way in which Israel remembers its fallen soldiers to the American form of commemoration. During such a day in Israel, all businesses, public transportation, entertainment venues, schools, and even the army are "closed" for the day. The entire collective, physically and psychologically, participates in the meaning of the day which was designed to honor and remember those who gave their lives so the collective can live. There are no special sales on cars, shirts, or electronics, and the day is not commemorated through broadcasts of an all-day marathon of M.A.S.H. episodes. It is a silent day in which the Israelis use the memory of the fallen to look at the present and imagine the future. [10]

Israelis are not Jews and Jews are not Israelis

In the recent film *The Believer*, the main character is a young Jewish man in New York who becomes a neo-Nazi skin-head. When confronted by some of his Hebrew school friends he accuses Jews of being weak and without dignity.

"But what about the Israelis," a Jewish friend attempts to contradict him; "Jews are not Israelis and Israelis are not Jews," the skin-head replied.

For Israelis the issue of memory is a deeply existential experience that is life defining and affirming. When growing up in Israel during the 1960s, next to the pictures of Theodor Herzl and David Ben-Gurion that hung above the blackboards in our public schools, a Biblical phrase from Deuteronomy was also displayed: "If I forget thee, O Jerusalem, let my right hand wither." We young Israelis didn't forget our historical place and responsibilities and neither did countless generations of Jews before us who swore to remember our collective past. As young Israeli soldiers we swore our loyalty to the nation on top of Masada in order to incorporate the memory of ancient "fighting" Jews into the new Israeli collective consciousness. Memory was everywhere and carefully designed; I lived on a street that was named after the Zionist poet and writer Berl Katzenelson; I attended a public school that was named after Joseph Hayyim Brenner, another Zionist revolutionary who was murdered by local Arabs during the riots of 1921; my high-school was located on Syrkin street named after the Zionist thinker Nahman Syrkin who combined socialism and nationalism; and I belonged to a local chapter of the Labor Zionist youth movement *Ha-Noar Ha-Oved* (The Working Youth) that was named after Ber Borochov, a Marxist Zionist.

It is for obvious reasons that the Holocaust provided the most intense need to address the role of memory in contemporary Jewish history. The phrase 'Never-Again' became the charge given to the new fighting children of Israel and we responded accordingly, even if at times it seemed to others (including non-Israeli Jews) too excessive. Witness the recent bombing of southern Lebanon by Israel in response to the killings and abduction of its soldiers. We hold the memories of powerlessness, humiliation, and ultimate objectification in front of our open eyes so we never experience them again. To the dismay of many distinguished Jewish thinkers such as Martin Buber,

Yeshayahu Leibowitz, and Immanuel Levinas, the Holocaust created new values in the form Judaism took in Israel. The Israeli values of nationalism, secularism, and military heroism are now threatening Jewish values developed over 2000 years of passivity and spiritual isolation. As the first Israeli generation, we have attempted to live ordinary lives and in fact, created a new one. We do not forget what the German murderers and their collaborators did to our families and culture, and we also do not forgive. To the disappointment of many of my non-Jewish colleagues in America, we Jews are not religiously or morally obligated to forgive. We do not believe that forgiveness with or without genuine apology will contribute to the amendment of the world in the style of Nelson Mandela and Desmond Tutu. In fact, demanding Jews to forgive (not forget) the transgressions of others upon them, is in itself another form of continuous violence.[11] Those who insist on forgiveness argue that by not forgiving the German criminals and their collaborators, as well as the mostly silent free world, the Israeli-Jews are now contributing to the spread of violence around the world. By not forgiving the Nazis, the Israelis developed a vengeful and militant culture which, in its attempt to defend Israel's survival, led to more violence, i.e., the Palestinian/Israeli conflict.

The Jewish View of Memory

Generally speaking, Jewish faith is grounded in the requirement to remember the past and God's kindness towards them. Indeed, Jewish history provides nearly 5000 years of collective memories starting with the original covenant between Abraham and God, and continuing through the exodus from Egypt, the destruction of the first Temple in 586 B.C.E., the destruction of the second Temple in 70 A.D., the 11th century Christian Crusades, the 14th century Spanish Inquisition, the 17th century excommunication of Spinoza, the 19th century pogroms in Russia; the 1889 Dreyfus Trial in France, the 1896 publication of Herzl's *The Jewish State*, the 1939–1945 Nazi Holocaust, the 1948 creation of the first Jewish State in 2000 years, the ensuing wars with the Arabs, to only name a few.

The original job of determining what is remembered and how it is remembered fell on the early rabbinic establishment after the exile of 70 A.D. According to David G. Roskies, past events "were disassembled and reassembled according to biblical archetypes: the Flood, Sodom and Gomorrah, the *Akedah* (the binding of Isaac), the Exodus, Sinai, the breaking of the tablets, the destruction of the Temple, the Exile, [and] the restoration of Zion."[12] What is central for the thesis of this book, however, is Roskies' further claim that "the rabbis never treated the individual as worthy of memorialization. There was no place for heroes … it was liturgy that became the central repository of group memory."[13] What ultimately has been established as worth memorialization "was not the factual date but the meaning of the desecration."[14] This approach to memory, he correctly observed, led to the creation of the archetype of *Kiddush Ha-Shem* (the sanctification of God's Name) during collective persecutions such as the Crusades, the Russian Pogroms, the Holocaust, and the death of every Israeli soldier. In the aftermath of the Holocaust, he offers, new archetypal models for memory have emerged or reinvented, such as *Hurban* (total destruction); *Shoah* (to be consumed by fire); *Gvura* (Heroism); *Yizkor* (In Memorial); *Nekama v-Mered* (Revolt and Revenge); *Leda* (Rebirth), and others.

> And so while the link between memory and covenant has been irrevocably broken, while individual actions are now celebrated along with those of the collective, while old archetypes are displayed by new ones, and while visual images supplant the written word, it would seem that group memory and archetypal thinking are still a viable form of Jewish self-expression.[15]

A similar sentiment regarding the importance of group and archetypal memory, and against individual heroes, is expressed by Peter Ochs when he writes that,

> For classical Judaism, individuality is a passing thing. Something is individual only while it serves a purpose. Once the purpose is fulfilled, or aborted, the individual evaporates, or is remembered not as an individual but as an exemplary instrument of action. In memory … individuals lose their evanescent character, becoming ideas or images of possible rather than actual individuals.[16]

Indeed, there is something admirable about the priority of the collective in Jewish ethics and its reluctance to recognize individuality as a given of human existence. It isn't surprising then, that historically, creative Jewish thinking usually seemed to converge with the modern philosophical expression of communalism, i.e., the priority of the social over the individual. Unlike Christianity's personal and private redemptive relationship in which the individual alone is judged by God during the ultimate Judgment Day, redemption in Judaism is always a social and collective undertaking. The coming of the Messiah in Judaism is directly contingent upon the time in which all Jews will engage in *Teshuvah* (return).[17] Even the giving of the Ten-Commandments and the actual encounter with Divinity itself, we ought to remember, were public events witnessed by the entire nation of Israel.

In my view, the values that are expressed by accepting the priority of relations are those that constitute the essence of humanism, and they are infinitely more ethical and humane than arrogant and vulgar individualism. Indeed, Martin Buber expressed this essence of biblical Judaism when, re-imagining the first line of Genesis, he wrote: "In the beginning is the relation."[18] The notion of individuality in its most vulgar expressions is merely, to use John Dewey's phrase, "a way of feeling." It is the psychological state of alienation which was mistakenly taken by philosophy as a metaphysical fact about our nature. In fact, if one views the essence of communalism as a philosophical attempt to articulate the possibilities of human freedom, freedom from objectification, from the commoditification of everything, from a loss of genuine subjectivity and spontaneous creativity, then communalism is consistent with what Buber called the spirit of Israel. For Judaism, wrote Buber, "unity, not division and separation, is the purpose of creation."[19] It is the overcoming of modern and past class, national, regional, economical, educational, and political distinctions and divisions. As such, Buber described the early attempts at communal living in Israel as "Paths in Utopia." The *kibutznick* (the cooperative farmers), is "the new type of man ... who can translate ideas into life, who along with the national idea will satisfy the longing for a just communal life."[20]

As an Israeli, I must agree with Buber's above understanding and I wish to make a further claim. Socialism and Labor Zionism, as originally envisioned by the Kibbutz Movement, was the closest Zionism came to be a model for the rest of mankind. The movement's values in relations to the land, its people, and politics reflected an essentially humanistic ethical vision. In the early days of the movement, kibbutzim that were formed by the youth movement *Ha-Shomer HaZair*, actually anticipated a visit by leading Soviet communists so they could show them how real communalism works. It is my view that Israel's Kibbutz movement was the most unique and significant ethical contribution Zionism made to mankind. It is still, in many Israelis' eyes, the real and humane spirit of Israel.

While I wholeheartedly share in the commitment to the priority of relationships over singularity as a metaphysical category, one should be cautious not to confuse metaphysical assumptions with the daily and individuated lives of ordinary people. We need to be careful not to confuse the false notion of individuality as a description of a private ego or self, with the true reality of individuated experiences, what William James called "Reals of Experience." There is the obvious danger that in our passion to reject the "myth of privacy" and embrace the ethical values involved in the priority of relations, we will neglect the irreducible experiences of ordinary men and women. While it is warranted to hold that ordinary experience is best captured by a relational anthology, the existential and individuated experience is still part of that reality. Even more specifically, it is not inconsistent to maintain that the reality of personhood emerges out of its relations with the environment (both physical and ideational), and also acknowledge that the experience of personhood is individuated. "Let us not pretend to doubt in philosophy what we do not doubt in our hearts," correctly recommended the American pragmatist Charles. S. Peirce.[21] We must be cautious that our ethical sentiment about our relational nature, which is certainly warranted by contemporary knowledge, does not blind us to the irreducible reality of individuated existence. As the Existentialists correctly reminded us, ignoring the individuation of personal experience will result in the formation of "herd" mentality, the repression of natural tendencies, loss of personal freedom, and inauthentic existence, i.e., bad-faith.

The point I wish to make is that when using memory to solidify and make cohesive a community, the role of persons should not be eclipsed by the larger lesson of the event. As Israelis we remember the collective sacrifice of all soldiers who were killed on behalf of our survival. But, it will be a mistake to overlook the individual soldiers who paid the ultimate price, especially those who acted heroically. Indeed, the Holocaust and the wars against the Arabs developed a tradition of individual memory that is in total opposition to the rabbis' traditional emphasis on collective memory. But there is no need to view such a development as an ethical transgression but rather as a correction and moral development. Overlooking the tremendous sacrifice of extraordinary individuals, as well as the complexity of heroism, objectifies people and runs the risk of loosing what Buber called the "living center" of the community.

What contributed to the existence of a "living center" (*thick* relations) in the Israeli-Jewish community is due in part to the members' shared participation in the nation's continuous struggle to survive. As I write these words, the fighting between the terrorist group Hezbollah and the IDF are raging out of control. Again, the children and grandchildren of Holocaust survivors and other persecuted Jews are defending their lives against a fascistic and religious movement that swore to eliminate them. Israeli national education, folklore, literature, art, military service, and common fate became the process by which *thick* relations were created. Furthermore, military service for Israelis is not a separate estate that, as in other nations, attracts mostly misguided nationalists. As the current fighting in Lebanon clearly shows, Israel has not yet achieved the envious position of many democracies that possess secure and legitimate boarders, and where military service mainly involves checking passports at the boarder. Since all Israelis, men and women alike serve in the military, I can attest to the fact that extraordinary ethical obligations exist in the IDF between soldiers and between soldiers and their commanders. To forget the name of a comrade-at-arm is a national disgrace and ethical failure. Those who lost their lives have paid the highest price for the collective. But unlike their Arab enemies, Israelis do not sacrifice for the glorification of death but for the affirmation and sanctification of life itself, i.e., so others may live.

I recognize that the very existence of a military culture may be repugnant to many of my contemporary liberals and progressives the world over. I myself felt this way when my youthful dreams were replaced with green uniforms and loss of personal freedom. Yet, I am realistic enough to recognize that military service provides a society with some irreplaceable values, habits, and skills. I often observe with sadness my students' poor skills and habits of cooperation, responsibility, brotherly and sisterly love, national and communal loyalty, and ultimately the willingness to sacrifice for the collective good. The reason for their extreme individualistic ethics is clearly the result of an upbringing that lacked any experience of national service. Where else can they acquire the above skills that will enable them to serve something larger than their own hedonistic tendencies? For many, even their religion prefers individual salvation over a collective one.

William James, himself a pacifist, correctly argued that so far, those who object to the existence of the military have found, "no moral equivalent" to the values and skills embodied in military service. The contemporary pedagogical attempts to "engage" students as citizens and members of a larger community, is a poor substitute for the actual engagement involved in military service. Shared responsibility and collective accomplishments are forms of conduct that must be grounded in physical and intellectual habits and skills. It cannot be established in a classroom, in one semester, or through the mere transmission of ideas and information. To be a genuinely transformative lesson, habits and skills must be formed through lived experiences, not merely by grasping information about such qualities. Through military service, argues James, the young person's qualities "acquire dignity when he knows that the service of the collectivity that owns him needs them. ... Martial virtues must be the enduring cement; intrepidity, contempt of softness, surrender of private interests, obedience to command, must still remain the rock upon which states are built. ... to get the childishness knocked out of them, and to come back into society with healthier sympathies and soberer ideas ... they would be better fathers and teachers of the following generation."[22] To the dismay of many, James' argument has been proven true by actual results as befits pragmatism. With no mandatory national service or alike, American culture inevitably turns towards hedonism as the morality of choice, i.e., the person who dies with the most toys wins. Indeed, even left-wing American intellectuals who champion collective responsibility disguise their hedonistic morality by adopting pseudo-political views about absolute privacy, freedom from the collective "big brother," or delusional ideas about non-violence and forgiveness.

What is ethically so significant in the relationships between brothers and sisters in-arms is their developed and more expansive sense of themselves as social beings. The reference "in-arms" does not necessarily entail violence or unjust wars against defenseless nations but rather, the collective's attempt to develop in its citizens the skills necessary for a nation. As James observed elsewhere, intellectual loyalty is far from sufficient to make a free society flourish since intellectualism rarely brings about concrete growth in the collective experience. When one serves the collective through military service, he/she learn with their bodies a different sense of family than the traditional and egotistic one in which blood members are just an enlarged agent of selfishness. The new Israeli society is a group of people who are connected deeply by values they have acquired during their national service.

Memory and National Identity

Turning to the core question of this book, we want to know whether *the Israeli-Jewish community has similar ethical obligations with regards to the victims of the Holocaust, especially those who died as martyrs,* i.e., Moshe Y. Lubling. We are not asking the universal question of philosophical ethics regarding whether or not future generations, Jews and non-Jews, ought to ethically remember the Holocaust and its victims. This, of course, is a larger question regarding the nature and future of human morality. Our question is directed at the ongoing process of Holocaust memorialization in the Israeli-Jewish community which allows for the marginalization, and even denial of individual actions and heroism. Should the post-Holocaust Israeli community, with its memorial museums and research institutions, be ethically condemned for not remembering the name of my grandfather who died during the Holocaust as a fighting hero?

As we established above, the concept of memory always had a central role in Jewish cultural history. In fact, it is the memory of its unique past that established Jewish identity through centuries. As such, not only does a community of *thick* relations have the ethical obligation to remember the names of those who died on its behalf, it also has a practical obligation to maintain its identity. The latter can be sustained, to be sure, only if events, persons, and practical lessons are remembered and nourished. The Israeli-Jewish community has such a psychological and ideational identity that imposes unique ethical obligation to nourish and protect this identity. The community's continuous survival wholly depends on its ability to maintain a consistent identity over time despite challenges and upheavals.

The philosophical treatment of the issue of identity over time, although usually directed towards individual's identity rather than the collective, reveals important insights about the collective's identity. By the identity of the person philosophy refers to the constant quality of personhood that exists overtime.[23] But it is not conceptual identity that we are after in this book but the living identity that carried a people for centuries and that still unites millions around the globe. It is the ideational continuity that makes an Israeli's heart tremble when she watches pictures of funerals for Israeli soldiers killed in the latest war against Hezbollah. In these pictures an Israeli does not just see the immediate loss of life and potential; what is also seen are centuries of funerals and victimization. The piles of dead bodies near a burial pit in Treblinka are not of other people but of themselves throughout time and space. What I existentially experience as the connection between me and the fallen Israeli soldiers is the identity that was established by personal acts of consciousness through collective memories.

Generally speaking, there are two possibilities for the establishment and existence of identity overtime; either through physical continuity or psychological continuity. I exclude the possibility of spiritual continuity since, in all honesty, I do not know what it means. To say that it is the spiritual entity (soul) that accounts for identity overtime is not to say much philosophically. The term is an empty tag for something we know nothing about, or to use John Locke's phrase, it is something, "I know not what." Furthermore, using physical continuity to account for identity is obviously problematic since physical materials are constantly changing their very formation. If we use physical continuity as a criterion for identity, then every time the physical materials that constitute the object change, the object establishes new identity. [24]

On the other hand, the psychological criterion for identity overtime usually involves the existence of memories and does not require physical or conceptual identity. Hence, John Locke argued that the ability to see oneself as a unified whole is grounded in the function of consciousness, "… and as far as this consciousness can be extended backwards to any past action or thought, so far reaches the identity of the person."[25] In other words, as far as the person can extend her memories to past "action or thought" so far extends the identity of such person. A simple case of forgetfulness, therefore, could cost someone her identity. I suggest that while such a notion of identity might face some philosophical difficulties, it nonetheless serves as a paradigmatic example for the reality concerning collective identity and memory.

An act of collective forgetfulness such as in the case of Moshe Y. Lubling may cause the collective to lose its identity overtime. This continuous identity involves a series of archetypal memories, as well as daily and annual rituals, the Torah that was communicated orally from one generation to another, the usage of the Hebrew language, and a 2000 year old longing for a return to their homeland. The Jews that were murdered by the Nazis and their many collaborators are, psychologically and ideationally, the same community as the ones that existed before the exile in the year 70 A.D. Along the same lines, then, we can argue that a community that cannot recollect its past actions or thoughts will lose its identity; it will either become a different community, or no longer a community at all.

Moshe Y. Lubling and Labor Zionism

It is not the claim of this book, however, that all Jews or Zionists have the ethical obligation to remember my grandfather's actions. It is much more specific—it is only aimed at the Zionist community in Israel and its diverse ideologies. My grandfather did not die heroically so Jews can live freely and capitalistically in Argentina, Canada, or the USA. What motivated his actions was a great passion towards an independent Hebrew nation with a social-democratic political system, not just another Jewish colony in other people's lands. The issue of identity through memory in Israel, however, is complicated and involves three competing cultural and educational paradigms; the national, ethnic, and civic.[26] These paradigms, furthermore, reflect the original three basic forms of Zionism—Political Zionism, Revisionist Zionism, and Cultural Zionism. The national/political paradigm started with the pre-state pioneers and culminated with the contemporary image of the Israeli. The political/national paradigm has been the most influential, and to a large extent, is responsible for the creation of the State of Israel. Its platform involves the claim that there is no other solution to the dangers of anti-Semitism but the political and practical one, that is, by the creation of an independent Jewish nation like all other nations. The original leader of the movement was David Ben-Gurion; a Russian Jew who literally walked to Palestine all the way from Russia. His ideology was shared by Moshe Y. Lubling and it involved a mixture of Democratic Socialism and Labor Zionism. From the creation of the state in 1948, Political Zionism built the nation's health, education, military, agricultural, and welfare systems, as well as created the nation's cultural milieu. Practically speaking, the State of Israel would not have come into existence without the socialistic vision of Political and Labor Zionism. Martin Buber, although not a Political Zionist, expressed the best in the latter's ideology when he responded to Gandhi's objection to the Jews "imposing themselves on the Arabs."

> Our settlers do not come here, as do the colonists from the Occident, to have natives do their work for them; they themselves set their shoulder to the plow, and they spend their strength and their blood to make the land fruitful ... Together with them (the Arabs), we want to cultivate the land ... to "serve" it, as the Hebrew has it ... We have no desire to dispossess them; we want to live with them. We do not want to dominate them, we want to serve with them.[27]

Labor Zionism was not merely concerned with the creation of a Jewish State but with the creation of a new Jewish society. They saw themselves as liberated from a 2,000 year-old "ghetto" mentality. They desired to overcome their historical and cultural detachment from productive physical labor and an ordinary sense of life. They sought to strengthen their souls and bodies, both as Jews and as new citizens of the modern political world. They believed that they were setting a global example for a healthy and just community life. Their goal was to create a new breed of Jews; secular, proud, militant, earthy, and politically independent.

I certainly share in this paradigm of identity and its treatment of memories; my forbidden first name attest to this shared identity. The name *Yoram* did not name any of my relatives who died in the Holocaust. Its usage meant to signal the beginning of a new life, diametrically different from the religious life of the Diaspora. *Yoram* was the name of the second king of Judaea who sinned against God and it was forbidden for Jews to use his name for over 2000 years. My name meant to represent the anti-traditional and anti-religious attitude of Political/Labor Zionism. In particular, it meant to represent our parent's rebellion against a religious tradition of weakness and dependency. Witness the following statement by Uri Avneri, the editor of the Israeli Magazine *Aolam Azea* (This World), a peace activist, and a former member of the Israeli *Knesset*, that represents the entire sentiment of the nationalistic paradigm:

> My name is biblical, Uri, meaning light. Avner, or Abner, was the field marshal of King David, I gave it to myself. Like most of my age group in what was then Palestine, I changed my name immediately on reaching age eighteen. With this one act we declared our independence from our past; we broke with it irrevocably. The Jewish Diaspora, the world of our parents and their background—we wanted nothing to do with. We were a new race, a new people, born the day we set foot on the soil of Palestine. *We were Hebrews, rather than Jews; our new Hebrew names proclaimed this.*[28]

A similar sentiment was recently expressed by the famous Israeli writer Yoram Kanyuk[29] who put it this way: "In our view, and in the view of our teachers who had immigrated from East-Europe, Jews were ridiculous figures from the stories of Mendelie the Book Seller and Peretz ... they were 'Jews' and in the other side there were us."[30]

In essence, Labor Zionism displayed the urgent psychological need of the early pioneers to transform some of their traditional and negative characteristics. Indeed, the psychologist Jay J. Gonen has observed that the newly emerging Jews found two particular exiled characteristics repugnant. "These were the *schnorrer* and the *luftmensch,* or the beggar and the pipe dreamer ... While Zionism's major battles against these two images were won, the war is not over.[31] Not only is the struggle of this paradigm of identity far from over, in actuality it has lost grounds to the Ethnic Paradigm and suffered a number of fatal blows in the last forty years. Take for example the issue of "Jewish work" so much emphasized by the early Labor Zionists. Since the occupation of the West-Bank and Gaza in 1967, the Jewish work force virtually disappeared. Palestinians, in a twisted and tragic sense of historical humor, were forced to build the Jewish nation they had always resisted. Subsequently, Palestinians were replaced by Russian immigrants who, in turn, have been replaced today by workers from Eastern Europe, the Far-East, and Africa. In merely fifty years of existence, the new Hebrew nation lost its Jewish work force and has regressed towards its exiled characteristics.

The national paradigm in Israel involved the intentional forgetfulness of the powerlessness experienced by Diaspora Jews; only memories of heroism were sanctioned as worth remembering. For Labor Zionists, Zionism was not a continuation of Jewish history, but a revolt against it. In fact, Zionism is not a Jewish matter at all! It is, by definition, an anti-Jewish movement that attempted to break away from historical Jewish memory and identity. They did not wish to remember the mostly passive Jewish behavior during the Holocaust but only the few incidents in which Jewish heroes fought back, i.e., Moshe Y. Lubling. Recall the earlier admonition by Israel Galili that the paradigm in which the *Judenrat* existed should never be rehabilitated since "such thoughts can destroy the nation's soul." Rather, what should be remembered, argued Yitzhak Gruenbaum, are "those who went to their death while resisting."

Labor Zionism's sense of redemption was umbilically connected to the land and its giveness through work and engagement, and not by means of power, claims for unique rights of ownership, and the exclusion of the local Arabs from equal participation in determining the land's future. Their Zionism, like biblical Judaism, consists of their relations to others and to the place and not in confrontations and insistence upon metaphysical uniqueness and its implied rights. ***This is the paradigm of identity and memory that has*** *direct obligation to remember the name and actions of Moshe Y. Lubling.* As our previous discussion demonstrated, Moshe Y. Lubling was an active leader of several Labor Zionists organizations in Poland and was actively engaged in preparing socialist Jewish groups to immigrate to British controlled Palestine. He was secular and intellectually an enlightened Jew who sought political freedoms and just communal life. But most importantly, he was a fighter who refused to be led as a "lamb to the slaughter" and died fighting.

However, Labor Zionism's dream of a new Jewish person is in danger of evaporating into the desert air like the sweat of their labor. The promise of redemption through working the land has been turned, at times, by other Zionist ideologies into a fanatical territorial nationalism with an almost complete disregard to democratic and moral standards, not to mention rational and pragmatic political considerations. The most significant regression, however, has been the systematic destruction of the love of cooperation as manifested in the early years of the *kibbutz*, national education, and military service. The love of cooperative relations is in danger of being replaced with an individualistic and economically monadic universe that celebrates right-wing economical programs that enslave individuals and destroy families and communities. Despite it all, Labor Zionism did succeed in transforming the moral, psychological, ecological, and existential health of the Israeli-Jews, and by implication, world Jewry. It produced and contributed many ameliorative qualities that are consistent with Judaism's commitments to heal and redeem the world. Indeed, there are many redeeming qualities in cooperation, love of work, self-reliance, deep sense of the land, and collective justice. Labor Zionism, as a process of self-becoming, has provided the healing that was contained in its original promises.

Not shared by Moshe Y. Lubling was the second Zionists ideology, that of the Revisionists/ethnic paradigm. The revisionists agreed in principle with the political solution to the problem of anti-Semitism, but rejected the compromise over territory and a national socialist ideology. Their platform involves free market capitalism, strong military, no national educational system, no welfare system, and strong nationalism. Their original claim was for a Jewish State across both sides of the Jordan River, the "Greater Israel" they called it. Today this form of Zionism is manifested by the Right-Wing Likud Party and their religious partners *Gosh Emunim*—the Settlers' movement. Since 1976 the Revisionist movement did its best to destroy all that has been built and accomplished by Labor Zionism. Their first assault was against the *Kibbutz* movement by cutting all governmental support to the cooperative farms. The same farms that defined the boarders of Israel, that sustained the nation's food supplies, that provided all of the nation's military heroes, that gave the nation's its culture and folklore, and that stood for the uniqueness of the Jewish revival, were now being abandoned by the new government. Throughout the coming years the revisionists succeeded in destroying the universal health care system, the educational system, and the unique cooperative culture created by Labor Zionism.

Even more tragic is the marriage that was created between the revisionist ideology and Religious Zionism. Their only common ground is the notion of a greater Israel and the rejection of Labor Zionism. Revisionism rejects Labor Zionism because of its socialistic ideology and religious Zionism rejects it because it is anti-Jewish. Since the religious right in Israel is predominantly messianic in vision, the consequences of this marriage have been tragic and irreversible. After 100 years of Labor Zionism, the ethnic Zionist ideology is threatening to turn Israel back into a big Jewish Ghetto of *schnorres* and *luftmenschen*, of middlemen and bosses, and into a religious community that does not work but lives on charity and governmental support. It is a movement of zealots that believe in a magical sense of history in which God or the messiah will rescue the Jewish people, regardless of their apparent impractical political practices. In fact, prior to the establishment of Israel in 1948, Labor Zionism regarded revisionism as an impediment to peace and to the establishment of the state. They also regarded its members as "gangs of which no one elected or empowered" who are not only immoral and nationally irresponsible, but suicidal since their only political direction involved the use of power. "They employ threats and violence against the settlement and they do everything in their power to force military control on the land. They are not concerned with abandoning human life as long as they increase the tension … Aren't the revisionists concerned with the total closure of the Jewish settlement and its institutions?"[32] Matters haven't changed much from these dreadful days in which the revisionists engaged in acts of terrorism against the British Colonial power and the local Arab residents of the land. There is also no doubt in my mind that they are responsible for the murder of the former Labor Zionist, and Israeli Prime Minister Yitzchak Rabin.

While grounded in the Revisionist movement, the ethnic paradigm in Israel developed in earnest only after the 1967 Six-Day War. This paradigm sought, very successfully we must acknowledge, for an integration of nationalism with a revived religious vision. While individuals like Yoram Kanyuk embody the perspective of the national paradigm, Moshe Y. Lubling's nephew, the late Professor Harold Fisch, embodies the perspective of the ethnic paradigm. As we recall, Professor Fisch was the former Rector of

Bar-Ilan University in Israel and one of the intellectual leaders of *Gush-Emunim*, the intellectual umbrella for the settlers' movement. [33] While this family relationship might seem irrelevant at first, it does provide a vivid example of the interconnected identity of the new Israeli-Jewish collective. [34]

Professor Fisch's ideological thesis is that the historical journey of Judaism operates within a separate and unique ahistorical "calendar." Consequently, such a calendar makes Israelis one people with one special destiny. [35] The calendar reveals three defining moments in the new Israeli culture underscoring the messianic culmination of the present day; they are the Holocaust, the 1967 Six-day War, and the 1973 Yom-Kippur War. For Professor Fisch and others in the Greater Israel political camp, (especially the former Prime Minister Menachem Begin), the wars with the Arabs were a direct continuation of the Nazi attempt to exterminate the Jewish people. [36] This Jewish "calendar" is nothing other then the historical blueprint for the return of the Messiah and final Jewish redemption. For Professor Fisch, Zionism was primarily "the child of Jewish prophetic history." The latter is "a divinely bestowed revelation that imposes upon the Jewish people the unconditional obligation to return to Eretz Israel and restore the broken covenant with the Lord of Israel." Put differently, argued Rubenstein, "Eretz Israel was not meant to be a place of refuge for human refuse wanted by no other nation. Nor was Eretz Israel regained solely by human agency. God restored Eretz Israel for redemption of Israel, and, through Israel, of all of mankind." [37]

The destruction of European Jewry, the return of biblical land to Jewish hands in 1967, and the miraculous victory in the 1973 Yom-Kippur War are all manifestations of God's restoration promise through the coming of the messiah. [38] According to Fisch, from the Holocaust we learned "that work as such does not necessarily make us free, and that mankind, in descending into its own primitive depths, does not discover the path of salvation." [39] The Six-Day War "was a moment in which the story of Israel suddenly acquired meaning, a moment of truth for every one. What was revealed then was the truth of the Covenant as a continuing reality comprising divine promise and human achievement." [40] Finally, the Yom-Kippur War "was the War of the Day of Atonement. It was the war that 'made us one': it made us not only one people, but a people subject to a special destiny, to special stresses, to special existential perils, a people with one calendar which stretches back from creation ... to the future." [41]

While I cannot share the religious context of Professor Fisch's understanding of Jewish Identity, I share his sentiments regarding the momentous nature and shared consciousness of the events. Indeed, the Holocaust taught us that nations with secular religions such as Nazism and Communism did not liberate the collective spirit. Communities without a humanistic/spiritual center are much quicker to join book burning and psychotic plans for final solutions. We have also painfully learned that we are not part of the Gentile "calendar" and that our collective fate must be as an independent nation. I share Professor Fisch's expression of a collective sense of destiny that Israelis shared in the aftermath of the Six-Day and Yom-Kippur Wars. Even a secular pragmatist like me experienced the intensity of the national and historical connectivity when I first touched the remains of the Second Temple, or stood with captivating amazement at the sight of Mount Sinai. I also share his depiction of the unifying nature of the Yom-Kippur War, when hundreds of thousands of Israelis living abroad jumped on airplanes and returned to defend their community. However, where Professor Fisch sees these events as moments in the forthcoming redemption, I see them as moments in the ongoing national struggle for identity described above.

Finally, I agree with Fisch's understanding of Judaism as an ethnic community but for utterly different reasons. Let me anticipate some objections regarding any account of Jewish particularity with regards to identity and ethical responsibility. The claim that Jews possess a unique essence that separates them from the rest of humanity should be rejected together with all other metaphysical claims of ethnic essentialism. However, there are particularities in Jews that are imposed from without and are not contained from within. As Jean-Paul Sartre observed; what "serves to keep a semblance of unity in the Jewish community," is their common situation, "that is, they live in a community which taken them for Jews."[42] Indeed, the world would not allow us not to be Jews, and if we did not exist, the Gentile world would have created us. If left alone, I am afraid to say, Judaism would have disappeared centuries ago.

The Civic/Cultural form of Zionism is the third paradigm of identity and memory in contemporary Israeli culture. I believe that my grandfather would have shared its humanism while rejecting its apolitical solution to the problem of anti-Semitism. It is represented today, according to Uri Ram, by the thoughts of Professor Yehuda Elkana of Tel-Aviv University.[43] His position, however, is merely a re-statement of Ahad Ha-Am's and Martin Buber's unique brand of Zionism. Professor Elkana rejects the ethnic paradigm of Professor Fisch and calls for a multi-ethnic democracy in Israel. The rejection is grounded in the true and simple fact that a nation of political and ethnic particularity cannot also be a democratic and fair community, and he is entirely correct. *Gus-Emunim's* ideology of the Greater Israel and the language of "Holy Jewish Land" or Jewish "calendar" are no different than similar claims by radical Islam that all of Arabia is Holy Islamic Land or by the Germans' reference to their culture as the autobiography of God, e.g., Hegel. Elkana and others acknowledge that in the journey Zionism took some necessary emphasis on ethnicity was necessary and important to maintain. But now that Israel is no longer in its pioneering stage, the national and ethnic paradigms should no longer play a part. Post-Zionism's identity must now be based on the democratic values of inclusiveness and equality. Obviously, such a political move would have the potential to turn Israel into an Arab country with a Jewish minority that is again vulnerable to the whims and discrimination of others.

Elkana also rejects the way Holocaust memory has been used in the Israeli culture. It is neither sufficient nor helpful, Elkana argues, to simply use the categorical imperative - **remember**—without spelling out what precisely ought to be remembered. As a result, young generations of Israelis interpreted the imperative to mean toughness and lack of moral sensitivity. In particular, Elkana rejects the national and ethnic argument that the Holocaust provided, or should provide, an ultimate lesson for the citizens of Israel, i.e., to be able to defend themselves, period. "Any life lesson," he argues, "or life perception the source of which is the Holocaust is a disaster ... for a society which wishes to live in relative calm and relative security as all societies."[44]

There is not much that can be objected to in Elkana's position except to say that so far the various forces in the world do not consider us an ordinary society like all others. Observe Iran's president Ahmadinejad's latest two-day conference on Holocaust evidence and Zionism's "crimes against the Palestinian people," or the global condemnation of Israel over the tragic killing of 68 Lebanese civilians last summer and the consequent charges of "crimes against humanity." Yet, the world is virtually silent while Iraqi Sunnis and Shiites are killing each other for the tune of over 1000 civilian casualties a week. I suggest that the Holocaust still provides important lessons to remember. The fact that at times Israeli politicians, military leaders, or soldiers behave improperly against the Palestinians is not a sign of the nation's moral breakdown. Elkana seems to forget that if Jews are not a unique ethnic group but a society like all others, then there is no need to judge the society for the misguided behavior of a few. Every society has individuals that embarrass the national consciousness, but no one reacts to such individual embarrassments as Jews and Israelis do. I have encountered very few Australians in my life who seem unable to go on living or enjoying life because of what their ancestors have done to the aborigines. Other societies seem to accept the fact that reality is imperfect and involves deep acts of injustice that cannot be erased. Jews, however, cannot help blaming themselves for the acts of the few *as if* we are somehow ethnically the same people.

As a Labor Zionist, Moshe Y. Lubling would have shared the hopes and dreams of all ideologies in which no artificial categories such as economic class, religious belief, or place of origin, define human beings. He too would have wished for an aesthetically anarchistic world in which individuals and groups engage each other through mutual agreements, and a world without central governments that are, by their organizational structure, always coercive and objectifying. But, he would have also argued that such senti- mental thinking is the material for artistic expression, and not for ensuring the immediate survival of ordinary men and women stigmatized by others as the universal scapegoat. As such, the continued unity of the Jewish people does not rest on some metaphysical uniqueness that is innate. Such talk is philosophical nonsense and belongs to a different type of discourse that I personally do not share. However, the psychological element in Jewish identity overtime is two-fold. First, the collective memory that has been past from one generation to another through symbols, commemorations, worship, language, and hope; and second, through the conditions and situations imposed by others. Considering the latter, I would argue that the militant and rough character of Israeli-Jews, for better or worse, was not created for its own sake in a vacuous universe but in the face of situations others imposed upon them. Starting with the Holocaust and the world's view of the Jews as dispensable objects, and ending with the current demonization of Israel by Arab and European interest, has created the contemporary Israeli Jew. Such imposed reality has everything to do with the psychological element in the identity of the Israelis. In fact, these situations have much more to do with the creation of cultural identity and use of memory then the personal com- mitments of Israelis to the national, ethnic, or civic ideologies.

As I pointed out above, the civic paradigm of identity and memory had its beginning in the thoughts of the Jewish writer and Zionist Ahad Ha'am. It can be said that in practice and influence it is the weakest of the three major aspects of Zionism, although intellectually it provided the most profound expression of Jewish humanism and philosophical brilliance. From its beginning, Cultural Zionism argued that the land of Israel should not be used for a political solution to the Jewish condition in Europe. Political Zionism, it argued, is only concerned with the revival and survival of the Jewish physi- cal existence. Instead, the land should first become a spiritual and cultural place for the revival of the Jewish spirit. As the founder of cultural Zionism, Ahad Ha'am and his followers argued that what truly require transformation are the Jewish soul and its shattered spiritual existence. He pointed out that in Hebrew the words for 'soul' (*nefesh or neshama*) are descriptive of an interconnected duality between the body and its spiritual aspects. Political Zionism, he maintained, by only being concerned with the body, will endanger the revival of the Jewish people by splitting its very character. Ahad Ha'am's cultural Zionism was an attempt to heal the soul of the Jewish people before they entrusted into the world of realpolitik. It is commonly held in Israel that while Ahad Ha'am tried to become the therapist of his people, he ended up being merely a preacher.

As I mentioned earlier, the conflict between Political and Cultural Zionism rests on the deep psychological need to transform traditional Jewish life, i.e., the mentality of the *Shtetil*. Martin Buber, one of my all-time favorite Jewish intellectual heroes, was also a leading member of *Yihud* (unification), a dissenting Zionist movement that promoted a cultural and humanistic understanding of the Zionist goal. While Buber supported Ahad Ha'am's cultural agenda, he also supported and shared many of the convictions and ideas held by Labor Zionism, most notably A.D. Gordon and his idea of redemption through work of the land.[45] Buber understood what very few Zionists did, that collective life—socialism—is a Jewish idea and a value. Judaism's ultimate purpose, he held, is to overcome all dualism, all divisions, all classes, and all political authority. Indeed, the *kibbutz* movement and Labor Zionism came closer to this vision than the revisionists and their religious and zealot partners.

Political power alone, he observed, inevitably leads citizens to view the state as an end in itself which contributes to the objectification of people, their interests, and the environment. Such objectification allows, and may even encourage, unjust and immoral conduct. Zionism, as merely a political solution to the problem of anti-Semitism leaves little room for the practice of unique Jewish values. A nation that regards physical existence as an end in itself cannot practice supernatural ethics; the latter is to be understood as Judaism's cosmic moral commitment to improve the earth's condition.

For Buber, Judaism imposes different requirements on its members than any other religion. Like Plato's lover of wisdom, the Jewish people's experience is a continuous pedagogical journey replete with metaphysical, ethical, aesthetical, epistemic, and most importantly, civic implications. Unlike the American people or the Polish people, that despite their individual and collective religious faiths, they do not constitute both nations and communities of faith; the Jewish people do! As a community of faith we are bound by the spirit of Israel, which means that we must follow the way of justice and truth. As a nation, our conduct must follow the spirit and meaning of our election. The dysfunctional character of the Diaspora Jew, therefore, will never be healed by the mere creation of a nation without also serving its unique commands.

For Buber it is the duty of the State of Israel to carry the burden of bringing God's lived Presence back into the world. Its public conduct must always be constrained by the humanistic commitments imposed upon it by the original covenant. Zionism, as the modern revival of the Jewish people, must be a movement with axiological and humanistic goals which are first, to overcome all divisions and second, to lead the world in the formation of healthy "relational spaces."

Indeed, for Zionism and the State of Israel to be truly redemptive, they must carry forward God's incomplete work of creation (I use the term 'God' in its widest sense). It cannot be assumed that this work is made complete merely by the Jewish people's arrival to the Land of Israel. Their survival and redemption depends on the continuous humanistic work left after creation. Not merely *Tikkun Olam* is required of the Jew since Tikkun assumes a previously fixed state of the world (Olam). For Zionism as Humanism, it is the continuous creation of the 'New' through Truth and Justice that constitutes their relation to the ancient and living God of Israel. However, while I share much of Buber's Zionism, I can not share his dialogical optimism. It assumes a certain good-will in the world that cannot be supported by ordinary experience. If it was possible to 'dialogue' with Hitler or Arafat, then the world would not have been this world.

Locating the Good in the Quality of Relations

There are several objections to the argument that communities of thick relations, like the Israeli-Jewish collective, have the obligation to remember those who died on their behalf. First, there is the charge by the philosopher Richard J. Bernstein[46] that to locate the source of the ethically good in the quality of relationships is not sufficient to support an ethical obligation. Such an ethical criterion does not explain the ontology of the ethical value but merely expresses a personal preference for one modality of relations over another. In other words, to argue that a community which centered on care and respect through memory is an ethically preferable community than one that does not is merely a statement of personal taste. Ethical obligations must have a universal grounding force that is more than merely the specific and unique tradition of Jewish or Israeli history. The latter might have specific cultural preferences with regards to memory and the nature of collective life, but that does not imply universal obligations. In short, the quality of relations is neither a necessary nor a sufficient reason to obligate anyone to remember other peoples' names and actions.

In response we must say that philosophically the objection is correct. If the object of philosophical ethics is to locate universal obligations in human conduct, then the mere quality of human relations is not sufficient to establish such universality. But, neither Margalit nor I are attempting to argue for the universality of the obligation to remember, the contrary is our argument. The argument is that individuals who are members of communities with thick relations, like the Israeli-Jewish collective, seem to display an obligation to remember the names of others. The reason for such practice, furthermore, is the consequent creation of a unique collective space. The objection overlooks the context and unique background within which the question about memory is asked. That is, that within the historical context of Jewish history, the space that defines a community is the ultimate criterion for ethical evaluation, what Martin Buber called "the in-between."

What ought to be remembered, I contend, should not be determined by what is philosophically and universally obligatory but rather by the collective vision and values of the community. The latter usually determines which individuals or events best represent their identity and its proper continuation in the future. The reason why the Israeli-Jewish community made a conscious effort to "bracket" (not forget) the more painful memories of the Holocaust, is because these memories do not serve the future identity of the state. It is not the memories of the few corrupt groups of *Judenrat* or the passivity with which many Jews accepted their fate that should inspire the new character of the Israelis. As Israelis, our future identity had to be associated with *G'vurah* (heroism) rather than the personal and psychological implications of the *Shoah,* as is the case with generations of children of survivors who are not Israelis. Whatever one might feel about Israel's response to the Holocaust, its future identity through survival is radically different than the future identity and survival of Jews elsewhere.

The second objection involves the ambiguous meaning of the "we" that have the obligation to remember. In response we can use Emerson's observation that man cannot be expressed as a fact but only as a suggestion. As such, the "we" that ought to remember involves a two-fold suggestion. First, it is the "we" of an ethical ought for all those who value the ethical space created by communities of thick relations. This meaning of "we" refers to those who are able to practice ethics from within the naturalistic conditions under which they live, and not from an abstract and formal position. Second, it is the "we" of an already established community of thick relations which in the case of Moshe Y. Lubling involves the Labor Zionists collective in particular, and Zionism in general.

Finally, one can object that the ethics of memory makes "too much" of the distinction between thick relations and thin relations, or between ethics and morality.[47] Indeed, the reason why I make "too much" of this distinction is because I want to highlight the differences between formal and situated ethical obligations. The idea that I make too much of the difference between, on the one hand my obligations to my father, and on the other hand my obligation to all God's children, is empirically mystifying since it flies in the face of ordinary experience. Those who share this objection would want us to believe that our deep sense of kinship is essentially unethical. There are no "objective" reasons why my father, as a human being among others, should be more valuable to my life than an unknown person somewhere. This philosophical attempt to negate ordinary practices that have been grounded in centuries of instinctual living is precisely why Nietzsche referred to universal moralists as "deniers of life." It is this spectatorial practice of philosophical ethics that have made the study of ethical conduct irrelevant to most ordinary individuals. When the conception of God was such that people could no longer relate to it, they proclaimed God's death; the same should apply to an ethical conception that is foreign to the irreducible experience of ordinary people. Ordinary experience cannot acknowledge, relate to, follow, or be comforted by a God that turns the other cheek, forgive its enemies, lack feelings of revenge and anger, and asks his children to act the same. Ordinary individuals also cannot relate to an ethical conception of human conduct in which people are obligated to care for unknown people in the same way they care about their immediate family, friends, and nation. A God's eye viewpoint about ethics might be what is intellectually desired for a perfect universe, but not for the daily conduct of ordinary men and women.

Therefore, to object to the particularity and locality of ethical relationships is a philosophical move that confuses the press of ordinary experience with logical and formal notion of necessity.[48] In principle, if life is sacred and all living things are of equal importance to the Creator, then it goes without saying that I should remember and care equally for everyone. However, this is philosophical nonsense since, as Dewey taught us, ethics start from ordinary human practice which hardly allows individuals to live without kinship and special preference to those with whom they share history and identity. It is attention to the common and local that sharpens our insights into the nature of conduct, not an escape from it. What is at issue here is the condemnation of a collective for forgetting the name of Moshe Y. Lubling, which reveals an ethical sentiment that exists among people with thick relations. Furthermore, the ethics of memory attempts to explain why individuals who are in thick relations *ought* to remember the names of others, and not, why we should remember those that we have only humanistic relationships with. In a perfectly ideal universe, unlike this one, it would have made sense for America to enter WWII in 1939 and save the lives of millions of Jews, Gypsies, and Slaves. In reality, however, the American public was against entering the war in order to save the victims; as a result close to 60,000,000 people lost their lives. Is America responsible for their death? Indeed, in the best of all possible worlds, if America would have entered the war in 1939 and saved countless lives and communities, then this would have constituted moral behavior *par excellence*. But this is not the way the world works and the reason is that no individual or collectives can have relationships of care with all existence. This is why thick relations are different and impose different obligations upon their members. The Israeli-Jewish community, and in particular the national paradigm of identity, has the obligation to remember the name of Moshe Y. Lubling. But ethical obligations cannot be enforced, they are voluntary and they reflect the quality of the community. An ethical community is one that does not only have relations of care and responsibility for the living but also to those who died in its name.

NINE

Returning to the Scene of the Crime

What happened to Jews in Poland after the war may not be, intrinsically, much of a story. That a quarter million people were no longer welcome by the majority population in a country their ancestors had lived in for centuries was not very unusual by the standards of the epoch. As ethnic cleansing goes, the murder of some 500 or 1,500 people should not have raised many eyebrows, either ... And yet, half a century later we ask ourselves with dismay, How could there be anti-Semitism in Poland, of all places, after Auschwitz.[1]

—Jan T. Gross, *Fear*

Since 1995, I have visited Treblinka and Poland numerous times with my parents and my wife Lynne, with my Elon University students, and with my brother, Moshe, and his wife Varda, also a child of Holocaust survivors. Unlike my father, I wanted to visit Germany, Austria, and all other European countries in which Jewish communities were wiped off the face of this earth. It is still not clear to me why I am being drawn back to the scene of my family's murder. There is nothing that can possibly attract me to Poland and to its people. Meeting the Polish people and other European citizens made it clear to me how the Holocaust happened, in particular after meeting the Polish people. I could clearly understand how nearly three million Jews could have been dragged out of their homes in every village, town, and city in Poland, while the population was waiting to take over their property.The phenomenology of space in Poland is of unique interest to me. For me, it is emotionally dark, empty of soul, heavy with guilt, racked with insecurity, and intellectually bankrupt. I recently participated in a philosophical conference in Europe where I met several Polish intellectuals. Immediately upon discovering that I am a Jew from Israel, they approached me and began complaining about Israel's treatment of the Palestinians. Here are individuals who represent the nation that confiscated, stole, and did not protect its three and a half million Polish Jews. The first opportunity these intellectuals had to speak freely in an international philosophical dialogue, all that could come out of their mouth was a complaint about the way the Jews behave.

I have visited the town of Wolbrom several times and stood across the street from my great grandfather's house, the place in which my father was born. Looking at the house, I noticed that there is still a business on the first floor and a family that lives on the second floor, just as my murdered family. I never attempted to enter the house or even stand close next to it. So far, every visit I made to Wolbrom ended with an uncomfortable set of circumstances. During my first visit, while walking in town with my parents and wife, my father was pointing to several apartments in the center of the town where his mother's family used to live. Some local bar-sitting Poles saw my father pointing his finger at the building and they immediately got up and started to walk towards us. My father asked me to leave immediately and my American wife was shaking in her L.L. Bean shoes.

I did not want to leave! I wanted these individuals to approach me; I wanted them to know that we have survived. More than anything else, I wanted them to know that I am an Israeli; a proud child of a destroyed local Jewish family who will not run away. I looked at the coming drunks and thought about what a former Israeli Chief of Staff said during the 50th commemoration ceremony at the Auschwitz death-camp. When asked by a journalist what goes through his mind as he stands in Auschwitz, he responded: "… that we arrived here fifty-years too late." I wanted these Polish residents of Wolbrom to know that although I came here fifty-years too late to save my family, I will not retreat now! My family was waiting for me in the car while I remained standing with my camera taking pictures of the buildings. They circled me and began to ask questions; I looked straight into the eyes of those surrounding me and for a few minutes we were engaged in a staring contest. I continued to take pictures and walked away from the group.

I returned to Wolbrom three more times. Both visits with my students ended in confrontations with the local Polish residents. In both cases, they objected to my students' presence in the town and their picture taking of my grandfather's home. In both cases my students exploded with anger and pushed the locals away. During my last visit in 2003 with my brother, our rental car was vandalized. The locals just stood on the sidewalk watching us as we tried to comprehend the situation; all around us we could hear the word 'Jew' being repeated again and again.

The Fisch family's House in Wolbrom, Pinchas Lubling birthplace

I also returned several times to the town of Czestochowa. It is a holy city that houses the Black Madonna relic in Sanya Gori, a magnificent Church surrounded by tremendous walls that once kept Napoleon's army from invading the Church. During the Holocaust, the Church survived untouched and saved many individuals from the hands of the Nazis; none were Jewish. As a matter of fact, during my last visit to the Church a priest pointed my attention towards a painting of a nun.

"She will be canonized soon" he informed me.

"Why, what did she do to deserve such an honor," I asked?

"She saved the souls of over 5000 Jewish children in Auschwitz," he answered proudly.

"What do you mean saved their souls?"

"Oh, she was allowed to baptize them before they were tossed into the flames," he said.

I could feel the blood rushing quickly into my head. "Did I hear him correctly? Did he just say 'saved their souls'? " I could see in my mind the

Ukrainian guards in Auschwitz standing next to a pit with burning flames shooting into the sky, the suffocating smell of burning flesh and the screams of naked children about to be burned alive. The guards are continuously drinking cheap vodka to numb the few emotions and feeling they may still have. I could see the nun putting her hands on the children's head to bless them while the guards are laughing and throwing the "saved" children into the flames; talking about Christian involvement and guilt during the Holocaust years.

My return to the Jewish Ghetto in Czestochowa was a frightening experience. How ordinary the streets appear, as if nothing ever happened to the 50,000 Jews who lived here. As we approached Katedralne Street I could feel the bystanders' eyes following our every step. They knew precisely why English speaking individuals were visiting this area of town. They all knew that this area was part of the Large Jewish Ghetto before it was liquidated on September 22, 1942. As we approached the number 11 building, I could tell that my father became increasingly nervous and apprehensive. We cautiously entered the courtyard and located the first floor apartment in which his family last resided. Very quickly a group of locals gathered around us and one woman turned to my father and asked: "Are you here to claim back your property? There is nothing here that belongs to you; no Jews ever lived here."

Pinchas was astonished by the locals' behavior but not surprised. He put his arms around me and started to walk me through the deportation process. "The trucks arrived at the Ghetto early in the morning," he recollected, "and the soldiers jumped out and took different positions near every corner. Others started to circle the Ghetto, guns in hand and the anticipation of another day of killings. The commandant of the liquidation arrived in his officer's car followed by an entourage of motorcycles and other cars. From the other cars a group of local religious leaders emerged dressed in their gowns and shiny crosses; they were discussing the operation with the Germans to make sure that the deported Jews did not pass by the local church. The Germans were yelling orders to block the streets next to the church while they were setting their tables and other materials for the selection. The trains arrived and stood quietly next to the Monastery at the end of the avenue. At 8:35 A.M. the order was given to round-up the Jews."

I imagined hearing the first group of families as they were ordered out of their apartments. I could hear the guards yelling at the frightened Jews and soon the unmistakable sound of machine guns. I genuinely could hear all this in my mind.

The ground apartment in the Czestochowa Ghetto—the last residence
of the Lubling family before the deportation to Treblinka, 1995

"Stay with your mother Reja, no matter what, do not get separated, I heard my father saying," continued Pinchas, "he already discussed the deportation several times with me, I knew exactly what to do in case we got separated. My father thought that I had the best chance of surviving."

"I was watching the river of people, mostly families carrying their measly possessions in bed sheets on their backs," explained Pinchas as he walked with me through Katedralne Street. I could feel my legs giving-up from weakness. I felt sick to my stomach. "The guards would pass by the deported Jews and indiscriminately level blows at the women and children. Blood was everywhere," he said.

"Where, where did they do it," I asked while looking around to see if there were any marks left in that spot.

"If a child cried," my father continued, "the guard would toss them into the snow and fire their automatic guns at the children. The snow was red with blood and the sidewalk quickly resembled a slaughter house."

…It suddenly happened. A group of guards reached number 11 on Katedralne Street. They had wooden sticks in their hands and an insane look in their eyes. Some had their boots covered with red snow and mud.

…Quick, do it quick, they yelled at my family," Pinchas remembered.

The exact site of the *Aktion* in which the Lubling family separated during the liquidation of
the Large Ghetto in Czestochowa; to the left stood the train to Treblinka, 2000

… My father recognized some of the guards from the work details. He
knew the nature of these beasts.

Pinchas suddenly stopped at the end of the street. "Here, right here is
where the selection took place."

…You two, over here," the Commandant ordered my mother and sister.
Within a few seconds they were dragged into the stream of people heading
for the trains. I turned my head for a second to look at my mother and sister
for the last time and I could see the cruelty inflicted upon them by the
guards. I watched the Ukrainian guards hitting them with sticks and pushing
them towards the trains near the monastery."

I looked in the direction my father pointed out to me, but all I could see
were new stores and a crowded street. I looked at the rooftops from which
the local residents poured urine over the deported Jews. The avenue looked
ordinary and unassuming. I could spot the monastery and the railroad tracks
next to it. This is the place; here is where it all happened. I felt ill again, there
was no sign or mark to indicate that my father's family was separated here;
that right here, on this exact spot, my grandmother was beaten by a Ukrainian guard…right here, where this cheap shoe store is now standing.

"What is your profession? The Commandant barked at my father and me," Pinchas continued. "We are plumbers, we have been plumbers all our lives, we have our own tools, my father responded in German."

...Go straight, he ordered, and we proceeded forward towards a row of standing trucks, right there where the Pharmacy stands now. In the trucks we found others from the Ghetto, we were all men with able bodies."

"Where did they take you?" I asked my father.

"The steel factory next to the Jewish Cemetery," Pinchas responded.

We started to walk back to our car, but I had difficulties leaving the place. I wanted to discover something, to understand more, to reconnect with my family, but there was nothing. Just ordinary streets with Polish people living and owning Jewish houses and businesses. There was no sign of the slaughter and theft of lives and property.

But nothing could match my return to Treblinka, the scene of my grandfather's heroic death. The experience truly resists human expression, especially a linguistic one, but I will do my best. An hour north of Warsaw through fruitful agricultural farms you reach the town of Malkinia and right next to it is Treblinka. The place seems frozen in time. Most houses are still without running water and most farmers have no other means of transportation than a horse and cart. With their pale white faces they follow every passing car wondering to themselves ... "how did they all survive?" These individuals live right next to the scene of the most horrific crime in modern history; they saw it, they smelled it, they profited from it, and they allowed it to happen. The few bars in town are the same bars that were frequented by the SS and the Ukrainian Guards after a hard day in the camp. It is here that they purchased the Vodka with the money they stole from the victims and that they drank while operating the gas chambers. The faces of the local Poles reflected all this horror.

You soon drive next to an abandon old sign reading TREBLINKA which the residents forgot to remove after they changed the name of the town. Very soon you drive on an unmarked gravel road and without any preparation you arrive at a small parking lot hidden in the woods. A small wooden kiosk sells a few Polish books and posters about the death camp. A visitors' book is laid on a small chair outside the kiosk where one can write a few words about the visit. Across the parking lot, a farm is still standing while its habitants are watching the few visitors that arrive daily.

As I walked deeper into the woods the silence became painfully vivid. The birds are not singing in these woods anymore. It seems as if all life has been dragged out of these woods; as if the birds were too embarrassed to act normally around these woods. The silence was painful and in a Zen fashion it actually screamed. On the right side a row of concrete slabs were laying on the ground representing the missing railroad tracks that brought nearly a million Jews to slaughter. If you made a left onto a stone walkway you found yourself on the path the Nazis sarcastically referred to as "The Road to Heaven." The stones are purposely sharp and uneven designed to inflict as much pain upon the victims as possible and to occupy their attention so they do not escape. At the end of this misery lane stood the gas chambers. I could imagine standing on both sides of the chambers where the Ukrainian duo sadists, Ivan and Nicholas, with their big butcher knifes and vicious dogs, cutting off women's breasts while the dogs locked their jaws on men's genitals. On the other side of the gas chambers stood the crematory where some prisoners extracted the gold teeth of the dead Jews, while other prisoners carried their bodies to the pit to be burned.

"If I am not mistaken, this is where the Ghetto was standing," I cautiously walked towards the spot and stood silently to take it all in. I was standing on holy ground, arguably the biggest single burial site in history, where nearly a million Jewish men, women, and children, including my grandfather and his family were murdered, burned, and their ashes buried. I walked on each part of the space so I might stand in the same spot my grandfather stood.

Now, I am not a religious or spiritual person, my life after the Holocaust made such an engagement or experience impossible for me. As a radical empiricist, I usually shy away from talk about souls, spirits, or reincarnation. I am also sure that what I felt and experienced in Treblinka was introduced into my mind by my own pre-reflective intentions. But, as with many other places in Poland, I felt that I was there before. I felt it all, I saw it all, I knew where everything was, and I could feel my grandfather's "presence" facing me at every turn.

I looked at the trees that separated the bare spot that once was the camp and the surrounding woods and waited. I wanted to know if the trees could tell me what they saw, do they remember my grandfather? He was a thin and tall young man with a thunderous voice, piercing eyes, and a face that expressed only one emotion—that of *Nekama*—of revenge? This is the most significant spot on earth for me; here my future soul was born.

I slowly walked away from the place where the camp once stood. I could still smell the burning bodies; I could hear the screams of the doomed Jews who were led to the gas chambers. I could experience the chaos of the new coming transports, the cries of the children, and the brutality of the guards. I left and the camp kept following me, in my dreams, my conversations, my teachings, and my every conscious moment. I finally internalized my grandfather's death as my own; in Treblinka I died as well. Do not pay attention to my life-like appearance; I have died many years ago in this place. The place that birds don't sing and flowers do not grow; the place in which, to paraphrase Elie Wiesel, not only men and women died, but the very idea of the person, of the human being, died as well.

It is ironic, as well as tragic, that it took the Holocaust to save me from the fate of remaining a Diaspora Jew. I presume that it is true that some individuals through their heroic death *zivo lanu et achaim* (have ordered us to live); to live freely, proudly, and independently in our land. My grandfather's heroic life and death has provided the spiritual revival of the Jewish people in Israel, whether or not they are being so informed by the "official" narrators of the Holocaust.

The philosopher as a young Zionist, Israel 1961

NOTES

Introduction

[1] Elie Wiesel, *Night,* trans. Stella Rodway (New York: Bantam Books, 1960), p. 65.

[2] Tom Segev, *The Seventh Million* (New York: Hill and Wang, 1993), pp. 109–110.

[3] Benjamin Beit-Hallahmi, *Original Sins* (New York: Olive Branch Press, 1993), p. 134–5.

[4] Benjamin Orenstein, *Hurban Czenstochow* (West Germany: Central Farwaltung fun der Czensochower Landsmanszaft in der Amerikaner Zone in Dajczland, 1949), (Yiddish), p. 172.

[5] Berl Katznelson, "After a Conversation on the Diaspora," 6 June 1944. *Works of Katznelson* (Tel Aviv: Mapai, 1950, (Hebrew), XII: 218.

[6] Cf. Sidney Hook's remarks that there is a "convergent set of hypotheses" discoverable in the writings of Dewey and Karl Marx. See his *John Dewey: An Intellectual Portrait* (New York: John Day, 1939), p. 174.

[7] Eugene Kogan, *The Theory and Practice of Hell* (New York: Berkley Publishing Group, 1980), p. 111.

[8] H. Leivick, *Ein Treblinka bin eich nit Gevain* (New York: Dorech Publishing, 1945), (Yiddish), p. 11. This poem was translated by Yaacov Dovid Shulman.

[9] Alan M. Dershowitz, *Just Revenge*, (New York: Warner Books, 1999), p. 201.

[10] Ehud Olmert, "I am Speaking to You," Chanel 2, Israel, July 31, 2006.

[11] The same officers of the Karlsruhe later fought allied forces near Normandy. One of the German University visited was Heidelberg where Jews had been expelled.

[12] William James, "Pragmatism's Conception of Truth," in *The Writings of William James*, ed. John J. McDermott (Chicago: The University of Chicago Press, 1981), p. 441.

[13] Sidney Hook, *The Hero in History* (Boston: Beacon Press, 1943), p. 29.

[14] Martin Buber, "Hebrew Humanism," cited in *The Writings of Martin Buber*, ed. Will Herberg (New York: Meridian Books, 1956), p. 296.

Chapter I—Holocaust Historiography

[1] See Andreas Huyssen, *Present Pasts: Urban Palimpsests and the Politics of Memory* (Stanford: Stanford University Press, 2003); *Twilight Memories: Marking Time in a Culture of Amnesia* (New York: Routledge, 1995).

[2] Ben Jacobs, *The Dentist of Auschwitz* (Lexington, KY: The University Press of Kentucky, 1995), p. 101.

[3] Similarly, a testimonial book and subsequent movie by Jack Eisner, a survivor of the Warsaw Ghetto and Majdanek, stretch even the imagination of his own hired editorial assistant who later wrote that, "a number of us who read the early manuscript felt that believability was one of its greatest problem … Jack had performed so many heroic deeds and had so many close brushes with death that he tended to stretch his credibility. Caroline Latham, *Publisher Weekly*, September 12, 1980, p. 48.

[4] Cited in Tom Teicholz, *The Trial of Ivan the Terrible* (New York: St. Martin's Press, 1990), p. 270.

[5] Ibid.

[6] Binjamin Wilkomirski, *Fragments,* trans. Carol Brown Janeway (New York: Schochen Books, 1996).

[7] Ibid., cited from the back cover of the paperback edition.

[8] Israel Gutman, cited in Elena Lappin, "The man with two heads," *Granta* 66 (summer 1999), p. 46

[9] Avishai Margalit, *The Ethics of Memory* (Cambridge, Mass: Harvard University Press, 2004), p. 174.

[10] Jean-Francois Steiner, *Treblinka* (New York: A signet Book, 1967), p. 171.

[11] In his book Steiner depicts the killing of "Ivan the Terrible" at the hands of the revolting prisoners. However, in 1984 and after, Steiner claimed that he based his knowledge of the event on Eliyahu Rosenberg's testimony in which he described the killing of the notorious guard. The testimony was contradicted by him in 1987 when he identified John Demjanjuk as the notorious guard. Steiner was also forced to admit that much of the events depicted in his book were imaginative, in particular, conversations or thoughts attributed to individuals or among prisoners.

[12] Jean-Francois Steiner, *Treblinka* (New York: A Signet Book, 1967), p. xxii.

[13] Ibid., xiv.

[14] Tanhum Grinberg, "The Revolt in Treblinka," cited in Alexander Donat, editor, The *Death Camp Treblinka: a Documentary*, pp. 216–17.

15 Samuel Willenberg, "I Survived Treblinka."

16 Stanislaw Kon, "The Treblinka Revolt."

17 Barbara Amouyal, *The Jerusalem Post,* August 17, 1986.

18 "Sir, - I was deeply astonished to read Barbara Amouyal's front-page article of August 17, which is based in part on an interview with me. Many hundreds of the 20,000 testimonies held in our archives were extensively used in Nazi war criminal trials, contrary to what Amouyal wrote. I told Amouyal that survivors wrote their accounts for the record of history. I cannot understand why she made of it that survivors wanted 'to be part of history.' I said there are some—fortunately very few— testimonies, which proved to be inaccurate. Why did Amouyal make them out to be a large number?" Shmuel Krakowski, Letter to the Editor, *Jerusalem Post*, August 21, 1986.

19 Portland's *Dan Gannon* was attacking Michael Berenbaum for not producing documents to prove that gas chambers existed. He writes: "If he (Berenbaum) refers to 'eyewitness testimony', he should know that even Shmuel Krakowski—Director of archives at Israel's Yad Vashem Holocaust Documentation Center—reports that over 10,000 'eyewitness testimonies' to Nazi atrocities have been found to be FALSE at Yad Vashem alone!" The Nizkor Project have recorded that in 1995 the misrepresentation of Krakowski's remarks were still present in Keven Schmid's BeWise web site, as well as in 1996 on Arthur Butz web site where he writes: "A historiographically important item is found in the Jerusalem Post (17 August 1986 in the regular daily edition, pp. 1, 4). The Yad Vashem Archives in Jerusalem hold thousands of such testimonies. Its director at the time, Shmuel Krakowski, admitted that 'over half' of the testimonies are 'unreliable' because the 'survivors' relied on their imaginations and were never in the places they claimed, or relied on stories they heard rather than things they witnessed." The misrepresentation of Krakowski is still being used to challenge eyewitness testimonies.

20 David L. Norton and Mary F. Kille, *Philosophies of Love* (New Jersey: A Helix Book, 1971), p. 2.

21 Robert Braun, "The Holocaust and Problems of Historical Representation," *History and Theory*, Vol. 33, No. 2. (May, 1994), p. 175.

22 "…when historians claim that history is a combination of science and art, they generally mean that it is a combination of *late nineteenth century* social science and *mid-nineteenth century art*. That is to say, they seem to be inspiring to little more than a synthesis of modes of analysis and expression that have their antiquity alone to commend them … Many historians continue to treat their 'facts' as though they were 'given' and refuse to recognize, unlike most scientists, that they are not so much

'found' as 'constructed' by the kind of questions which the investigator asks of the phenomena before him. It is the same notion of objectivity that binds historians to an uncritical use of the chronological framework for their narratives." Hayden White, "The Burden of History," *History and Theory* 5 (1966), p. 127.

23   John Dewey, *The Quest for Certainty*, cited in *The Later Works of John Dewey*, ed. Jo Ann Boydston (Carbondale: Southern Illinois University Press, 1984), p.164.

24   Ibid., p. 163.

25   Carlo Ginzburg, "Checking the Evidence," *Critical Inquiry*, Vol. 18, No 1. (Autumn, 1991), p. 84–85.

26   In this context, the Holocaust scholar Deborah E. Lipstadt observed that deniers never work within an intellectual vacuum but usually adopt intellectual currents that they can manipulate to their advantage. The Deconstructionist/post-Modernist/neo-Pragmatist intellectual current is a case in point. According to Lipstadt, starting in academic circles during the 1960's, a critical literary was developed arguing against the fixed meaning of texts and for the interpretative legitimacy of the reader in determining the meaning of the text. As a result, it became politically and intellectually improper to talk about, let alone establish, historical narratives as objectively true. "In academic circles some scholars spoke of relative truths, rejecting the notion that there was one version of the world that was necessarily right while another was wrong." Deborah E. Lipstadt, *Denying the Holocaust* (New York: The Free Press, 19930, p. 18.

27   Hilary Putnam, *Truth and History* (Cambridge, Mass: Harvard University Press, 1981), p. 54.

28   The prime example for such shortcoming is the neo-pragmatist philosopher Richard Rorty, who located the wisdom of American pragmatism in its rejection of foundational metaphysics, but neglected to appreciate the pragmatists' reconstructive duties. As all other neo-Pragmatists and post-Modernists, Rorty failed to grasp what John Dewey so clearly grasped, that is, that since knowing is an interactive activity that goes on in the world, it is equally capable of deconstructing existing realities as well as reconstructing new ones. And, while deconstructing traditional language and assumptions is necessary for philosophy, it cannot be an end in itself without incriminating itself as aristocratic.

29   John Dewey, *The Quest for Certainty*, cited in *The Later Works of John Dewey*, ed. Jo Ann Boydston (Carbondale: Southern Illinois University Press, 1984), p. 160.

30   I owe this phrase to my friend and mentor Dr. Arthur Lothstein.

31 John Dewey, *Art as Experience* (New York: Minton, Balch & Co., 1934), p. 153. My Italic.

32 Hilary Putnam, *The Many Faces of Realism* (LaSalle, Illinois: Open Court, 1987), p. 36. The fact that we cannot know things-in-themselves was Kant's view although he continued to use it philosophically; Putnam's point, on the other hand, is much stronger.

33 Ibid., p. 37.

34 Carlos Ginzburg, "Checking the Evidence," p. 83.

35 Robert S. Frey, "Is Objectivity Morally Defensible in Discussing the Holocaust," cited in Problems *Unique to the Holocaust*, ed. Harry James Carges (Kentucky: Kentucky University Press, 1999), pp. 98–109.

36 Martin Broszat, "A Plea for the Historization of National Socialism," in Baldwin, ed. *Reworking the Past,* 77–87.

37 Samuel Moyn, *A Holocaust Controversy: The Treblinka Affair in Postwar France* (Waltham, Mass: Brandeis University Press, 2005), p. xix.

38 Benjamin Nathans, *Beyond the Pale: The Jewish Encounter with Late Imperial Russia* (Berkeley, CA: University of California Press, 2002), p. 14.

39 John Dewey, *Ethics*, cited in *The Middle Works of John Dewey* (Carbondale: University of Southern Illinois University, 1983), p. 292.

Chapter II—Twice-Dead

1 See Jean-Francois Steiner, the author of *Treblinka* seems to have made such an accusation in his interview to *Le Nouveau Candide* on March 14, 1966. His interview was displayed on the front page of the magazine under the heading: THE JEWS: WHAT NO ONE EVER DARED TO SAY.

2 Witold Chrostowski, *Extermination Camp Treblinka* (London: Vallentine Mitchell, 2004), p. 26. According to a Polish eyewitness, Lucjan Puchala, "there were 2–3 trucks full of Jews that were daily brought in to the camp. The SS men and Ukrainians supervising the work killed a few dozen people from those brought in to work everyday. So that when I looked from the place where I worked to the place where the Jews worked, the field was covered with corpses."

3 Samuel Willenberg's writes the following conversation with one of the camp's *Baumeister*: "Just before you came here from Czestochowa, the German gunned down most of the prisoners `who used to sort the clothing of the ones they'd murdered before in the gas chambers. They took lots of men from our transport in order to fill the depleted quota, and

they organized us into something resembling a camp ... The only reason there are lots of Czestochowa people here is that they were the first transport to arrive after the massacre of prisoners like ourselves." See *Revolt in Treblinka* (Warsaw: Jewish Historical Institute, 1984), pp. 18–19.

[4] The account was first published in Hebrew in 1956 in *Sefer Milkhamot Hage-taot,* eds. by Yitzhak Zukerman and Moshe Basuk (Tel-Aviv: Hakibuts Hameuchad Publishing House, 1956).

[5] Alexander Donat, ed., *The Death Camp Treblinka: A Documentary* (New York: Holocaust Library, 1979), p. 282.

[6] Ibid., p. 15.

[7] Israel Gutman observed that "most of the acknowledged leaders of Polish Jewry left the areas of the country that fell under Nazi control. They left during the brief war in Poland in September 1939 and at the beginning of the occupation. The tradition parties and the public institutions that had represented and guided the Polish Jewish community between the two World Wars were left without contact with party headquarters abroad and without any guiding forces within the country itself. See "Youth Movement in the Underground and the Ghetto Revolts," cited in *Jewish Resistance during the Holocaust—Proceeding of the Conference on Manifestation of Jewish Resistance Jerusalem, April 7–11, 1968* (Jerusalem: Yad Vashem Press, 1972), p. 260.

[8] Yisrael Gutman writes: "...the adherence of this or that member to the JewishFighting Organization did not derive from his personal, individual understanding of the need to fight or from any personal trait that led him to active fighting. In many cases, joining a fighting organization was a natural continuation of the member's path in the youth organization, and it cannot be taken for granted that as an individual he would necessarily have linked up with a fighting formation ... Before anyone else the youth movements came to understand and recognize the unprecedentedly terrible reality, and they had the courage to draw the necessary conclusions.

The youth movements possessed organizational instruments and the human material which had developed and been nurtured in the educational cells and which measured up to the special and most formidable mission." Ibid., pp. 270, 281.

[9] Benjamin Orenstein, ed., H*urban Czenstochow* (West Germany: Central Farwaltung fun der Czenstochower Landsmanszaft in der Amerikaner Zone in Dajczland, 1948), (Yiddish).

[10] Ibid., p. 190.

[11] Tzvi Rozenvayn writes that the "... the chairman of the Worker's Council, Moshe Lubling ... died later *as the leader of the uprising in*

the death camp Treblinka." See "The Hunger Strike in the Czestochowa Ghetto," cited in *Tshenstokhov: Naye tsugob-material tsum bukh "Tshenstokhber uiden,"* ed. David Singer Samuel (New York: United Relief Committee in New York, 1958), p. 47, (Yiddish).

[12] Benjamin Orenstein, H*urban Czenstochow* (West Germany: Central Farwaltung fun der Czenstochower Landsmanszaft in der Amerikaner Zone in Dajczland, 1948), pp. 186–192. Translated by Yoram Lubling. My Italic.

[13] Ibid.

[14] This is not the only reference to Galewski, the camp-elder, as responsible for the cruel death of many prisoners. While Galewski is mentioned by different survivors as a later member of the Organizing Committee, only Marian Platkiewicz identifies Galewski as the leader of the revolt. See his testimony "Revolt in Hell," cited in *Plotzk: A history of an Ancient Jewish Community in Poland*, ed. Eliyahu Eisenberg (Tel Aviv, Israel: Hamenora Publishing House, 1967), (Yiddish), pp. 544–552.

[15] S. Naiger, *Kiddush Ha-Shem* (New York: "CYCO" BICHER-FARLAG, 1948), (Yiddish), p. 535. It is not clear to me who Mr. Dorsman is and how he came to know about Treblinka. It seems that he was originally from Lublin, Poland, and was connected with Jewish resistance in Czestochowa. Chances are that he was among those who remained in Czestochowa after the liquidation and either knew or heard about him.

[16] Refael Mahler, ed., *Tshenstokhover Yidn* (New York: United Czestochower Relief Committee and Ladies Auxiliary, 1947), (Yiddish).

[17] Samuel David Singer, ed., *Tshenstokhov; naye tsugob-material tsum bukh "Tshenstokhover yidn"* (New York: United Relief Committee in New York, 1958), (Yiddish).

[18] Ibid., pp. 47–51. My Italic; the article was only recently translated by Mark Froimowitz for the Yizkor Book Project.

[19] Liber Brener, "The Truth about the Czestochowa Ghetto", in *Bleter Far Geshikhte,* January-July, 1955, (Yiddish), p. 180.

[20] Samuel David Singer, ed., *Tshenstokhov,* p. 51.

[21] Meilech Bakalczuk is the author of the 1958 book, *Memories of a Jewish Partisan* (Buenos Aires, Argentina: Central Association of Polish Jews in Argentina, 1958).

[22] Maier Shimon Gshori, ed., Volbrom Irenu (*Our Town Wolbrom*) (Tel-Aviv, Israel: The Organization for Wolbrom Survivors in Israel, 1956), (Yiddish and Hebrew), pp. 542–544.

[23] *Sefer Czestochowa* (Jerusalem: The Encyclopedia of the Diaspora Press, 1967), (Yiddish and Hebrew), pp. 301–304.

24   Glazer actually uses a slightly different spelling for most of the figures in
      Treblinka. The last letter of the last name Lubling was changed from a
      'g' to a 'k'. Unfortunately, my attempt to clarify this misspelling came
      too late; in 1997 Mr. Glazer committed suicide after the death of his be-
      loved wife. However, there are good reasons to believe that he was sim-
      ply wrong about the spelling not the person. First, Mr. Glazer was
      writing his account without ever seeing the actual spelling of the name
      Lubling. It is completely possible, and highly logical, that he was spell-
      ing the name phonetically and not from actual knowledge of the spelling;
      phonetically, of course, the two pronunciations are the same. Second, the
      name Lublink is a uniquely Dutch and Christian name. We know that
      there were no transports of Dutch Jews to Treblinka, especially not of
      Christian Dutch citizens. According to records, seventy percent of all
      Jews deported from the Netherlands were sent to Auschwitz, the rest to
      Majdanek and Sobibor, never to Treblinka. Third, there are no other ref-
      erences to the name 'Lublink' in any archive or database on Treblinka
      while there are numerous references to 'Lubling'. Fourth, Glazer identi-
      fied Lublink as a Jew working in the area where the properties of the
      victims was sorted which is precisely the work that Moshe Lubling   was
      doing in Treblinka according to other testimonies. The working group
      associated with sorting the properties of the victims was normally be-
      tween 12–18 people. What are the chances that there were two individu-
      als with almost identical names, both instrumental in the organization
      and leadership of the revolt, one Polish Jew and the other a Dutch
      Christian?

25   Richard Glazer, *Trap with a Green Fence: Survival in Treblinka*, trans.
      Roslyn Theobald (Evanston, Illinois: Northwestern University Press,
      1995), p. 64.

26   Ibid., p. 66.

27   Ibid., p. 84.

28   Ibid., p. 105.

29   Ibid., p. 138.

30   Ibid, pp. 140

31   Ibid., pp. 141.

32   Ibid., p. 144.

33   Ibid, pp. 140–148. My Italic.

34   Elie Wiesel, *Night,* trans. Stella Rodway (New York: Bantam Books,
      1986), p. 37.

35   Ibid., p. 104.

36   Ibid., p. 82.

Chapter III—The Son Survives

1 My father claims that the letter was addressed to him while others claim that it was first received by Aron Gelberd. Pinchas recollects that the letter was personal while others remember it as a call to the underground organization to take-up arms against the Nazis in Czestochowa.

2 Sefer Czestochowa, p. 304. The testimony regarding this letter exists in the 1948 book *Hurban Czenstochow* and 1967 book *Sefer Czestochowa,* but no researcher found it of interest. This explains why, to this day, the Treblinka researchers are not clear as to when precisely the idea of the revolt surfaced and by whom. Knowing about this historical letter, read by several living survivors, could have shed light regarding the timeline of the resistance activity. Yitzhak Arad has wrongly concluded in 1980 that "when and within which group the idea of the rebellion first occurred cannot be stated with any certainty." Again he attempts to portray the uprising as mysteriously spontaneous: "It seems reasonable to assume that the idea occurred to several groups at more or less the same time in talks among the 'court Jews' and among 'square Jews.'" See *Proceedings of the Fourth Yad Vashem International Historical Conference*, Jerusalem, January 1980. Cited in *Jewish Virtual Library.* Arad then goes to list the leaders of the "organizing committee" as Dr. Chorazycki, Kurland, Zelo Bloch, Salzberg, and Sudowicz … no mention of Moshe Y. Lubling from Silesia, his letter, and the scores of survivors' testimonies

3 The account was first published in a Jewish-Polish Newspaper *Dos Naye Lebn*, Warsaw, May 10, 1945.

4 Richard Glazer, *Trap with a Green Fence*, trans. Roslyn Theobald (Evanston, Illinois: Northwestern University Press, 1995).

5 The aspect of collective witnessing is significant for Judaism since, unlike Christianity, its beginning was also public. In Sinai the Jews received the Torah in public, for all to witness, while Christians received their holy charge through the disciples' private conversations with God.

6 Plato, *The Apology,* in *Great Dialogues of Plato*, translated by W.H. D. Rouse (New York: New American Library, 1956), p. 434.

7 Reuben Ainsztein, *Jewish Resistance in Nazi-Occupied Eastern Europe* (London: Paul Elek, 1974), p. 916.

8 Ibid., p. 916 note # 45

9 Yitzhak Arad, "Jewish Prisoners Uprising in the Treblinka and Sobibor Extermination Camps," in *Proceedings of the Fourth Yad Vashem Inter-*

national Historical Conference, Jerusalem, January 1980, Seventh Session.

[10] Isaiah Trunk, *Jewish Responses to Nazi Persecution* (New York: Scarborough House, 1979), p. 264.

[11] Yitzhak Arad, *Proceedings of the Fourth International Historical Conference* Jerusalem, January 1980, Seventh Session.

[12] Yitzhak Arad, *Treblinka: Hell and Revolt* (Tel-Aviv, Israel: Am Oved Publish-ing, 1983).

[13] On May 3, 1995 Esther Aran wrote the following: "Dear Prof Lubling: Thank you for your letter and for the enclosed material. I am sure that the testimony given by your father together with the material that he has brought us and the material sent by you will bring the facts to the awareness of researchers who use our date base. There are no plans to publish a second edition of the Encyclopedia of the Holocaust at the moment. Should this be done in the future, we shall take your comments into consideration when preparing the new edition."

[14] A Picture of the Tombstone was printed in *Sefer Czestochowa*, published in Israel in 1967.

Chapter IV—Moshe Yehoshua Lubling

[1] Volbrom Irenu, *A Yizkor Book*, p. 542.

[2] Harold Fisch, *A Zionist Revolution* (New York: St. Martin's Press, 1978), pp. 58–59.

[3] It is among the ranks of this movement that in 1990 a group of young religious Jews plotted to destroy the Al-Aksa Mosque in Jerusalem in order to purify the Temple Mount. It was also a member of this ideological movement that assassinated Israel's former Prime Minister Yitzchak Rabin. *Gush Emunim*, Rubenstein argues, "constitutes a continuing nightmare for those who hope for at least minimal Israeli-Palestinian co-existence." Even more, while not suffering directly from the Holocaust, members of *Gush Emunim* do not view Eretz Israel as a "place of refuge for human refuse wanted by no other nation. Nor was Eretz Israel regained solely by human agency. God restored Eretz Israel for the redemption of Israel and, through Israel, of all of mankind." Richard L. Rubenstein, *After Auschwitz* (Baltimore: John Hopkins University Press), pp. 216–17.

[4] In August 1929, Arabs launched multiple attacks against the Jewish community in British controlled Palestine. A Total of 133 Jews were killed and 300 wounded. More than 8000 Jews became refugees. The British reacted by closing newspapers and disconnecting international

communication. In October the same year several Arabs were convicted of the killings during the riots and were either executed or sent to long prison incarceration.

5 Indeed, addressing the Holocaust, John Dewey wrote: "There are issues in the conduct of human affairs in their production of good and evil which, at a given time and place are so central, so strategic in position, that their urgency deserves, with respect to practice, the name ultimate and comprehensive. These issues demand the most systematic reflective attention that can be given. It is relatively unimportant whether this attention be called philosophy or by some other name. It is of immense importance that it be given, and that it be given by means of the best tested resources that inquiry has at its command." John Dewey, *The Problems of Men* (New York: Philosophical Library, 1946), pp. 11–12. For more see Alan Rosenberg's article "The Holocaust as a Test of Philosophy," cited in *Echoes from the Holocaust*, eds. Alan Rosenberg and Gerald E. Myers (Philadelphia: Temple University Press, 1988).

6 While it is not the place to address this issue, I must point to it as a future agenda for Holocaust Studies. Indeed, much was written on the topic but very little was done to address its concrete consequences, personally and collectively understood.

7 Pinchas Lubling's testimony; YVA 0.3/8412

8, The comedic duo, it should be pointed out, left Israel after a while since Israelis rejected the Yiddish language that brought the Polish Ghetto into Israel.

9 See Jean-François Steiner *Treblinka* (1st Chapter) for a brilliant depiction of such confusion.

10 YVA 0.3/8412

11 YVA 0.3/8412

12 Dr. Binyamin Orenstein, "Destruction," cited in *Hurban Czenstochow*, p. 42. This article was recently translated by Mark Fromowitz for the Yizkor Book Project.

13 Jean Amery, *At The Mind's Limit: Contemplations by a Holocaust Survivor on Auschwitz and its Realities*. Translated by Sidney Rosenfeld and Stella P. Rosenfeld (Bloomington: Indiana University Press, 1980), p. 10.

14 Dr. Binyamin Orenstein, *Hurban Czenstochow*, p. 88. Translation by Yoram Lubling and Aron Tyson Smith.

15 YVA 0.3/8412

16 Smuel Willenberg, *Revolt in Treblinka* (Warsaw: Zydowski Instytut Historyczny, 1992).

17 YVA 0.3/8412

[18] Ibid.
[19] Dr. Binyamin Orenstein, *Hurban Czenstochow*, p. 190. Translated by Yoram Lubling and Aron Tyson Smith.
[20] Dr. Binyamin Orenstein, *Hurban Czenstochow*, pp. 171–2. Translated by Yoram Lubling and Aron Tyson Smith.
[21] In the original obituary for Moshe Lubling in *Hurban Czenstochow* the writer asserts that Pinchas Lubling was killed in the small ghetto in Czestochowa.
[22] YVA 0.3/8412
[23] YVA 0.3/8412
[24] Ibid.
[25] Ibid.
[26] Cf. The Stockholm Syndrome.
[27] YVA 0.3/8412

Chapter V—The Need to Reconstruct the Treblinka Revolt

[1] Samuel Rajzman, "The End of Treblinka," cited in Alexander Donat, *The Death Camp Treblinka- A Documentary* (New York: Holocaust Library, 1979), p. 251.
[2] Alexander Donat, Ed. *The Death Camp Treblinka: A Documentary* (New York: Holocaust Library, 1979), p. 15. My italics.
[3] Tanhum Grinberg, "The Revolt in Treblinka," cited in Alexander Donate, ed. *The Death Camp   Treblinka*, p. 215.
[4] Samuel Rajzman, "The End of Treblinka" Ibid., p. 242.
[5] Israel Kastner was a member of the Committee for Rescue and Assistance in Hungary. In 1944 the Committee negotiated the famous "Goods for Blood" deal with the SS which proposed the exchange of Hungarian Jews for 10,000 trucks loaded with goods from the West. He negotiated with Adolf Eichmann and ultimately succeeded in rescuing selective members of the Hungarian Jewish community. In 1955 Kastner was put on trial in Israel and was found not-guilty. The judge, however, acknowledged that Kastner's negotiations accelerated the killings of Hungarian Jews, and that he "sold his soul to the devil". In 1957 Kastner was murdered in Israel by another survivor, he stabbed him in the back.
[6] Yisrael Galili, "He Who Distinguish between Sanctity and Abomination," (Hebrew), *Lamerchav* (July 2, 1954).
[7] Yitzhak Gruenbaum, "A Sign for Generations—A Miracle for Generations," (Hebrew), *Hamishmar* (June 2, 1954).
[8] Binyamin Orenstein, H*urban Czenstochow*, p. 189.
[9] Alexander Donat, ed. *The Death Camp Treblinka*, p. 283.

10 Richard Glazer, *Trap with a Green Fence,* trans. Roslyn Theobald, (Evanston, Illinois: Northwestern University Press, 1995), p. 57.

11 In Richard Glazer's *Trap with a Green Fence* he describes the special attention that was given to non-Polish Jews. He writes: "In a show of patriotic sentiment toward the few 'hard-working boys from Bohemia' who had somehow landed among the 'pack from Poland,' Sergeant Suchomel ... a member of a German-speaking minority in Bohemian Krummau ... has soup and oranges sent to Zelo from the German mess." (p. 80–81); or the negative view of the Polish Jews by the Czech prisoners: "... the Poles ... [have] been that way all their lives—selling bad water, hustling, and defrauding." (p. 81); finally, notice a verbal conflict between Hans, a Jewish foreman of Germanic origin with the Polish Jews: "You pack –filthy Poles! I hate you, if you have to know, just like I hate them. I hate you for all your deceit and trickery ... wallowing in their own shit, just wallowing in their own shit..." Ibid., p. 94.

12 Samuel Willenberg, *Revolt in Treblinka* (Warsaw, Poland: Zydowski Instytut Historyczny, 1992), p. 217.

13 Lucy S. Dawidowicz, *The Holocaust and the Historians* (Cambridge: Harvard University Press, 1981), p. 119. In addition to the Polish historians, a number of Jews who remained in Poland after the Holocaust are now coming out of their shamefulness and behave as Holocaust scholars. They all suffer from what I call the "Professorial Syndrome." After allowing themselves to return and live with the same people who cheered while Jews were deported to their deaths, they now wish to re-write Holocaust history as proud citizens of the Polish nation.

14 Diane L. Saltzman, Director, Collections Division, in a letter to Dr. Yoram Lubling. Dec. 30, 2004 she writes: "After speaking with several historians in the Museum's Center for Advanced Holocaust Studies, as well as contacting a colleague in Warsaw who, in turn, consulted the director of the Museum at Treblinka, no additional..."

15 Jan T. Gross, *Fear:* Anti- Semitism in Poland after Auschwitz (New York: Random House, 2006)

16 Jan T. Gross, *Neighbors*: The Destruction of the Jewish Community in Jed-wabne, Poland (New York: Penguin Press, 2001)

17 Richard Lukas, "Jedwabne and the Selling of the Holocaust," cited in Anthony Polonsky & Joaana B. Michlic, eds. *The Neighbors Respond: The Controversy over the Jedwabne Massacre in Poland* (New Jersey: Princeton University Press, 2004), p. 430. The article was originally published in the *Polish-American Journal*, May 2001.

18 Ibid.

19 Ibid., 433

[20] Ibid., p. 431

[21] Ibid., 432

[22] Adam Michnik, "Poles and the Jews: How Deep the Guilt?" Cited in Anthony Polonsky & Joaana B. Michlic, eds. *The Neighbors Respond: The Controversy over the Jedwabne Massacre in Poland* (New Jersey: Princeton University Press, 2004), p. 435. The article was originally published in the *New York Times* 17 March 2001.

[23] Ibid.

[24] Ibid., 438

[25] Leon Wieseltier, "Washington Diarist: Righteous," p. 441; originally published in *NewRepublic*, 9 April 2001.

[26] Ibid., pp. 443–4

[27] Ibid., p. 449.

[28] While I accept the proposition that Jews may live anywhere they want, I simply cannot understand why Jews would want to live in a country that includes Auschwitz and Treblinka?

[29] James E. Young, *Writing and Rewriting the Holocaust: Narrative and Conse-quences of Interpretation* (Bloomington and Indianapolis: Indiana University Press, 1990), p. 176.

[30] Richard Glazer, *Trap with a Green Fence, trans. Roslyn Theobald* (Evanston, Illinois: Northwestern University Press, 1995), p. 105.

[31] Samuel Rajzman, "The End of Treblinka," cited in Alexander Donat, *The Death Camp Treblinka* ed. (New York: Holocaust Library, 1979), pp. 245–6.

[32] Samuel Willenberg, *Revolt in Treblinka* (Warsaw, Poland: Zydowski Instytut Historyczny, 1992), p. 170.

[33] USHMM Archives RG-50.030*0185, 1988, p. 11.

[34] Samuel Willenberg, *Revolt in Treblinka* (Warsaw, Poland: Zydowski Instytut Historyczny, 1992), p. 52.

[35] Jan T. Gross, *Fear: Anti-Semitism in Poland after Auschwitz* (New York: Random House, 2006), pp. 41–42.

Chapter VI—The Treblinka Revolt

[1] See Central Commission for Investigation of German Crimes in Poland (New York: Howard Fertig, 1982), pp. 95–109.

[2] During the Fourth Yad Vashem International Historical Conference in 1980 Arad suggested the following: "There is no way of knowing the exact number of prisoners who successfully escaped and found places to hide. According to various estimates, about 60–70 of the Treblinka escapees were still alive at the end of the war. It may be assumed, how-

ever, that a larger number escaped during the uprising but that some met their death under various circumstances in the year between the uprising … and the liberation of all of Poland. Thus, of the 850 prisoners in the camp, it is probable that at least 100 escaped and successfully eluded the pursuit forces. This estimate is higher than figure generally accepted until now. (See for example: *The Death Camp Treblinka –A Documentary,* Alexander Donat, ed. New York, 1979. A list of sixty-nine survivors is given in this work, but it contains mistakes and duplication. Testimonies of twenty-seven of the survivors are in my possession.).” Seven Session, Chairman: Bela Vago.

3   Stanislaw Kon, “The Treblinka Revolt,” cited in Alexander Donate, ed. *The Death Camp   Treblinka—A Documentary* (New York: Holocaust Library, 1979), p. 225.

4   Yitzhak Arad, *Belzec, Sobibor, Treblinka* (Bloomington and Indianapolis: Indiana University Press, 1999), p. 277. The one testimony referred to is by the survivor Oscar Strawczynski and in Gitta Sereni’s book *Into the Darkness,* London, 1974, p. 182.

5   Cited in Alexander Donat as “The Treblinka Revolt,” pp. 224–130.

6   Aria Kudlik, “The Revolt Freed Me,” cited in *Sefer Tshenstokov* (Jerusalem, Israel: The Encyclopedia of the Jewish Diaspora, 1967–19680, Vol. 1, p. 167. Also see YVA 0.3/550

7   YVA 0.3/550

8   YVA 0.3/550

9   Samuel Rajzman, “The End of Treblinka,” cited in *The Death Camp Treblinka—A Documentary*, ed. Alexander Donat (Holocaust Library, 1979), p. 240.

10 Ibid.

11 Jewish Historical Institute in Warsaw—ygn.301/5041

12 Chiel Rajchman, USHMM Archives RG-50.030*0185—December 7, 1988, p. 9.

13 Ibid., p. 10.

14 YVA 0.33/4821

15 YVA 0.3/3131

16 YVA 0.3/556

17 Alexander Donat, *The Death Camp Treblinka—A Documentary* (New York: Holocaust Library, 1979), p. 291.

18 Jankiel Wiernik, “One Year in Treblinka,” cited in *The Death Camp Treblinka—A Documentary,* ed. Alexander Donate (New York: Holocaust Library, 1979), *p.* 178.

19 Notice Samuel Willenberg’s account of Chaskel in Treblinka. “His assignment was to stand outside camp headquarters and carry out petty

errands. ... Whenever he appeared he aroused alarm. At the sight of him, conversations were broken off and the prisoners withdrew into themselves, ... Chaskel and a fellow named blau had set up a partnership and were aided in their evil business by a gang of assistants to whom all feelings of comradeship were alien." (Ibid, pp. 205–6). Also, Jankiel Wiernik writes that, "Another amazing character trait of the Germans is their ability to discover, among the populace of other nations, hundreds of depraved types like themselves, and to use them for their own ends. In camps for Jews, there is a need for Jewish executioners, spies and stool pigeons. The Germans managed to find them, to find such gangrenous creatures as Moyshke from near by Sochaczew, Itzik Kobyla from Warsaw, Chaskel the thief, and Kuba, a thief and a pimp, both of them born and bred in Warsaw." (Ibid., p. 161).

[20] Jankiel Wiernik, "One Year in Treblinka," cited in *The Death Camp Treblinka—A Documentary,* ed. Alexander Donat (New York: Holocaust Library, 1979), p. 148.

[21] Ibid., p. 159.

[22] Jean-Francois Steiner, *Treblinka* (New York: Simon and Schuster, 1967), p. 187.

[23] USHMM RG-50.030*0033

[24] Moshe Y. Lubling's son Pinchas contradicts this testimony and claimed that the letter was delivered to him first and was shared with others in the resistance movement later. Regardless, the letter remained with Pinchas until 1945.

[25] Aaron Gelberd, "Nineteen Days in Treblinka," cited in *Sefer Tshenstockhov*, ed. M. Schutman (Jerusalem, Israel: The Encyclopedia of the Jewish Diaspora, 1967–8), Vol. I, pp. 160–164.

[26] YVA 0.3/1846, p. 8—This is taken from a supplementary testimony provided by Mr. Goldfarb in 1979 to Arad. In the interview Arad reflects the difficulties in understanding the leadership of the resistance in Camp II, Treblinka. He says: "It is difficult, then, to say who were the organizers or the organizer. This is one of the problems that I confronted when I am trying to describe the situation. This is to say, with regards to Camp I—about this we have data. We know that there was Chorazycki, and that there were other people around him. In other words, over there matters are more or less clear." (p. 5).

[27] YVA 0.3/1846, p. 13 of supplementary testimony

[28] YVA 0.3/1846, p. 26 Original Testimony

[29] Tanhum Grinberg, "The Revolt in Treblinka," cited in Alexander Donate, ed. (New York: Holocaust Library, 1976), p. 215. My Italic.

[30] Ibid., p. 217.

31 Ibid., p. 218.
32 As I pointed out earlier, the death of Dr. Chorazycki also marks the general time in which, until the publication of Glazer's book, I thought Moshe Y. Lubling was killed as well.
33 It should be noted that some suggested that Moshe Y. Lubling worked in "sorting the clothes of the victims." See his obituary in *Hurban Czenstochow.*
34 YVA 0.3/2267
35 USHMM—Transcript of Isadore Helfing's interview for Wentworth Films, Inc., 3.9.1992, p. 12.
36 Ibid., p. 22.
37 USHMM—Abraham Kolski tape interview, March 29, 1990.
38 Richard Glazer, *Trap with a Green Fence*, trans. Roslyn Theobald (Evanston, Illinois: Northwestern University Press, 1995), pp. 141–142.
39 YVA M. 49. P/118
40 Abraham Krzepicki, "Eighteen Days in Treblinka," cited in Alexander Donat, ed. *The Death Camp Treblinka* (New York: Holocaust Library, 1979, pp. 77–146. The original transcript can be located at the Jewish Historical Institute in Warsaw (file # 290)
41 YVA 0.3/4181, p. 5.
42 YVA 0.3/4181
43 USHMM RG-50.030*0132—July 10, 1990.
44 Ya'akov Miller, "Eyewitness Testimony 47. The Uprising in Treblinka," cited in *Jewish Responses to Nazi Persecution,* ed. Isaiah Trunk (New York: Stein and Day, 1979), p. 262. According to Trunk "the veracity of this testimony is confirmed by A. Gurevitch, secretary of the Cultural Committee, Eschwege.
45 Stanislaw Kon, "The Treblinka Revolt," cited in Alexander Donat, ed. *The Death Camp Treblinka—A Documentary* (New York: Holocaust Library, 1979), p. 229.
46 Ya'akov Miller, "Eyewitness Testimony 47. The Uprising in Treblinka," p. 263
47 Ibid., p. 351
48 Ibid., p. 264
49 YVA M.49.P/106
50 Marian Platkiewicz, "The Revolt Liberated Me," cited in *Plotzk: A History of an Ancient Jewish Community in Poland*, ed. Eliyahu Eisenberg (Tel-Aviv, Israel: Hamenora Publishing House, 1967), p.548.
51 Samuel Willenberg, *Revolt in Treblinka* (Warsaw, Poland: Zydowski Instytut Historyczny, 1992), p, 137.
52 Marian Platkiewicz, "The Revolt Liberated Me," p. 549.

53 See the testimony by Wolf Shneiderman, YVA 0.3/560
54 Marian Platkiewicz, "The Revolt Liberated Me, p. 550.
55 YVA 0.3/556
56 Marian Platkiewicz, "The Revolt Liberated Me," p. 547.
57 YVA 0.3/4039
58 Ibid.
59 Ibid.
60 YVA 0.3/4039—Mr. Rosenberg's file in Yad Vashem contains a number of testimonies given in different times, including his 1948 testimony to the Jewish Historical Institute in Warsaw, 1961 testimony for the Eichmann trial in Israel, 1968 testimony to the Israeli Police, and 1979 testimony to Yad Vashem.
61 As I noted elsewhere, Rosenberg's account of the Treblinka Revolt and his participation in it was, in part, the basis for Jean-Francois Steiner's 1966 book *Treblinka*. Unfortunately, it was also Rosenberg's testimony that, in part, led Steiner to conclude that the Treblinka prisoners did not revolt until they realized that they themselves will be killed.
62 YVA 0.3/1586, p. 14
63 He also provides the information that Galewski had difficulties walking and had special shoes made for him. This fact may explain why Galewski, although succeeded to escape, could not walk any further and committed suicide in the forest.
64 YVA 0.3/1586, p. 18.
65 YVA 0.3/560
66 Samuel Willenberg, "I Survived Treblinka," cited in *The Death Camp Treblinka—A Documentary,* ed. Alexander Donat (Holocaust Library, 1976), p. 196.
67 Samuel Willenberg, *Revolt in Treblinka* (Warsaw, Poland: Zydowski Instytut Historyczny, 1992), p. 138.
68 When writing his account after the war, Willenberg still was not aware of Galewski's role in the uprising. He writes that "he was cautious and did not want to take part in any underground activity." (Ibid., p. 190)
69 Ibid., p. 197
70 Ibid., p. 203
71 YVA 0.3/4181
72 Witness the following exchange between Arad and the Treblinka survivor Sonia Lewkowicz in 1979. Arad—"When did talk about a revolt started in Treblinka?" Lewkowicz—"I heard about preparations for an uprising from the time I arrived at the camp on December 1, 1942." Arad—"How did the uprising in the Warsaw Ghetto influence the people and when did the news reach you?" Lewkowicz—"As far as I can

remember we didn't know about the uprising in the Warsaw Ghetto … I didn't know and others didn't know either … [the Ghetto Warsaw Uprising] was not the turning point. We didn't know. I am complete certain of that." YVA 0.3/4181

[73] This summary is based on Samuel Willenberg's account in *Revolt in Treblinka* (Warsaw, Poland: Zydowski Instytut Historyczny, 1992).

[74] Stanislaw Kon, *Opstand in Treblinka* (Amsterdam: Uitgave "Stichting M.S. Fonds"—Sliedrecht, 1945).

[75] Stanislaw Kon, "The Treblinka Revolt," cited in *Anthology of Holocaust Literature*, eds. Glatstein, Knox, Margoshes (Philadelphia: The Jewish Publication Society of America, 1969), pp, 319–325.

[76] Ibid., p. 282

[77] Gitta Sereni, *Into the Darkness* (London: 1974), pp. 241–242

[78] Alexander Donat, ed. *The Death Camp Treblinka—A Documentary* (New York: Holocaust Library, 1979), p. 80.

[79] Samuel Willenberg, *Revolt in Treblinka,* p. 280

[80] This charge was categorically rejected in 1966 by Samuel Rajzman and Karl Unger.

[81] Samuel Rajzman, "The End of Treblinka," cited in Alexander Donat, ed. *The Death Camp Treblinka: A Documentary* (New York: Holocaust Library, 1979), p. 242.

[82] The blue print with a dedication by Weinstein was recently sold on e-bay.

Chapter VII—Monday, August 2, 1943

[1] Ian MacMillan, *Village of Million Spirits: A Novel of the Treblinka Uprising* (New York: Penguin Book, 1999), p. 5.

[2] Richard Glazer, *Trap in a Green Fence* (Northwestern University Press, 1995), p. 140

[3] Yitzhak Arad, *Proceedings of the Fourth Yad Vashem International Historical Conference*, Jerusalem, January 1980 (Jerusalem, Israel: Yad Vashem, 1984), pp. 6–7.

[4] Based on the testimonies by Richard Glazer, *Trap with a Green Fence* Evanston, Illinois: Northwestern University Press, 1995), pp. 138; 142–143; Samuel Willenberg, cited in Alexander Donat, ed. *The Death Camp Treblinka—A Documentary*, p. 210 and Samuel Rajzman also cited in Alexander Donat, ed. *The Death Camp Treblinka—A Documentary, p.* 244

[5] Based on testimony by Richard Glazer, *Trap with a Green Fence*, pp. 138, 140–141; and the testimony of Alexander Kudlik, cited in the 1967 *Sefer Czestochowa*, p. 166.

[6] Based on Taigman's testimony at the Eichmann trial, ARC website; Strawczynski testimony [YVA 0.3/3131]; Glazer, 140; Grinberg in Donat, 220–221; testimony of Eugeniusz Turowski [YVA 0.3/556], 2; testimony of Leon Perelsztajn [YVA M.49.P/106], 1).

[7] Based on the testimony of Wiernik, cited in Donat, pp. 186–187; Dr. Arad, *Belzec, Sobibor, Treblinka*, p. 289; testimony of Eliyahu Rosenberg [YVA 0.3/4039], 3; and the testimony of Sonia Lewkowicz [YVA 0.3/4181], 4).

[8] Based on a claim by Arad in *Belzec, Sobibor, Treblinka*, p. 287 (Arad gives no citation for this claim); also based on the testimony of Marian Platkiewicz in *Plotzk*, p. 549

[9] See Arad's *Belzec, Sobibor, Treblinka*, pp. 288–289; also the testimony of Eliyahu Rosenberg [YVA 0.3/4039], 13).

[10] See Richard Glazer's *Trap with a Green Fence*, p. 142; Samuel Willenberg in Donat, p. 210; Stanislaw Kon in Donat, p. 229; Arad's *Belzec, Sobibor, Treblinka*, pp. 287, 291; and Marian Platkiewicz's testimony in *Plotzk*, pp. 549–550

[11] See Arad's *Belzec, Sobibor, Treblinka*, p. 287; testimony of Marian Platkiewicz in *Plotzk*, p. 549

[12] Stanislaw Kon's testimony in Donat, p. 229; testimony of Eugeniusz Turowski [YVA 0.3/556], 3; testimony of Kalman Taigman [YVA 0.3/1586], 6, 12.

[13] See Arad's *Belzec, Sobibor, Treblinka*, pp. 244, 288; Willenberg's testimony in Donat, pp.208–209; Glazer's *Trap with a Green Fence*, pp. 138–140; testimony of Kalman Taigman, [YVA 0.3/1586], 14; testimony of Wolf Schneidmann [YVA 0.3/560], 4.

[14] See Richard Glazer, *Trap with a Green Fence*, p. 140

[15] See Willenberg's testimony in Donat, p. 209; Grinberg's testimony in Donat, p. 221; Arad's *Belzec, Sobibor, Treblinka*, p. 290; Strawczynski testimony [YVA 0.3–3131]; testimony of Wolf Schneidmann [YVA 0.3/560], 4; testimony of Leon Perelsztajn [YVA M.49.P/106], 3).

[16] Richard Glazer, p. 140

[17] See Arad's *Belzec, Sobibor, Treblinka*, p. 290; Strawczynski testimony [YVA 0.3/3131]; Samuel Willenberg, *Revolt in Treblinka*, p. 144.

[18] See Arad, *Belzec, Sobibor, Treblinka*, p. 291; Marian Platkiewicz testimony, *Plotzk*, pp. 549–550; Richard Glazer, *Trap with a Green Fence*, p. 143; and Samuel Willenberg, *Revolt in Treblinka*, p. 144.

[19] See Arad, *Belzec, Sobibor, Treblinka*, p. 291

20 See testimony of Wiernik in Donat, p. 187; Arad, *Belzec, Sobibor, Treblinka*, p. 292; testimony of Sonia Lewkowicz [YVA 0.3/4181], 5).

21 See Wiernik's testimony in Donat, p. 187; also Arad, *Belzec, Sobibor, Treblinka,* p. 292.

22 Arad, Belzec, Sobibor, Treblinka, p. 292.

23 Ibid., p. 293.

24 See Arad, *Belzec, Sobibor, Treblinka,* pp. 291, 293; Samuel Willenberg's testimony in Donat, pp. 210–211; Nahum Grinberg's testimony in Donat, p. 221; and Samuel Rajzman's testimony in Donat, p. 244.

25 See Willenberg's testimony in Donat, p. 211; Kon;s testimony in Donat, p. 230; testimony of Strawczynski [YVA 0.3/3131]; testimony of Kalman Taigman [YVA 0.3/1586], 14, 17).

26 See Richard Glazer, *Trap with a Green Fence*, p. 144; Willenberg's testimony in Donat, pp. 211–212; Samuel Willenberg, *Revolt in Treblinka,* pp. 144–145; testimony of Alexander Kudlik [YVA 0.3/550], 168).

27 Stanislaw Kon, "The Treblinka Revolt," cited in Alexander Donat, ed. *The Death Camp Treblinka—A Documentary*, p. 230

28 Samuel Moyn, *A Holocaust Controversy: The Treblinka Affair in Postwar France* (Waltham, Mass.: Brandeis University Press, 2005), p.3

29 Jean-François Steiner, *Treblinka* (New York: Simon and Shuster, 1967), p. 187

30 Cited in Samuel Moyn, *A Holocaust Controversy: The Treblinka Affair in post-war France* (Waltham, Mass: Brandies University Press, 2005), p. 23.

31 Ibid., Boruine Frenkel wrote that "Steiner is a criminal ... for accusing the Jews for collaborating." See p. 94.

32 Cited in Tom Segev, *The Seventh Million* (New York: Hill and Wang Publishers, 1993), p. 400. "Often I, like many Jews, find at the bottom of my soul a dull sense of pain because I didn't kill Hitler with my own hands."

33 Although Steiner first saw in the Treblinka revolt the new spirit of Judaism he later expressed disappointment in the Israeli culture for its rejection of traditional Judaism. For a similar sentiment see *Kedma,* a movie by Amos Gitai.

34 Ibid., p. 114.

35 Yeshayahu Leibowitz, "Heroism," cited in *Contemporary Jewish Religious Thought*, eds. Arthur A. Cohen and Paul Mendes-Flohr (New York: Charles Scribner's Sons, 1987), p. 363.

36 Ibid., p. 365.

[37] John Dewey, "Force and Coercion," in *The Later Works of John Dewey*, ed. Jo Ann Boydston (Carbondale: University of Southern Illinois, 1990), Vol. 10, p. 246.

[38] For more see Yoram Lubling, "John Dewey and the Problem with Pacifism," *Contemporary Philosophy,* Vol. XXVI No. 5&6, 2005, pp. 17–23.

[39] Albert Einstein, *Ideas and Opinions* (New York: Bonanza Books, 1971), p. 106–7.

[40] See the film *Manhattan*

[41] See Emil L. Fackenheim, *To Mend the World* (New York: Schocken Books, 1989), p. 130.

[42] Richard L. Rubenstein, "Buber and the Holocaust," *The Michigan Quarterly Review* (September 1978), p. 399.

[43] See BT Av. Zar 2b.

[44] Richard L. Rubenstein, "Buber and the Holocaust," Ibid., 395.

[45] Notice the continuous criticism of the Israeli use of force by Jewish intellectuals such as Noam Chomsky, Michael Lerner of *Tikkun*, and groups such as the California Jews for Justice who calls for the indictment of Israeli leaders for crimes against humanity. Personally, such perspective from Jewish individuals stretches even William James' notion of "vicious intellectualism." To be a member of the most hated and discriminated group in Western history, and to hold at the same time that there is virtue in passivity, boggles the mind of the present writer. It reflects a deep sense of denial resulted from living an entire life without danger in the United States. In the same way that there can be no atheists in a foxhole during combat, there are also no pacifists in the Jewish community's struggle to survive in Israel.

Chapter VIII—The Ethics of Memory

[1] Dahn Ben Amotz, *To Remember and Forget* (Tel-Aviv, Israel: Mah-tziot Publishing House, 1980), p. 54. In Hebrew.

[2] In particular, I refer to the Yad-Vashem Holocaust Museum and research institute in Israel, its former director Yitzchak Arad, who wrote the only extensive research book on Treblinka, and to the U.S. Memorial Holocaust Museum in Washington, D.C.

[3] Avishai Margalit, *The Ethics of Memory* (Cambridge, Mass. Harvard University Press, 2002).

[4] This example is based on actual events in Israel. See Avishai Margalit, *The Ethics of Memory*, p. vii.

[5] Avishai Margalit, *The Ethics of Memory,* p. 23.

6 Alexander Donat, *The Death Camp Treblinka—A Documentary*, p. 279
7 See Martin Buber's discussion of responsibility in *I and Thou* and Aristotle's discussion of Friendship in the Nicomachean Ethics.
8 See Jose' Ortega y Gasset, *On Love: Aspects of a Single Theme,* trans. Toby Talbot (New York: Meridian Books, 1957), pp. 85–104.
9 Avishai Margalit, *The Ethics of Memory* (Cambridge, Mass: Harvard University Press, 2002), p. 69.
10 Post-Sixties American culture is a perfect example of a community of communications, as Christopher Lasch astutely observed in his 1979 book *The Culture of Narcissism*. For most of my middle-class American students and colleagues, the war in Iraq, September 11, and the Katrina catastrophe were all experienced as television shows, i.e., as communications. Generally speaking, contemporary young Americans have no existential connection to the war or its casualties, nor do they know America's unique identity and responsibility to others. In fact, the large majority of college students and faculty have never served or volunteered to serve the collective; no national service, no military service, no political service, not even administrative service.
11 I owe this insight to my colleague Steven Schulman of the philosophy department at Elon University.
12 David G. Roskies, "Memory", cited in *Contemporary Religious Jewish Thought*, eds. Arthur A. Cohen and Paul Mendes-Flohr (New York: Charles Scribner's Sons, 1987), p. 582.
13 Ibid., p. 582–3.
14 Ibid.
15 Ibid., p. 585.
16 Peter Ochs, "Individuality", cited in *Contemporary Religious Jewish Thought*, eds. Arthur A. Cohen and Paul Mendes-Floher (New York: Charles Scribner's Sons, 1987), p. 484.
17 The term denotes the act of decision in its ultimate intensification; the decisive turning point in man's life. The individual undergoes a renewal of awareness and a total reversal of practice in the midst of the normal course of life.
18 Martin Buber, *I and Thou,* translated by Walter Kaufmann (New York: A Touchtone Book, 1970), p. 69.
19 Martin Buber, "Hebrew Humanism," cited in *The Writings of Martin Buber*, ed. Will Herberg (New York: Meridian Books, 1956), p. 294.
20 Martin Buber, "On National Education," cited in *The Writings of Martin Buber*, p. 288.

[21]   Charles S. Peirce, "Some Consequences of Four Incapacities," cited in *Philosophical Writings of Peirce*, ed. Justus Buchler (New York: Dover Publications, 1955), p. 229.

[22]   William James, "The Moral Equivalent of War," cited in *The Writing of William James*, ed. John J. McDermott (Chicago: University of Chicago Press, 1977), pp. 668–69.

[23]   The quest for identity reveals a logical paradox since identity overtime involves the deeper problem regarding the phenomena of change. To say that X yesterday is identical to X today is to say that X is both the same and different. Although X is now a day older, which will make her a totally different object than X yesterday (different space and time), X today is also "mysteriously" identical to yesterday's X. How can an object be the same and different at the same time is the essence of the philosophical paradox of change, and by direct implication of identity.

[24]   First, it is impossible to establish physical continuity between the Jews of the biblical period and the Jews who survived the Holocaust, even with DNA science. That such inability to show physical continuity is impossible constitutes the essence of the compliant by anti-Zionists that the European Zionists are not the "same people" as the ones who lived on the land two thousands years ago. Some anti-Zionists will go as far as to argue that the Jews of Europe are ordinary Slaves who formally converted to Judaism around 700 A.D., as described in Judah Halevi's *The Kuzari*: "… we know from historical records (that the King of Khzars), became a convert to Judaism about four hundred years ago." If this is true and most European Jews are converts (which is factually false), then indeed one can argue that such national identity **overtime** cannot be established. Of course, some physical continuity of Jewish existence in the holy land throughout the two thousand years of exile can be established to some degree. See Judah Halevi, *The Kuzari* (New York: Schocken Books, 1964), p. 17.

[25]   John Locke, *An Essay Concerning Human Understanding* (New York: Dover Publication, 1980), Vol. I, p. 449.

[26]   Uri Ram, "National, Ethnic, or Civic? Contesting Paradigm of Memory, Identity and Culture in Israel," *Studies n Philosophy and Education*, 2000), pp. 405–422.

[27]   Martin Buber, "A letter to Gandhi," cited in *Pointing the Way* (New York: Harper Press, 1957, p. 145.

[28]   Uri Avnery, *Israel without Zionism* (New York: Collier Books, 1968), p. 4. My Italic.

29 It is believed that Yoram Kanyuk was the first child in Israel to be named
    Yoram. The name was suggested to his father by the famous poet Hay-
    yim Nahman Bialik.
30 Yoram Kanyuk, "Cruel Junction," (Hebrew) *Politika* 17, 1987), p. 8.
31 Jay J. Gonen, *A Psychohistory of Zionism* (New York: New American
    Library, 19750, p. 7.
32 *Ha-Chuma,* February 5, 1947. In Hebrew.
33 See Richard L. Rubenstein, *After Auschwitz* (Baltimore: John Hopkins
    University Press, 1922). In the second edition (1992) of this important
    book Rubenstein identifies Professor Harold Fisch as the leader of a new
    Zionist response to the Holocaust. See pp. 216–220.
34 In 1968, Rabbi Solomon Fisch, Professor Fisch's father and my grand-
    mother's brother, gave a talk about the "Greater Israel" during my Bar-
    Mitzvah celebration in Israel. The movement started immediately after
    the 1967 war.
35 Harold Fisch, *A Zionist Revolution* (New York: St. Martin Books, 1976),
    p. 94.
36 Witness the following public letter written by Amos Oz to Prime
    Minister Menachem Begin in 1981 during the war in Lebanon. Cited in
    Tom Segev, *The Seventh Million* (New York: Hill and Wang Publishers,
    1993), p. 400.
    "Adolf Hitler destroyed a third of the Jewish people, among them your
    parents and relatives, among them my relatives. Often, I, like many Jews,
    find at the bottom of my soul a dull sense of pain because I did not kill
    Hitler with my own hands. I am sure that in your soul a similar fantasy
    hovers. There is not and will never be a cure for this open wound in our
    souls. Tens of thousands of dead Arabs will not heal that wound. But,
    Mr. Begin, Adolf Hitler died thirty-seven years ago. Unfortunately or
    not, it is a fact: Hitler is not in hiding in Nabatea, in Sidon, or in Beirut.
    He is dead and gone."
37 Richard L. Rubenstein, *After Auschwitz* (Baltimore: John Hopkins
    University Press, 1992), p. 217.
38 Moses Maimonides wrote: King Messiah will arise and restore the
    kingdom of David to its former state and original sovereignty. He will
    rebuild the sanctuary and gather the dispersed of Israel. All the ancient
    laws will be reinstituted in his days. See Moses Maimonides, *The Code
    of Maimonides: The Book of Judges,* trans. Abraham M. Hershman (New
    Haven: Yale University Press, 1949), chapter. 11, p. 238.
39 Harold Fisch, *A Zionist Revolution* (New York: St. Martins Press, 1978),
    p. 59.
40 Ibid., 21.

[41]   Ibid., 91.

[42]   Jean-Paul Sartre, *Anti-Semite and Jew*, trans. by George J. Becker (New York: Schocken Books, 1965), p. 67.

[43]   Cited in Uri Ram, "National, Ethnic or Civic? Contesting Paradigms of Memory, Identity and Culture in Israel," *Studies in Philosophy and Education* 19: 2000, p. 418.

[44]   Ibid.

[45]   Gordon's vision expresses the highest sense of personal and collective redemption through labor of the land. "If we do not till the soil with our own hands, the soil will not be ours—not only not ours in a social, or a national, but even in a political sense. The land will not be ours and we shall not be the people of the land. Here, then, we shall also be aliens just as in the lands of the Diaspora ... It is only to the degree that we here possess settlements and farms in which the work is done wholly by us that we shall become citizens and natives of the land ... You will derive pleasure from every task that you undertake ... You will then know in your heart that that there is in work such spiritual wealth of which you can see only the barest fringe." Cited in A.D. Gordon, *Selected Essays*, trans. Frances Burnce (New York: League for Labor Palestine, 1938), pp. 60, 250, 251.

[46]   Richard J. Bernstein, "The Culture of Memory," *History and Theory*, Theme Issue 43 (December 2004), pp. 165–178.

[47]   Ross Poole, review of Margalit's The Ethics of Memory, *Ethics*, July 2005, pp. 834–838.

[48]   Richard J. Bernstein, *John Dewey* (New York: Washington Square Press, 1967). It is surprising that Bernstein who in 1967 wrote a biography of John Dewey will fail to appreciate the locality and situated nature of ethics.

Chapter IX—Returning to the Scene of the Crime

[1]   Jan T. Gross, *Fear: Anti-Semitism in Poland after Auschwitz* (New York: Random House, 2006), p. 258.

INDEX